Mandalay
to
Norseman

by Thomas (Tom) D.W. McCulloch

Printed in Victoria, Canada

National Library of Canada Cataloguing in Publication Data

McCulloch, Tom, 1925-
     Mandalay to Norseman / Tom McCulloch.
ISBN 1-4120-0071-8
     1. McCulloch, Tom, 1925- 2. Mandalay (Ship) 3.
Norseman (Ship) 4. Merchant mariners--Canada--Biography.
5. World War, 1939-1945--Personal narratives, Canadian. I.
Title.
D811 M25116 2003   940.54'8171   C2003-
901469-X

TRAFFORD

This book was published *on-demand* in cooperation with Trafford Publishing.
On-demand publishing is a unique process and service of making a book available for retail sale to the public taking advantage of on-demand manufacturing and Internet marketing.
On-demand publishing includes promotions, retail sales, manufacturing, order fulfilment, accounting and collecting royalties on behalf of the author.

Suite 6E, 2333 Government St., Victoria, B.C. V8T 4P4, CANADA
Phone   250-383-6864   Toll-free   1-888-232-4444 (Canada & US)
Fax   250-383-6804   E-mail   sales@trafford.com
Web site   www.trafford.com   TRAFFORD PUBLISHING IS A DIVISION OF TRAFFORD HOLDINGS LTD.
Trafford Catalogue #03-0434   www.trafford.com/robots/03-0434.html

10   9   8   7   6   5   4   3   2   1

My brother Gordon Carmichael McCulloch, whose photograph appears in Figure 7, was the last of the McCulloch family of Greenock still resident in Scotland. We had discussed the progress of this undertaking over the telephone on several occasions over the past half-year. His comments were always pithy and pointed and were much appreciated by the author. Even as a child, he knew how to prick any display of pomposity exhibited by his sibling. I looked forward to presenting a copy of *Mandalay to Norseman* to him when we visited Scotland later in the year.

Unfortunately, he passed away on March 26, 2003.

His career followed the land while I followed the sea, but we met from time to time over the years in Malaysia, where he spent many successful years in the agricultural industry, and of course in Scotland and in Canada.

I miss him ver much indeed and dedicate this book to his memory.

Table of Contents

List of Illustrations

Foreword

Tom McCulloch's account of life at sea during the Golden Years when Great Britain had the largest Merchant Fleet in the world is a good read. It was of particular interest to me because he joined the *Mandalay* as I was about to leave and go up for my Second Mate's ticket.

No other ship has had the sentimental appeal that *Mandalay* had. God only knows why, as conditions aboard were abominable, but Tom seems to have benefited from his experiences aboard her as I did, and I enjoyed reading about it.

His description of life on board cable ships was equally fascinating. No doubt his skills as a navigator were tested when searching for a break in the cable. Akin to looking for a needle in a haystack. I have always wondered how it was done. Now I have an idea of the difficulties.

This account vividly illustrates the hardships endured when a man is away at sea for long periods of time, which puts a strain on any marriage. The fact that conditions aboard cable ships were better than average and that they often visited remote and exotic ports did nor fully compensate for the lack of home life. Tom seems to have weathered the storm better than I did in similar circumstances.

After one long and particularly difficult voyage, I was ready to quit and become an insurance salesman until a mate chided me "Och, it's not a bad life, remember the first twenty years are the worst."

The book brought back memories of the good and not so good times at sea, but it also reminded me how fortunate I was to have experienced these Golden Years.

A.F. (Tony) Winstanley
Former *Mandalay* Cadet
Author "Under Eight Flags"
Master Mariner

Preface

For a number of years I had toyed with the thought of writing my memoirs. My wife and children encouraged me to do something, but other than a few attempts at recalling certain episodes that occurred during the war years, I just nodded my head and took refuge in muttering about being far too busy and perhaps one of these days.

I did feel that I had a story to tell. After all, I did go to sea in the British Merchant Navy in 1941 as a Cadet Officer when I was barely sixteen years old. Prior to that event, I was brought up on the banks of the Firth of Clyde, an eager spectator of the maritime scene as the clouds of war gradually enveloped the ports and anchorages I knew so well. I saw my share of action-packed moments and so had interesting and sometimes exciting matters to discuss.

My life at sea continued after the war, when I spent some time on deep-sea cable ships around the globe before emigrating to Canada in 1948. These days on cable ships were unique, a very special way of life that can bring back fond memories even today.

Recently, I have had more time on my hands with the successful conclusion of an overseas-based training project. It was an opportunity for me to settle down and write about the past.

I have therefore produced this first book, which covers the period from childhood through arrival in Canada. I have been as frank as possible about seagoing life and its temptations, making sure that my better half was aware of what I was writing and that my children would not be overly shocked by my revelations.

I hope this book meets with their approval.

Acknowledgements

Although the author did write this account of his life between 1925 and 1948, and the facts of the story as he remembers them are his alone, he gratefully acknowledges the help of a number of people who contributed to the publication of "*Mandalay* to *Norseman.*"

Firstly, to Captain A. (Tony) Winstanley for his encouragement and his generous foreword. I had promised my family a story one day, but it was Tony's example that finally spurred me into action.

Secondly, to my wife Doreen and my family, who let it be known loudly and clearly that they wanted a legacy before my grey matter turned to mush or solidified. Additionally, their comments during the writing phase were both encouraging and supportive as I strived for honesty in discussing my character defects.

I also wish to acknowledge the inspiration of Allan and Lorna Morrison, whose home on the Lyle Hill in Greenock with its magnificent view of the Clyde finally triggered off my decision to put pen to paper. To the McLean Museum of the Inverclyde Council, who provided me with pertinent views of Greenock, my hometown. To Alex Brown of Victoria, formerly of Greenock, who provided me with much background information on my hometown and gave the connection a human face. To Captain Angus McDonald of Halifax, another Paddy Henderson cadet, who provided me with much useful insight into the movements of the Henderson fleet. To Ian Ferguson of Paisley for his memories of serving as a Radio Officer on *Salween* and *Prome* during World War II. To John Hill of Hexham, Northumberland, for his photographs of several vessels that were my home at one time or another.

To the late Angus Paterson and his widow Anne who brought back strong memories of the Murmansk run when I visited with them in Edinburgh shortly before Angus' death in 1999.

Finally, to Claire Champod, who edited the book and helped pull everything together prior to publication.

Figure 1 - The old harbour, Greenock, constructed in 1772

Figure 2 - The Greenock Custom House in the 19th century

Chapter One

Childhood on the River Clyde

I first saw the light of day on the 26th January 1925 (would have been named Robert if my mother had arranged things properly and had me on Robbie Burns' birthday).

We lived on 22 Benview Terrace, high above Greenock and overlooking the Tail of the Bank of the river with the shoreline of Helensburgh and the Lomond Highlands on the horizon, and that was where I was born—the heir to little but that magnificent view.

Greenock lies on the south bank of the River Clyde about twenty-two miles down river from the city of Glasgow. The origin of the name Greenock is thought to derive from the Gaelic "grianaig" meaning "sunny," and this has been translated as "sunny place" or "sunny knoll." Another theory suggests that it took its name from a "green oak" tree that grew in the town centre. Above the town centre lies the Well Park which was once the site of the castle of "Wester Greenock," the home of the Shaw family whose connection to Greenock goes back many centuries.

Figure 3 - Greenock from the Cut

In the thirties as in the past, shipbuilding and its associated trades were of enormous importance to the town. In 1764, the first square-rigged vessel was built. It was appropriately named Greenock. By the end of the nineteenth century, Greenock shipyards were launching in excess of sixty thousand tons of shipping each year. The industry was adversely affected by the business depression after the First World War, but by the mid-thirties it was slowly recovering, spurred to some extent by the threat of another war. The names Denholm, Lithgow and Scott underlined the prominence of the industry.

Along with the growth of the shipbuilding industry went the establishment of engineering shops. Additionally, there was a broad range of manufacturing companies engaged in the production of rope, woollens, flax, paper and chemicals. In the thirties, the town supported several sugar refineries, a distillery and a brewery. The sugar was transported from the docks to the refineries by horse-drawn wagons that slowly moved their cargo up the many hills that dominated the town. The wagons became a magnet for small boys who would dart after the wagons and try to cut the gunny sacks of raw sugar.

The town had a number of famous sons and daughters. One was William Kidd, born in 1645 in Greenock. He was a seventeenth century British privateer and pirate who became celebrated in literature as one of the most colourful outlaws of all time.

Greenock's most famous son was of course James Watt. He invented the separate condenser for the steam engine in 1765. He was also responsible for carrying out improvements to the harbour in 1772. His name is commemorated in the town in a variety of ways, and perpetuated in the world at large by the "watt" unit of power.

"Highland" Mary Campbell (1763-86), lover of Robbie Burns, is buried in Greenock cemetery.

My father was Thomas Duncan McCulloch, a Renfrewshire Scot whose Ancestors came from around Tain in the Dornoch Firth to fight for King Alexander at the battle of Largs in the 13th century. The Vikings were utterly defeated and the McCullochs were rewarded with lands in Galloway and around the Solway Firth. With the advent of the industrial revolution in the 18th century, many McCullochs moved off the land to seek better opportunity in Ayrshire and Renfrewshire. Some of them moved even further, to North America and beyond. (In the little town of Pictou, Nova Scotia, I recently came across a house dedicated to a Thomas McCulloch, Presbyterian minister and academic, who came from Renfrewshire to the new world in 1802 and established himself in Pictou, going on to become the first chancellor of Dalhousie University, which he created with the support of the government and population of Nova Scotia.)

Figure 4 - My father as a member of Scotland lawn bowling team, 1938

Back to my father—of more humble stock! He was born in Greenock in 1888, the son of Thomas Duncan McCulloch and Elizabeth Craig Hughes. He had a sister, Jean. His father died young, leaving his mother widowed and with two small children to support —a bit of a struggle! My father went to work full time when he was just a little boy, and therefore had only a very elementary education. Then, like countless others, he joined the British Army as a private in 1915. His regiment was the Argyle and Sutherland Highlanders, and he saw action on the western front. Later in the First World War, he was transferred into the Royal Army Service Corps on medical grounds. He served briefly on the army of Occupation of the Rhineland before discharge in 1919.

He went to work at Delingburn power station and became senior clerk. He married my mother, Ellen Gordon Wyness, in 1924. His interests were varied. He loved to garden—even his little plot. He was an ardent lawn bowler at the Grosvenor Bowling Club, representing his club in many Scottish tournaments, and in later years was capped for Scotland several times in international competition. He was active in Church of Scotland affairs at one time. He continued to financially support his mother, even though it must have been very difficult while raising his own family. In addition, he also made sure that his family got a good holiday each year in Stonehaven, close to my mother's people. He was basically a kind man and generous to a fault when he responded to other folks' misfortunes. He was no saint—I once saw him clobber a man who mistakenly grabbed our luggage and threw them aboard the wrong train. He could also physically punish my brother and me if we had misbehaved, but it was never severe and no doubt completely deserved.

After all these years, I still think of him with much love and affection. When he died in Montreal in 1959, I felt completely bereft. I do not feel that I have attained his high standards of integrity and behaviour. I still miss him very much. Of several clear memories of him, the most vivid was his compassion when a little girl fell outside a dairy and spilled all the milk out of the metal container she carried. She was bruised, but even more she was terrified at having to go home without the milk. Dad cleaned her off and paid the dairy for a replacement pint, then sent her on her joyful way.

He was proud of both my brother and me, even when he did not understand our rebellious ways. He helped make it possible for me to be accepted as a cadet in the Henderson Line of Glasgow—my ambition! This, at a time when the merchant navy was suffering very heavy casualties, which must have been hard for him to do. He later used his influence to ensure that my brother got a good start in the agricultural world, which led to his appointment as an assistant manager of a rubber plantation in Malaya.

He and my mother loved to sing—she playing the piano accompaniment. They often visited Ulster when they were younger and could give a spirited rendition of "the Mountains of Mourne" at any party. However, that is enough about Dad for now. I will return to him later in the opus! My mother, Ellen Gordon Wyness, was also born in Greenock, in 1894. However, she was of northeast of Scotland stock, as indicated by her middle and last names. Her father, Thomas Wyness, came from the Ellon-Methlick-Fyvie area of Aberdeenshire, a farming community. Her mother, Maggie Wallace, came from the same part of Aberdeenshire. I never knew her—she died before I was born—but I remember my grandfather Thomas Wyness. He retired as a detective sergeant on the Greenock police force and often looked after me. I particularly recall rides on the local buses around town, up on the top deck on the front of the bus, being sustained by large amounts of peppermints! He and my stepgrandmother also took me to the circus in Glasgow to make up for my having to attend several company shareholders' meetings in their presence. I believe they were babysitting me while my mother looked after my brother.

Figure 5 - My mother, 1935

My mother was a telephone operator prior to her marriage. She and my grandfather lived on South Street and attended the Presbyterian West Kirk. My father lived with his mother, my grandmother Elizabeth, on Ann Street and attended the South Kirk. Neither of my parents was particularly religious, but they did their best to ensure that their offspring were exposed to the teachings of the Presbyterian faith.

My mother was a gentle person, but quite able to make her voice heard and her views known. She had a wide circle of friends, many of whom had gone to school with her. Compared with the poverty of my father's upbringing, she had better schooling and access to a higher standard of living. She was knowledgeable about a variety of things, played the piano rather well, was well read, served on good works committees, sang passably, crocheted, sewed, knitted and, for the amusement of her friends, read the tea leaves in their cups.

She loved our annual expedition to Stonehaven and the Ythan valley. The North Sea relaxed her and visits to her cousins in Aberdeenshire renewed her ties to the Wyness clan. Life was never dull on these safaris

Figure 6 - Stonehaven (Stainhai), our holiday home

and she is at the centre of my memories of these days. Once, while living with her Aunt Nellie at Chapelton, she displayed a most unusual and unladylike behaviour. There was a huge bang from the vicinity of the front door as cousin Nelson took a pot shot at a brace of pigeons flying by. Mother came flying down the stairs believing that I had suffered a terrible accident. Her relief on seeing Nelson holding the smoking shotgun turned to bitter recrimination when she realized that a loaded gun had been stacked in a corner of the hallway since our arrival and that her precious sons could have been in great danger if their curiosity had overcome their caution! The lady had become a tigress!

Mother insisted that her sons sport the Gordon tartan every Sunday. It was all right with us, but it did lead to fights with non-kilted ruffians from time to time. It was also, unfortunately, a magnet for predators. She was our true support in times of illness and stress—she never let us down. She was sadly missed when she passed away in March 1941.

After seventy-eight years, it is difficult to remember events in the nineteen twenties and nineteen thirties, but some things still lurk in my remaining grey cells, such as being quarantined with measles or scarlet fever and having to hand over my most precious teddy bear to some miserable wretch employed by the authorities. The first memory of real injustice!

Vague memories of grandma McCulloch who to me was a rather stern old lady. She was a stickler for time and on holidays would arrive at the railway station before it opened. When we arrived, she would be there, sitting on her trunk with her brolly at the ready. I think I was the favourite of stepgrandma Wyness, which ensured that my brother Gordon was the apple of grandma McCulloch's eye.

My father had a sister, Jean, who married Tom Moffat. They had two children who were slightly older than us—Jean and Tom wouldn't you

Figure 7 - The author on the right, with his brother Gordon

know. We visited infrequently and finally drifted apart after grandma McCulloch died intestate and left my father to clean up the mess. I last saw my cousin Jean during an air raid precautions drill in 1939. We nodded to one another and that was it. Scots really do carry on family feuds unto the third generation!

There was a somewhat similar split when grandpa Wyness died and stepgrandma Isobel inherited all the property. My mother never spoke to Isobel again and, as a result, I was deprived of a loving grandma. I remember seeing her once while out playing. She saw me and such a look passed between us that has remained with me always. I do hope that our passing leaves all of our extended family in loving connection with one another.

We attended the South Kirk where the Reverend McKerracher reigned. He was a controversial figure—unmarried and therefore the object of much attention and speculation among the ladies—and it was also rumoured that he had a drinking problem. That problem was solved when he became regimental padre to the local 5/7th Battalion Argyle and Sutherland Highlanders. I believe the poor man was captured by the Germans at Saint-Valéry when the 51st Highland Division was defeated in 1940, after the fall of Dunkirk.

We also attended Sunday school at the South Kirk and I recall taking part in a biblical play performed in the church itself. I was Gabriel, or a herald, or some other character clothed in white robes and clutching a horn or trumpet. I stumbled on the pulpit steps and brought down not only myself but also other members of the triumphant celestial choir. Talk about creating an impression!

The trials and tribulations of Clydeside were not unknown to us. Many men were out of work. Once, there was a huge parade of workers and ex-servicemen through the centre of town. It was not for nothing that we were known as Red Clydeside.

My parents seem to have lost some interest in the kirk, but my brother and I still struggled to attend Sunday school at mother's insistence. But it was a long walk from Dunlop Street to the South Kirk, particularly in winter, and we slowly but surely fell into the ranks of the non-believers. Still feel a bit guilty about it even after all these years.

My first school was Highlanders Academy, an old multi-story building with nary a Highlander in sight. We were taught and drilled like young soldiers. I do not recall much fun, but I managed to involve myself in several fist fights in the school playground.

Somehow Armistice Day sticks in my mind with serried ranks of children lined up for the solemn ceremony. Although Dad had been a survivor of the trenches, he never talked about it and so I could only visualize knights in shining armour and gleaming swords and banners instead of the horror and carnage of that battlefield before armistice was declared.

The only teacher I remember was a tall forbidding man called Carney who terrified my compatriots and me. He could wield the strap like the best of them, but he must have been a good teacher as many of his lessons have remained with me to this day. Later in life, I discovered that he and Dad knew one another well through lawn bowling.

From Highlanders Academy, I graduated to Greenock High School in 1937, which in those days was located on Dunlop Street, only a short distance from our home. It was a very new building, bright and airy with high ceilings and lots of gym and laboratory space, together with large playing fields. In my first class were Guthries, McNeils, Browns—all cousins or second cousins of mine through the grandma McCulloch connection. It was grand fun and enlivened our studies, sometimes to the despair of our teachers.

The world outside was changing and, in 1938, Prime Minister Chamberlain humiliated us all by signing a peace treaty with Adolph Hitler. I can still see my father's face when he received the news. He predicted war with Germany within a year and he was right on! The Munich debacle saw us assembling gas masks on the school grounds and in church halls. Thank God, they never had to be used. Meanwhile, I was being exposed to Latin, English literature, French, mathematics, science, geography, history, art and physical education among many other things. I even became adept at making and displaying puppets.

I was also learning to appreciate exposure to the females in our year, although we were strictly segregated in separate classrooms in years one through three. I did well in history, geography and English, but after a good start in Latin, fell rapidly from grace. Other subjects were so-so and, with falling interest levels, I became a subversive element, joining a growing group of discontents. Was it our fault, or was it poor teaching methods, or was it the impending threat of war that overshadowed everything? Probably a mix of all three!

1938 was a momentous year! In addition to the Munich affair, the Empire Exhibition was held at the Bellahouston Park in Glasgow, and various visits were made to the exhibition, of an official and unofficial nature. The official visits were as a member of the 5th Greenock Scout Troop to take part in various ceremonies, such as the grand opening with King George VI and Queen Elizabeth present, and other events with the dowager Queen Mary officiating. I well remember standing in parade as Queen Mary approached and passed in her huge black Daimler. She looked down at me directly I swear with her usual scowl, as if to say "What a dreadful little boy!"

Other times were more fun events, when we tried out every ride in the fun fair, ogled at the giraffe women from Burma with their long brass ringed necks, and wandered around the clachan trying to soak up ancient Scottish clan existence. With all the peat smoke and the dungeon-like dwellings, it must have been a miserable life. As a Lowlander, I could not help feeling some smug superiority—probably quite unjustified as we were originally from the edge of the Highlands from both sides of our family. On all of these visits, we stayed with mum's old friends the Fernies in Ibrox, not too far from Bellahouston. More on the Fernie sisters later.

Meanwhile, down at the Tail of the Bank off Greenock, we were treated to an awe-inspiring sight—a Royal Navy fleet review which highlighted such vessels as the aircraft carrier *Courageous*, the battleship *Rodney* and the battleship *Warspite*. I visited *Courageous* and *Warspite* and as a small boy was suitably impressed. I climbed in and out of gun turrets and engine rooms and navigating bridges in an absolute ecstasy of delight. I was also imbibing the very unique smell of a working ship—traces of steam, oil , galley odours, cordite and humans, faint rumbles, creaks, the thudding of distant pumps, bosuns' whistles, unintelligible tannoy announcements, the whole bustle of a live ship. It all confirmed for me what I wanted to do as soon as I was old enough.

The Lyle Hill was a wonderful spot to view all the shipping in the River Clyde estuary. From there we saw the *Monarch of Bermuda* on her trials.

Dad was actually on board during the speed trials but was more impressed with the padded detention cells than anything else. Obviously not a potential seafarer.

Just beyond where we lived was a glen that originated up in the Kilbarchan hills and moors. That glen was a constant playground for the children of the neighbourhood. Many a dam was constructed and fort erected before falling to another invading force of small boys. Above the glen, a waterway had been built to convey water around the edge of the moors from Loch Thom to a defunct paper mill above the town. It was and is known only as the "Cut."

From the Cut, wonderful panoramic views of the river and firth were available at every turn. From the Cut, we saw the *RMS Queen Mary* sail down the Clyde on her maiden voyage—later viewing her at close range from Hunters Quay and the Esplanade. It was a perfect day, even if poor Mum had to carry a bowl of trifle to sustain us all.

Figure 8 - The *RMS Queen Mary's* maiden voyage, 1934

In 1940, we saw *RMS Queen Elizabeth* from the same vantage points, but the weather was foul and all was clothed in the secrecy of wartime. My dad always maintained that the view from the Cut was the finest in the world—perhaps a biased outlook but with some justice. Many years later, when visiting in Canada, he was heard to say that perhaps the view from the Malahat above Finlayson Arm on Vancouver Island was its equal!

In 1939, I was still battling away in Greenock High School. Shortly after returning to school after the summer holidays, Germany attacked Poland and, on 3rd September, we declared war on Germany. Our world as we knew it was coming to an end.

The spring and summer had been grand. I had several girlfriends (who probably each had several boyfriends). My favourite was Effie, who was a regular smasher, but I spared time for Etta, Georgia and Jean. One of my few accomplishments was dancing both highland and ballroom, courtesy of high school instruction. It ensured my popularity with the lassies at school and stood me in good stead later in life. Football, or soccer as it is known today, was my other passion, which I played with vigour and determination, but lacked the brilliance that the game demands. I was a member of Stuart House (the other houses were Scott, Wallace, and Bruce) and regularly played against opponents in school and across the town. I still follow soccer games played around the world—World Cup, European Cup, Premier League, etc. Is not TV wonderful, especially when backed up by the internet? I swam at Cardwell Bay and Gourock pools in freezing seawater temperatures and explored the Inverkip Valley and the second and third Lanark.

Figure 9 - The Marchioness of Lorne approaching Gourock, 1937

I saw quite a lot of the Firth of Clyde in those days. Friends of mine who lived on Waverley Street, Douglas and Alec Brown, had access to the Clyde steamers through their father Captain Brown. Frequently, we would cycle down to Gourock, Wemyss Bay or Largs to join his ship and sail off for the day to such exotic ports as Helensburgh, Dunoon, Rothesay, Kilcreggan, Sandbank, Roseneath, Kilmun, Kilchattan, Millport and many others. What grand times these were.

Additionally, my dad would take me along with him on his bowling tournaments when we would go to Strone, Cove, Rhu, Garelochhead and Clynder, where I would act as scorekeeper for my dad's Grosvenor Club rink. The last trip that I recall pre-war was a high school cruise and dance around the Kyles of Bute in the summer of 1939. It was very exciting and romantic, with the orchestra playing "South of the Border" and other ballads of the day.

The story of the Clyde pleasure steamers is worth telling as they played such an integral role in our lives. It all started with Henry Bell and his *Comet* in 1812 while the Napoleonic wars were still raging. *Comet* was about forty feet in length. Fitted with a 4 hp engine and internal flue

Figure 10 - Rothesay Pier with *Neptune, Marchioness of Breadalbane,* and *Redgauntlet,* 1908

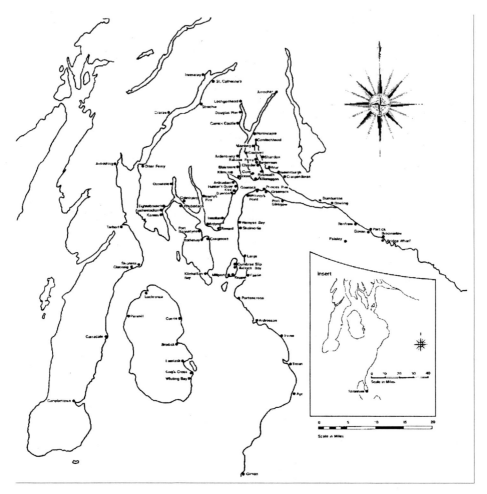

Figure 11 - The Firth of Clyde

boiler, she ran between Glasgow and Greenock and Helensburgh carrying passengers only. It took her four hours to steam the distance from Glasgow to Greenock, a trip that had previously taken forty-eight hours by oar and sail. It was said that on her maiden voyage the passengers had to wade in the water on occasion and push her off after grounding. It was also rumoured that two gentlemen passengers disembarked at Bowling fearing what they thought was an inevitable boiler explosion.

Within ten years, there were more than fifty steamboats plying the waters of the Clyde. By the end of the nineteenth century, more than three hundred passenger vessels were operating on the Clyde, its firth and attached lochs. Competition raged as coastal villages developed with the movement of wealthier people out of Glasgow. Many of these villages became resorts to serve the larger population of Glasgow, such as Dunoon and Rothesay. A holiday "doon the watter" was the ultimate goal of many Victorian families.

Specialized boats with owner/captains became common, running to such ports as Inverary and Ardrishaig, even some providing non-alcoholic cruises. There was also the highland Sabbath to overcome, so that steamboats could sail on their trade seven days a week.

Figure 12 - *HMY Victoria and Albert at the Tail of the Bank, 1847*
(Painting by William Clark)

The royal route was established in 1847 when Queen Victoria visited the Clyde. From the Tail of the Bank she sailed in the royal yacht *Victoria and Albert* to Ardrishaig on Loch Fyne, then through the Crinan Canal to Oban and the western highlands.

These were also the days of fierce and potentially dangerous races between steamboats of different companies to berth first at the many piers available so that they might pick up extra passengers or indeed deny the losing vessel a space at the pier. Rothesay was a particularly contentious port and sparked many a furious scene.

The advent of the railways into the pleasure steamer business eventually put paid to the owner/captains but did nothing to stop the rivalry and competition for the passenger trade. The Caledonian, the G&SW and the North British Railways all fought for a piece of the action from their shore bases at Greenock, Gourock, Wemyss Bay and, of course, Glasgow itself. In addition to supplying better and more comfortable ships, their cruise dining saloons became ever more opulent, and each vessel was equipped with a band to entertain the passengers. Out of Glasgow these were usually pipe bands, but down river they flaunted German brass bands with all the oompah-pah anyone could wish.

In 1914, many of these vessels were converted to minesweepers. Most of them survived the war and trade resumed normally again without, however, the German bands. The outbreak of war again in 1939 saw many of the pleasure steamers converted to tenders unloading and loading the many troopships gathered at the Tail of the Bank, or into minesweepers or anti-aircraft vessels. Sadly, many were lost in the conflict. The names of the Clyde pleasure steamers were many, but I will always remember the *Juno, Lucy Ashton, Duchess of Montrose, Jeanie Deans* and the *Waverley*. May they sail on forever in some celestial Firth of Clyde.

In addition to our land expeditions down the Kip Valley, well fortified with Mum's thick egg bap rolls, we explored the many side glens in the hills around Inverkip, always building a campfire with much ceremony and then dousing it with well aimed hoses of pee in a circle before departing for home.

In the hills above Inverkip was the Greenock boy scouts camp. Everton was a lovely spot, but difficult to get to with an ancient Rudge-Whitworth bicycle that weighed a ton. It was also the scene of a camping fiasco that put me off the camping scene for the rest of my life. The troop was under the direction of some rover scouts who supposedly knew all about camping lore. First of all we pitched tent on a slope just as the heavens opened and continued to come down in buckets for the following forty-eight hours. We never really got pitched properly on the slope and the rain poured down the hill and over and under the groundsheet, making life miserable for all concerned. Additionally, the campfires were washed out and we subsisted on cold gruel for most of the weekend. Needless to say, I never returned!

I restricted my scouting activities to learning to play the chanter and the tenor drum in the pipe band and to getting my nose banged about in several impromptu boxing events.

Around this time, the family attended the marriage of Dad's cousin, Hugh McCulloch, a wealthy contractor and developer who was marrying for the second time. The affair was held at the Grosvenor Hotel in central Glasgow and was very posh. I had not realized that there were so many well-to-do McCullochs in the world.

That summer of 1939 was also memorable when we visited Stonehaven and the Ythan Valley. The threat of war was visible everywhere. Troop trains carrying territorial regiments to their training grounds delayed our journey both to and from the north. With convoys of army lorries on the roads, war was in the minds of everyone! We however stayed as usual in Mrs. Gordon's small boarding house on Barclay Street in Stonehaven. The bathing pool was our second home, while Dad ruled on the bowling green. As in other years, charabanc tours to mystery spots were undertaken to Edzell, Loch Lee, and other spots. The great castle at Dunottar was also visited, together with trips along the Skatie shore to the high cliffs of Muchalls.

The "Over the Seas to Skye" painting in the hall on Barclay Street still sticks in my memory. Was Mrs. Gordon a Jacobite sympathizer, was it just sentimentality, or did she pick it up cheap at a sale? Just speculation after all these years. I never was a fan of the Stuarts—not James, or Charles, or the Old Pretender, or Bonnie Prince Charlie himself who brought ruin and disaster to the Highlands of Scotland.

Once again we visited with Aunt Nellie at Chapelton. Nelson Jamieson was on leave from his job as captain of a British India steamship. He had given Aunt Nellie a huge tiger skin (shot by himself) which now dominated the parlour. He enlisted me to carry his game bag on shooting expeditions around Chapelton, which soon filled up with pigeon, rabbit and hare. I was a mighty tired little fellow by the time the shoot was completed. Nelson's brother Monsie was always around, a quiet man but doing all the major work on the farm. He taught me how to catch rats in the barn and how to drown them in the river Ythan. We also visited with Mum's cousin Coral who was married to George Clark (another distant relative) at Middlethird Farm. The other Jamieson cousins of my mum's were Iris, outside Methlick, and Roslyn in Glasgow.

Returning to the Clyde in the summer of 1939, another sign of the war to come was the frantic activity encompassing the Greenock drill hall and barracks of the Argyll and Sutherland Highlanders. We no longer could wander up and peer into the drill hall but were held at bay by a large barbed wire fence. While the fence prevented civilian interference with the military activities being conducted therein, it did not stop the lassies from getting a good view of the young warriors as they boarded or unboarded their vehicles in full kilt regalia. Many a squeal went up as the lassies spotted a well-endowed member of the kilted brigade. Life was not all serious in those perilous times!

Chapter Two

The Upper Firth of Clyde

In retrospect, I was very lucky to be alive and well at such a time and in such a place. The Clyde River and Firth was and still is a most lovely part of the world. Mind you, it does need good weather to enable one to see it at its best. But even in midwinter it has grandeur, when the Highlands to the north meld into the grey skies and the mist. The Clyde is Scotland's principal river—106 miles long—rising in the green Lowther Hills on the Southern Uplands and flowing generally to the northwest through Glasgow and then southwestward to the Firth of Clyde.

In the thirties, the lower Clyde, flowing through the heart of Clydeside, was the industrial heart of Scotland. From the centre of Glasgow to Clydebank and beyond, either riverbank was occupied with cargo docks, shipyards, engine shops and more cargo docks. The depression in the late twenties and early thirties had hit Clydeside badly, but signs of recovery were everywhere by the late thirties. Further downriver, the ports of Dumbarton, Port Glasgow and Greenock were busy with trade and the building of seagoing vessels and their propulsion machinery. Other industrial activities that supported the growing population were the refining of sugar and the distilling of whisky.

From Erskine and Dumbarton, the dredged river widens somewhat as it proceeds westward, the land rises in elevation, and the scenery becomes quite breathtaking. Even the industrialization of the southern shoreline in the vicinity of Port Glasgow and Greenock cannot distract from the beauty of the hills and the river. Off Port Glasgow and Greenock, the river widens considerably into the area between Greenock and Helensburgh known to one and all as the Tail of the Bank.

Although the river was kept well dredged above the Tail of the Bank for Glasgow-bound traffic, deep draught vessels were unable to penetrate the upper river in safety and offloaded in Greenock or while at anchor. In those days, it was mostly the larger passenger liners that were affected.

Figure 13 - The Great Harbour and James Watt Dock, 1886

In the nineteenth century, the great harbour in Greenock would be filled with countless sailing vessels discharging cargoes of wool, sugar, grain, meat, tobacco, etc., from around the globe, then preparing to load coal and packaged goods for overseas destinations. What a sight it must have been—a forest of tall timber masts as far as the eye could see! In my boyhood, it was a backwater occupied by small training craft and numerous small nondescript vessels of various colours and states of repair—a sad comparison to the days of yore.

Just beyond Greenock on the south shore was Gourock, and nestled in Cardwell Bay just before approaching Gourock piers was the Royal Naval Torpedo Factory, whose products were suddenly in great demand as war appeared more and more imminent. Gourock was largely residential, but was also an important base for the many Clyde steamers that docked there to load and discharge passengers. It was of course the railway terminal for passenger traffic from Glasgow. Gourock was also a fun place for children and adults, with entertainment kiosks, Italian ice cream palaces, fish and chip shops by the dozen, putting greens, swimming pool and—the pièce de résistance—the Cragburn dancing pavilion, the mecca of all the young who could dance and of those who just wished they could.

Just beyond the Gourock pier, the shoreline trends to the southwest then to the south at the Cloch lighthouse, with lower land in the background in the vicinity of Inverkip, Wemyss Bay and Skelmorlie, and on into the seaside resort of Largs. Enough of the south shore of the Clyde for now.

As noted earlier, opposite Greenock the navigable river widens and the many offshoots of the Clyde start appearing. The first is the Gareloch with Helensburgh and Kilcreggan marking the entrance to the loch. This northern shore of the Clyde estuary, which eventually bends southward, is a complete contrast to the heavily industrialized and populated regions of Paisley through to Greenock. For hundreds of years, it had been under the sway of the Campbells. Indeed, Roseneath Castle belonged to the estate of the Dukes of Argyll. The last duke to own it was married to Princess Louise, a daughter of Queen Victoria. After she died in 1939, the castle was used as a HQ for US troops based there during the latter part of WW II. Roseneath Castle also features in the history of William Wallace—his jump on horseback from the small cliff known as Wallace's Leap in Scottish legend.

In early times, the people of the Gareloch and Roseneath Peninsula depended mainly on farming and fishing as a livelihood, mostly living in small clustered townships. With the advent of the paddle steamer in the early nineteenth century, it became possible for wealthy people in Glasgow, Paisley and other places to travel easily and quickly to various destinations on the Clyde coast.

A quote from the *Gazetteer of Scotland* in 1882 gives a good picture of the changing demographics of the area. "The parish of Rhu, village and parish on the west border of Dumbartonshire—the parish contains also Helensburgh town and most of Garelochhead village—measures 9 miles by 5 miles and comprises 20,126 acres, population 10,097. A belt of low shore and contiguous slope extending along all Gareloch from Helensburgh to Garelochead is thickly studded with mansions and villas, and has rich embellishment of wood and culture."

That description could well be applied to the late nineteen thirties
—nothing much had changed, except that steamer traffic no longer
depended on the rich but provided mobility to all. Holiday-related ferry
and cruise traffic flourished while the wealthy moved by motorcar or the
West Highland Railway. On the west side of the Roseneath Peninsula
was the entrance to Loch Long, a deep water loch that ran northward for
about twenty miles to Arrochar at its head. An offshoot loch, Loch Goil
commences halfway up Loch Long and, heading in a new direction,
terminates five miles or so up at Lochgoilhead. Both lochs are about one
mile wide and with high mainly treed lands on the western shore and a
lower more settled landscape on the eastern shore. In the late thirties, it
was travelled mainly by fishermen and yachtsmen. The small ferry port
of Strone was located on the western entrance to Loch Long and also
marks the entry into the Holy Loch, which can be clearly seen across the
Clyde from Gourock.

The Holy Loch is about a mile wide at its broadest part and between two
and three miles long at high water. The tide recedes for some distance at
its head. The loch's name clearly has some religious significance. Lots of
debate, but perhaps named after St. Munn, an Irish-born Celtic saint
who lived on what he called "the charmed loch" in Cowal in the 6th
century. Who knows? Nevertheless, a lovely spot just north of Dunoon.

I well remember travelling there to support my father's lawn bowling
activities in a small village called Sandbank on the south shore of the
Holy Loch. There was only limited seagoing activity in the late
thirties—a far cry from the Royal Navy submarine base of WW II or the
United States Navy nuclear attack submarine base during the cold war
with Russia from the sixties until the end of the eighties.

From the Holy Loch, the Clyde curves sharply southward with Dunoon as
the ferry focal point for that part of the river. Dunoon is at the heart of the
Cowal Peninsula. The name Cowal is a corruption of Coughail, one of
the sons of Fergus, king of the Scots who migrated from Ireland to create
the kingdom of Dilriada in mid-Argyll in the 6th century AD. With the
development of the clan system in mediaeval times, castles or fortresses
sprung up all over the Cowal Peninsula, one of the earliest being in Dunoon.

Dunoon castle was a royal castle under the control of the Earls of Argyll.
In 1472 a royal charter was granted to Colin Campbell, the Marquis of

Argyll, with a rental fee for the castle of one red rose. In the seventeenth century the Campbells moved to Inverary, and Dunoon castle was left to decay. However, in the early nineteenth century, wealthy Glasgow merchants built mansions in the area as the Clyde steamer service expanded. In 1868 Dunoon became a parliamentary burgh and the citizens prospered. In the late thirties, it was a mecca for the holidaymakers from up the river.

The Cowal Highland Gathering, the premier Scottish highland games, is held in Dunoon each year, with contestants flocking there from all over the Scottish diaspora.

From Dunoon, the shoreline of the Cowal Peninsula stretches south to Inellon and Port Bannatyne before curving northward into Loch Striven and the scenic Kyles of Bute. South of the Cowal Peninsula lies the beautiful Isle of Bute. The isle is about sixteen miles in length and has an average breadth of five miles. It is separated from the Cowal Peninsula by a narrow but navigable very scenic channel—the Kyles of Bute. The land on Bute is bleak and forbidding toward the Kyles, but with green fertile hills and valleys covering the remainder of the island.

The ferry terminal of Rothesay was the focal point for all of Bute in the late thirties. Rothesay Castle was constructed in the 13th century and was the island home of Scottish kings. During the wars of independence, it fell to the Sassenach but was retaken by Robert the Bruce in 1311. It became a royal burgh in 1400. With the coming of the paddle steamer in the early 19th century, it became the home of wealthy Victorian industrialists, then a popular tourist resort for trippers from Glasgow who thronged the isle.

During the summer months, the circumnavigation of the Isle of Bute through the Kyles was very popular and charabanc tours around the isle exposed the visitor to many historic sites but also to many breathtakingly lovely parts of the land and seacoast. Toward the southernmost point of Bute is the picturesque village of Kilchattan where I attended a church camp. It was a good place and lots of fun. We lived in huts, thank goodness, not miserable wet tents. The food was passable and we spent a lot of time messing about in small boats. Once we went fishing in the passage between Bute and the Little Cumbrae and I caught nothing but a bad case of mal de mer. But happy memories nevertheless.

When my time at the Camp was up, I travelled from Rothesay by paddle steamer to Wemyss Bay and then by train to Greenock—all on my own. My parents were happy to have me back, having no doubt worried themselves sick about what might have happened to me. Somehow or other I felt a sense of accomplishment—whether or not justified.

The isle of Bute, on the wester side of the River Clyde, represents the farthest extent of my childhood sojourns on the river. On the other bank, Largs, Millport and the Big and Little Cumbrae were as far as I ventured. Great Cumbrae lies about one and a quarter miles off Largs. The island is about three and a half miles long with a breadth of about two miles. The town of Millport has a population of three thousand souls. There is continual ferry traffic between Millport and Largs. Little Cumbrae Island lies a mile southwest of Great Cumbrae. It is about a mile long and half a mile wide. Population was about thirty souls in 1939.

Beyond my childhood travel limits was the main Firth of Clyde, flowing southward past Arran and Troon to the Ailsa Craig off Girvan—the famous Paddy's Milestone—and thence seaward between the Mull of Kyntyre and Coursewell Point on the Mull of Galloway. My journeys through these waters would come later, when I became a seafarer.

Chapter Three

The Impact of War

On September 1, 1939, Germany invaded Poland. Britain and France therefore declared war on Germany. Our world had changed forever. Actually, the signs of war were to develop slowly in my part of the Clyde. First, was the construction of an anti-submarine boom defence system in the vicinity of Cloch Point and the Cowal shore, followed by the presence of many more naval and merchant vessels in and around the Tail of the Bank. The shipyards and engineering shops geared up to full production.

The Royal Naval Torpedo Factory went to three shifts and the territorial battalions in the army joined the Fifty-First Highland Division in France. The liner *Athenia* was torpedoed off the North Channel between Scotland and Ireland. Then for a while things seemed to quieten down as winter approached.

In school, I was busy in my third year of high school, determinedly failing Latin, floundering in French, barely surviving in mathematics, but doing reasonably well in English, history and geography. My Latin teachers did their best with me, but when we moved on from Rome's wars with her neighbours to flowery speeches in the Senate and the declinations of Latin verbs, I rapidly lost interest.

My French teachers were a mixed bag. The only one I could relate to was an young exchange teacher from France. That was most likely because she was so lovely and nice that I was probably in love with her.

Alas, the others were somewhat pompous and dictatorial, thereby ensuring a lukewarm approach on my part to this most important part of my schooling. One teacher in particular got right up my nose. Her name was Miss Weir. She was a tiny woman but built like a pouter pigeon. When she handed out punishment for perceived offences, she had to mount a stool so that she could administer the strap to the boys who already at fourteen or fifteen years of age towered over her. I seemed to be one of her main targets—probably deservedly so—and once, in a spirit of bravado, I incurred her fury by continually moving my hands and arms out of the reach of her furious flailing. In doing so, I inadvertently pulled the strap from her hands and thereby earned a visit to the office of the rector. After being kept waiting for a long period outside his office, I was ushered into his presence. He duly chastised me verbally then proceeded to apply his own large strap to my hands and wrists. I never ever visited the rector again!

I was active in soccer and other school sports during this period and also took part in gym exercises. When I first came to the Greenock high school, our gymnastics instructor was an older ex-army man with a grim determined approach to physical training. It was not much fun. Then we got a new instructor whose name was Paterson, who adopted a different approach to physical exercise that made it much more fun. With the cooperation of the girls' physical training instructor, he encouraged cooperation between both groups in all sports activities.

Through such cooperation we male clods were made to learn to dance with female partners. We learned the tried and true Scottish numbers such as the Eightsome Reel and the Gay Gordons before moving on to the waltz, the quickstep, the slow foxtrot and even the tango. I did not realize it then but later came to know that I had a ready-made passport into the world of male/female relationships. (Greenock High School had separate classes for boys and girls in years one, two and three. In the senior years, four and five, the classes were mixed)

In English, we had a hot-tempered teacher called Murray. Known to us boys behind his back as "the Bonnie Earl of Murray." He was a good teacher but liable to fly off the handle at a moment's notice. On one occasion, he could not find his strap in order to inflict punishment on some poor soul (not me). He searched high and low for the missing strap while we sat back in our seats and rolled our eyes at one another as we realized that his strap had been thrown on top of his tall teacher's cupboard. We were threatened with all sorts of fiendish torture if we did not confess to hiding the elusive strap. A serious stand off was diverted when the dinner gong sounded. During the lunch recess one of our class sneaked into the classroom and placed the missing instrument on his desk. Honour was restored, the offending student forgiven, and the class resumed its studies of Shakespeare or whoever else it was that deserved our attention that day.

I also took art classes, but never could draw or shape or paint worth a damn. Even music lessons were beyond me, much to the despair of my mother, the pianist. There were, however, teachers who could impart history and geography to me, and that I thoroughly enjoyed.

In our spare time, we still spent hours each day in the glen and along the Cut, ranging as far as Shielhill glen and the "Roman bridge" and on down the Kip River to Inverkip. Once we disturbed the grouse on the moors above the Cut and were chased by a very irate gamekeeper who forced us away from the stone crossing bridges and made us attempt to leap the Cut in a single bound. As I recall, we did not quite make it, hitting the far bank with our bellies and then scrambling to our feet in terror before fleeing down into our local glen and then home. Needless to say, none of the foregoing was ever reported to our parents.

Other signs of war: the Clyde anchorages were protected by several batteries of land-based anti-aircraft guns, some based in the hills surrounding Greenock and down the Kip Valley.

In January 1940, I became fifteen years old—almost a man but not quite! In February 1940 the *RMS Queen Elizabeth* came down the Clyde from Clydebank to anchor off the Tail of the Bank. She was painted grey, which suited the dreadful wet grey day. Word of her passage passed rapidly from mouth to mouth and there were tens of thousands there to greet her at all the docks and shipyards and particularly at Princes Pier and the Greenock Esplanade.

The war had been taking a grim toll elsewhere, even if little was happening on the western front. The German attack on Poland was brutally successful, with large parts of the Polish army being destroyed. Then the Russians invaded Poland from the east, to fulfil their part of a secret German-Russian pact to share the spoils of Poland between them. Britain and France could do little to help their Polish ally. Almost all the UK war effort seemed to be taking place at sea. The battleship *Royal Oak* was sunk with heavy loss of life by a daring U-boat commander who penetrated the boom defences of Scapa Floe. German raiding vessels were active in the South Atlantic and Indian oceans, sinking and destroying many British and Allied merchant ships. One such raider was the pocket battleship *Graf Spee*. She was finally tracked down by the British cruisers *Exeter* and *Ajax* and the New Zealand cruiser *Achilles*. After a short but violent battle, she fled to neutral waters in Uruguay. Five days later, she sank herself by scuttling.

The disaster at Scapa Floe caused a large part of the Atlantic fleet to relocate in the firths and lochs of western Scotland, particularly to the Clyde anchorage off the Tail of the Bank, which afforded protection and proximity to maritime industry. The Gareloch, Loch Long and the Holy Loch all took on new significance.

The submarine menace was growing but controllable. The air war was non-existent, with little action by the Germans after the destruction of Poland, and the Royal Air Force confining itself to abortive leaflet dropping over western German cities.

However, on St. Andrew's Day (November 30, 1939), another war began which was to have fateful consequences for Britain and France. Russia attacked Finland on several fronts, claiming parts of Finland for itself as it had been in czarist days. Finland resisted strongly and the world was astonished to see Russia's huge army defeated in battle on every front. However, eventually Russia's preponderance of military strength prevailed and Finland sued for peace on March 12, 1940. Large chunks of Finnish territory were lost. Meanwhile in the west, where much sympathy was felt for the Finns, preparations were underway for a British/French Expeditionary Force to come to their rescue by way of a route across Norway and Sweden. An added bonus would be the interdiction of the German iron ore supply line from Narvik to Bremen. All this came to nought when the Finns surrendered.

However, the Germans were well aware of the potential threat to their iron ore supplies and had made and implemented plans of their own. On the April 9, Germany occupied Denmark and commenced the invasion of Norway. Planning must have been well advanced as, by late on the 9th, all the southern ports were taken either from the sea or by air. The Royal Navy was unable to intercept the German landings on the 9th, so they turned north for Narvik and finally, by the 13th, with the help of the battleship *Warspite*, sank all the German destroyers blockading the port.

Meanwhile, on the 11th, the first troopship convoy sailed from the Clyde for Trondheim and Narvik. Irish guards on *Monarch of Bermuda*, the first battalion Scots Guards on the Polish liner *Batory* and the Yorkshire Light Infantry and the Leicester Regiment on the *Empress of Australia*, together with the French Foreign Legion on board the *Général Paget*. German air power was predominant and the Allies and Norwegians had to abandon plans to retake Trondheim and were left occupying the approaches to Narvik in the north, around Bodo south of the Lofoten Islands, Namsos and Lillehammer on the middle coast. Further, heavy German land and air attacks caused Allied withdrawal from Andalens and Namsos on the 1st and 2nd May, thereby ensuring the capitulation of the remaining Norwegian forces in central Norway. A disaster was in the making!

Deep snow held up operations around Narvik and it was not until May 28th that the port was recaptured by a combined British, Norwegian, French and Polish brigade. Meanwhile, the sea war had gone on with considerable losses on both sides. The Allies were aided greatly by efforts of *HMS Glorious*, an aircraft carrier based on the Clyde, and equipped with Gladiators and Swordfish—ancient aircraft but gallant crews. She also delivered Hurricane fighters to the Trondheim area and received them on deck, a hazardous undertaking during the withdrawal. On the 8th June, it was decided to withdraw all forces from northern Norway as the German attack on the western front was rapidly becoming a rout of Allied armies and air forces. The withdrawal was successful, with all troopships returning safely to the UK. However, *HMS Glorious* was caught by the German battlecruisers *Scharnhost* and *Gneisenau* and sunk with great loss of life. Her two destroyer escorts were also sunk, but one managed to cause great damage to *Scharnhost* by torpedoes and a British submarine caused similar damage to *Gneisenau*, which enabled the troopship convoy to escape unscathed.

I have written about all of this because I felt part of it. The ships I have mentioned were all associated with the Clyde prior to the start of the Norwegian campaign. *HMS Glorious* I recall without any difficulty making her way down the Clyde anchorage to the boom defence barrier at the Cloch lighthouse. From the hills above Gourock town, she looked very elegant in her light grey paint that indicated her former base in the Mediterranean. I was proud to have seen her in all her power and deeply saddened at her sinking with such a huge loss of life.

Figure 14 - View from the Lyle Hill—The Free French Memorial

The seriousness of affairs had been brought even closer to home on the 30th April when the French destroyer *Maille Breze* blew up while anchored off the Tail of the Bank. The explosion was heard for miles around, and the death toll was horrific.

Aside from awe-inspiring events on the world scene and on the Clyde, my life in Greenock continued without undue incident. Besides school and scouts, I continued to deliver milk and rolls early every morning from the Co-op dairy and bakery, and also delivered cakes on Saturday morning. These chores gave me some extra pocket money that I probably spent on sweeties, lemonade, picture shows, comics and other intellectual pursuits. This also enabled me to start dating girls at a fairly early age and show off my prowess as a dancer.

I was too shy to become overly forward, but lust was in my heart, no doubt. One in particular I really liked—her name was Jean Ritchie—good looking, clever, with a good sense of humour. She lived at the other end of town from me. With bus service terminating about ten PM, it meant many long hikes home before that early rise for the dairy delivery. I suppose I was going steady.

I was not overly conscious of the great divide in Greenock when I was growing up. But the invisible barrier between Protestant and Catholic was a fact of life. The population of the town was roughly three quarters Protestant and one quarter Catholic. There were separate schools and even living areas, although that was changing slowly. The Protestant majority was largely composed of Scots from a Renfrewshire and Ayrshire background, while the Catholic minority were the descendants of Irish labourers who came over to Greenock during the industrial expansion period of the middle and late nineteenth century. There were occasional outbreaks of trouble over the years involving hotheads on either side, but in the late thirties these confrontations were few and far between.

A notable exception was on July 12, when large contingents of Orangemen from Northern Ireland and other parts of Scotland joined the parade celebrating King Billy's victory at the battle of the Boyne. These parades were a sight to see! Massive numbers of bowler-hatted Orangemen with huge banners depicting not just the battle of the Boyne but also the Orange dedication to the British cause in the battles of the Great War. Fife and drum bands hammered out tunes such as "The Sash My Father Wore" followed by many pipe bands playing the usual Scottish battle hymns and laments. All the public houses along the parade route closed their doors for self-protection, and the constabulary were out in force.

My family were not supporters of the Orange Order but we certainly were Presbyterian in upbringing and outlook and intermingled with those of our own background. I had one Catholic friend—Fred McCluskey, who lived in our neighbourhood—but I do not recall any others. There were Catholic girls in the adjoining Bow Farm district but, attractive as some were, we instinctively avoided them like the plague, without ever being instructed to do so by adults in authority over us. The great divide was all too real.

Many years later in Canada, I found myself in conversation with a lady of my age who was also a Greenockian. We animatedly exchanged memories of our youth until we suddenly realized that I was a product of my Protestant background and she was from the other side of the great divide. I believe it was a sobering and sad thought for both of us.

At the end of June 1940, my regular school days came to an end. After three years of high school it was obvious to all concerned that further study would not be appropriate for me. I wanted to join the workaday world and my parents reluctantly agreed. However, with the rest of the family, I took part once more in that wonderful annual holiday in Stonehaven and the Ythan Valley. We stayed longer than usual, as Dad felt Mum needed a longer break away from Greenock. It was the first sign of my mother's frailty and ignorant and self-absorbed me failed to register its seriousness. However, I remember it as a happy time!

The war had taken a turn for the worst after the debacle of the Norwegian campaign. The British Expeditionary Force had to be evacuated from Dunkirk under furious attacks from German armour and the Luftwaffe. On June 10 the Fifty-First Highland Division was compelled to surrender at St-Valéry, and on June 22 the French government capitulated to German military might, leaving Britain to fight on alone.

The signs of a country caught shortfooted were fairly obvious to most people. Through Stonehaven flowed many large military lorry and armoured vehicle convoys on their way south to strengthen the main army force in southern England which had left its transport and artillery behind in France. Fighter aircraft patrols were frequent along the coast, and the local papers were full of the names and photos of local lads killed or captured in France.

My brother and I indulged in the usual high jinks at the Stonehaven swimming pool while our parents bowled and took part in other adult pursuits. When we eventually left for our family visit to the farms along the Ythan River we were ready for a quieter time. As usual, we had a wonderful time and were well fed by Aunt Nellie at Chapelton farm. I little realized that this would be my last visit to Chapelton and that I would never see that grand lady again.

Chapter Four

Office Boy, Dog's Body, Preparing for Sea

Upon returning to Greenock in August, I went to work for Ross & Marshall as a lowly office boy. It was probably due to my father's influence that I got the job. He had a wide circle of friends. Ross & Marshall were a well-established shipping and stevedoring company, with offices located in the James Watt Dock. The partners in the firm were still active—Col. Campbell was the man in charge; Col. Marshall appeared to be more active as a tippler and often exuded the smell of strong spirits before departing early for his mansion down river in Skelmorlie. There were other adult employees: senior clerks, accountants, typists, engineers and stevedore foremen, marine superintendents, etc. I recall that the senior clerks wore winged collars and the accountants had eyeshades. An old-fashioned company about to be saddled with huge additional responsibilities.

When I joined the company, their main activities were in stevedoring and managing a small fleet of puffers. These small steamboats plied their trade between Greenock and the lochs and canals of the Firth of Clyde and beyond. They carried their cargoes of coal and sand and rock from Greenock and returned with fish and other goods such as whisky from the isolated western islands. They were a vital link in the commerce of the Clyde. The gangs of stevedores were mainly employed in handling oil and oilseed products, coal, sugar, and other cargoes that utilized the port facilities.

That was all to change just after I became Ross & Marshall's newest employee. The Tail of the Bank anchorage was designated an emergency port authority and small vessels from the continent that had fled the

German onslaught arrived in growing numbers to serve the new port. Additionally, as the bombing of harbours in the south escalated, large numbers of stevedores from the Thames estuary arrived in the Clyde anchorage and were deployed by Ross & Marshall. The fleet of small vessels from the continent, mostly Dutch, also came under the management of the firm. One I remember well. She was a typical Dutch scoot, diesel powered. She was called *Monica* and her cargo was fresh water for the many ships requiring her services. Her captain was also her owner, a typical Dutch arrangement I learned later.

Figure 15 - A Clyde puffer

I soon learned that though I might be called office boy, my duties were of a much more mobile variety. Communication in those days was still largely by the written word, and I was one of the conveyors of the written word, be it orders to ships' masters or stevedoring foremen, or clearance documents to the custom house, or waybills to be paid, or the delivery of fat packets of money to the stevedores who insisted on being paid in cash at the termination of each job. These and many other chores were my exposure to the grown-up world of commerce.

I soon learned my way around the docks and the adjacent shipyards and probably stank of the odours of the oilseed mills, the harbour detritus and the pall of coal dust that seemed to hang over everything. To compound the situation, the hammering noise of metal bashing and shaping and the smell and flash of welding torches together with merry tunes played by the rivetting machines, all added up to a sense of deliberate design-controlled chaos in support of the fight against the Germans.

My mother became an active volunteer in the war effort, serving visiting servicemen at a local women's auxiliary canteen. She also invited a number of naval men to our home for a meal and company. These chaps were all petty officers off the aircraft carrier *Furious* and kept in touch with us for a number of years after. I often saw *Furious* out in the Clyde. Sometimes she was accompanied by the battle cruiser *Hood*. I little realized then that the pride of the Royal Navy would be destroyed by the German battleship *Bismarck* in the space of seconds later in the war.

I had become determined to go to sea and become a deck officer and eventually be the captain of a ship. My early ambitions to be a chocolate seller at railway stations and the engine driver of the flying Scotsman had vanished. Looking back, my ambition probably stemmed from a combination of exposure to Nelson Jamieson, my mother's seafaring cousin, and the tremendous pull of the River Clyde and the activities that could be seen constantly and daily.

In September 1940, I began going to the James Watt School of Navigation in the evenings to partake of instruction in navigation and seamanship. My teacher was Captain Davidson who had formerly been with Paddy Henderson, a company I was to know well in the future. I believe I went to the school three nights each week and tried to absorb the intricacies of chartwork and coastal navigation. I learned about variation and deviation of the magnetic compass and how to plot a position on the nautical chart and to lay off a suitable course for the vessel to follow, also some rudimentary seamanship, some of which I had already been exposed to as a Boy Scout. It all stood me in good stead when I was taken on as cadet by the Henderson Line of Glasgow in the spring of nineteen forty-one.

Meanwhile, the war went on with increasing sinking of merchant ships that were vital to Britain's survival. In addition to London, many large industrial centres in England were attacked from the air and, in March 1941, it became the turn of Clydebank just upriver from Greenock. Many people were killed or injured in the bombing and large parts of Clydeside were devastated. Greenock had a few bombs to deal with as German aircraft became separated from their main attacking force.

The war had migrated from northwestern Europe to the Mediterranean, as Italy entered the war on Germany's side in the summer of 1940. Land battles were being waged in the western desert and in Eritrea, Somalia and Ethiopia, stretching British resources to their limits. Fighting had also taken place in Lebanon and Syria where Vichy French forces threatened British bases in Palestine. Also, the situation in southeast Europe was deteriorating rapidly. Italy's invasion and occupation of Albania in April 1940 had been followed by an attempt to invade Greece in October. The Greeks repelled the Italian invaders and, by November, were occupying large parts of Albania.

That same month the Royal Navy fleet air arm destroyed a large part of the Italian navy in Taranto harbour. In early 1941, Germany occupied Bulgaria, then used it as a springboard to attack Greece. The British position in the Mediterranean had become precarious.

At home, we were all on rations—but somehow my mother continued to cope. I do not recall doing without anything, but chocolate and ice cream went into the difficult to find column. Mentioning ice cream brings to mind an episode in Gourock the day after Italy declared war on Britain. Gourock had lots of ice cream parlours in the vicinity of the pierhead. That afternoon, a small number of agitators congregated close to the ice cream parlours (which were all owned by families with Italian-sounding names) and started to break the glass fronts before going on to pillage the premises. A large crowd of spectators appeared, unsure of what was happening. Then the police arrived on the scene and proceeded to sort out the perpetrators. I was only a bystander but I felt confused about what was going on. The agitators were obviously louts, but the ice cream shops belonged to Italians who were now our enemies—could this mayhem perhaps be justified in some way.

When I got home and told my father what had transpired, he set the entire affair in its proper perspective. One: there is no justification for vandalizing private or public property. Two: some of these Italians were

British subjects and had sons serving in the British Army. Three: the law must be upheld even if the police overly enjoyed their work. I have always regarded his comments as the underpinning of what must be the strength of our democratic society. Justice and fairness for all.

I probably was a typical self-centered youth at this time, with little thought for anyone other than myself. I believe I worked fairly diligently and that I earned the money that I was paid. Perhaps I did some things out of the goodness of my heart, but if so I surely do not remember. My view of religion was a trifle jaundiced, whether it was the Presbyterian version, the Episcopalian or—horror of horrors—the Roman Catholic. So I did not have a faith that I could fall back on in times of trouble. But at that age, I am sure I felt indestructible. I believe that I was not a bad person—no vices that I was aware of—but I had little in the way of any clear philosophy with which to tackle life at sea in an adult world.

I liked girls, but was inhibited enough that contact was friendly but chaste. I may have lusted, but warm kisses were as far as I progressed. Looking back, there were obvious signals that further advances might have been encouraged, but my puritan upbringing always got in the way. Anyhow, I liked some girls' company enormously and they reciprocated, which made these occasions very enjoyable. Dancing, particularly ballroom dancing, was an open sesame to female company if you were light on your feet. I think I put that talent to good use in later life.

I suppose these reflections come to my mind because around this period my mother became quite ill and had to be hospitalized. She seemed to partially recover and was being looked after at home when she passed away in March 1941. I was stunned because she had always been so strong and vital and now suddenly she was dead. My father and brother were devastated. Even now after these many years it is hard to contemplate. I dearly wish I had known her better, loved her more, and paid more attention to her over the years. However, that is the way of the world—if only!!

Shortly after my mother's funeral, I was summoned to Glasgow for an interview by Captain Cattenach, Marine Superintendent, P. Henderson & Company. Their offices were located at 95 Bothwell Street and were rather impressive compared with the utilitarian premises of Ross & Marshall. There were lots of beautiful models of ships, brass work of all sorts, and the occasional Burmese motif. Captain Cattenach was not a large man, but he did possess a rather formidable appearance to my probably overawed eyes. He questioned me closely about my experience and family background, neither of which seemed to impress him. He nevertheless instructed me that I would be hearing from him soon, warned me about the evils of drink and other temptations, and sent me on my way.

Figure 16 - The author as cadet, 1941

I immediately began preparing for my impending departure. Dad was a great deal of help ensuring that I was properly kitted out with serge dress uniforms, patrol jackets, uniform caps, jerseys, tropical kit, dungarees, shirts, ties, underwear, etc. The final acquisition was a large sea chest or trunk.

About the 20th April, I received my official orders, said goodbye to family and friends, and set off on the train for Liverpool. I believe Dad came along as far as Glasgow to make sure I did not get lost. The train journey to Liverpool was largely uneventful, although crowded, mainly with troops going in all directions—with Carlisle Station so packed it appeared to contain most of the British Army. Traffic was slower as we approached Merseyside, with rail tracks still under repair from the latest bombing raid. There was a very nice lady sitting opposite me who explained some of sights we saw. She was the wife of an engineer officer who was on a ship docked in Liverpool and she was on her way to join him for a few days. She appeared to think that I was very young to be going off to sea and wished me all the best in my endeavours.

We were late getting into Central Station in Liverpool, although there was still some daylight. All the taxis and other transport were quickly snapped up, so on the advice of my train companion I managed to hire a man with a small cart who loaded my sea chest on board and so we set off for the Liverpool docks. We were bound for South Sandon Dock where my ship, the *SS Mandalay*, was discharging cargo. The streets we traversed were largely deserted, with destroyed and damaged buildings on either side. In some places, the debris still spilled out into the street and made passage difficult for our small cart. A peculiar smell of decay and perhaps death pervaded the air, although the last heavy bombing raid had occurred in early April. We finally arrived on the Dock Road, which was easily identified by the high stone walls running along its length. We made ourselves known to the docks police on the South Sandon Dock gate and then trundled our way to the *Mandalay's* berth.

Chapter Five

Mandalay

My first sight of *Mandalay*, my future home, was a trifle disconcerting. She was partially discharged, but appeared to be covered with deep brown streaks over her black hull and tan upperworks. She also had a fair list to starboard and generally looked what she was, a disreputable tramp steamer but blessed with a beautiful name.

Somehow or other, I was divested of my sea chest, loaded on board, and shown to my quarters.

Figure 17 - *Mandalay*

Mandalay was an old ship, built in 1911 by Denny's of Dumbarton who built many of the company's ships. She was a three-island type vessel with five cargo holds and two deep tanks. She was about four hundred feet in length with a raised forecastle, midships, and counterstern. In peacetime, *Mandalay* would have had a crew of roughly seventy, but in wartime she carried a crew of seventy five—two additional radio watchkeeping officers and three naval staff to man the defensive weapons now mandatory. There were forty lascars in the crew and they were located in the forecastle. Midships was accommodation for the captain immediately below the bridge. The four cadets were housed on either side of the officers' saloon and pantry in two small cabins fitted with upper and lower bunks. The starboard cabin opened on to the weather deck, but the port cabin opened on to an alleyway leading into the saloon. A cabin housing the Indian butler or chief steward was located directly opposite the port cadets' cabin. I lucked out and got a berth in the port cabin.

The other deck officers and the engineers lived in midships cabins under the boatdeck. On the after end of the boatdeck, there were cabins for the radio operators, their equipment, and the naval personnel. There was no accommodation on the raised stern housing. It contained a steering flat and above it a gun deck to support an elderly four-inch anti-submarine weapon. The ship was powered by a triple expansion steam engine that could propel the craft through the water at the magnificent speed of ten knots. She was equipped with five-ton SWL Derricks, and two heavy-lift derricks, one at cargo hatch two and one at cargo hatch four.

Before proceeding further, I must mention my immediate impressions on viewing and boarding *Mandalay* that day. She was unkempt on deck as I have already indicated, but over all drifted the sweet smell of dates and figs—the source of the dark brown streaks on hull and upperworks. All caused, as I soon discovered, by the careless unloading habits of Liverpool stevedores. A large part of the ship's cargo consisted of figs and dates loaded when *Mandalay* visited ports in Turkey. Certainly the chaos and untidiness of the decks did not spill over into the accommodation, thank the Lord.

There were normally four cadets on board *Mandalay*. When I joined her in Liverpool, two had already departed on leave but two remained—Sutherland and Winstanley. Winstanley was ready to come ashore to study for his second mate's certificate of competency, having served his mandatory four years at sea. I must admit I was fascinated by him. Although only a small chap, he exuded confidence and worldliness, dapper in his shore-going uniform. He departed in a few days and it was to be fifty-odd years later before I would see him again, many thousands of miles away to the west of Liverpool. Another new cadet joined the ship at the same time as I did. He was a Welshman, Hubert Jenkins, a Conway boy. His father was captain of *Daldorch*, a newly acquired cargo steamer that had joined the Henderson fleet.

The mates and engineers were largely standby officers, and I cannot remember their names; however, one of the junior engineers had been a survivor from the sinking of the *Empire Citizen* (formerly the German vessel *Wahehe*) in February 1941. He was one of only five who lived to see another day. He told me about the cadet who survived, David Peebles, who apparently boasted to his companions that he would last longer as he could live off his extra fat. Unfortunately for David, he was lost later in the war when *Kambe* disappeared somewhere off the coast of West Africa, a mystery that has never been solved. Another engineer had been in the British Army in the retreat through France and had bitter memories of the unhelpful attitude of French civilians in the embarkation area around Rouen.

Our lascar crew were still a puzzle to me, as I was slowly learning their many roles in support of the proper functioning of the ship. Probably my earliest interface with the Indian crew members was through the butler and the stewards assigned to the officers' saloon. My tummy was way ahead of my mind as usual.

The discussion of food among former Paddy Henderson cadets raises differences of opinion even today. I, however, enjoyed the fare on *Mandalay* in 1941 and have fond memories of rice cakes and syrup for breakfast, together with fish kedgeree, followed by mulligatawny soup and curried lamb and chicken for other meals. These meals were served to us in the saloon by Indian waiters. We had to dress in uniform for meals, but otherwise wore dungarees for dirty deck and hold work, of which there was plenty. In particular, polishing the brasswork on the bridge and monkeysisland was a never-ending task. These tasks were soon to be put aside in the days that followed. But first a little bit of information about *Mandalay's* previous voyage.

She had sailed from Liverpool in August 1940, loaded with general cargo and military equipment bound for ports in Turkey. In peacetime, she would have simply voyaged through the Mediterranean, but that sea now being closed to British and Allied vessels, she was forced to circumnavigate the Cape of Good Hope and make her way north into the

Indian Ocean, the Red Sea and Gulf of Suez, then through the Suez Canal to the Aegean Sea and the Dardanelles. The first part of the voyage was in convoy, which was attacked by U-boats. When west of the Azores, *Mandalay* went its separate way, arriving at Durban, South Africa, on the 20th September, to coal bunker and adjust her degaussing gear. From Durban, she headed north up the Indian Ocean and Red Sea, then through the Suez Canal to Port Said.

There she joined a convoy that took them up into the Aegean Sea and thence to Turkey. After discharging her cargo in various ports, *Mandalay* loaded her cargo of boxwood, dried fruit, tobacco and aniseed and, in January 1941, sailed for Piraeus and Port Said and the Suez Canal. Next stop was Mombasa on the east coast of Africa, but not before having a lucky escape from a German raider. After completing bunkering in Mombasa, she made her way without incident to Durban—five long months since their outward-bound visit! The next brief stop was Capetown again, then northward into the South Atlantic heading for Freetown, Sierra Leone, the convoy assembly port.

The voyage home was not uneventful, nevertheless *Mandalay* docked safely in Liverpool on the 24th April after a period of nine and a half months away from home. I wondered whether my first voyage would be as long or as interesting. The cadets had already supplied me with all the titbits and events that had made the voyage memorable for each of them.

My arrival on board *Mandalay* must have been on the 25th or 26th April, and after quickly familiarizing myself with the shore ship routine, and among all the unloading confusion where I felt like a fifth wheel, I took early opportunity to see something of the great seaport of Liverpool.

The Dock Road and others running off it were relatively clear of debris, and buses were running in daytime but on a severely reduced schedule. Somehow or other, I found my way to the pierhead and all the main streets of the city. Lime Street, Grafton Street, Lord Street, South Castle Street, Church Street, all teemed with life. Magnificent buildings such as the Liver Building and the Liverpool Corn Exchange dominated the horizon. It was a vibrant city indeed. I decided to investigate further on the following weekend when I expected to be off duty. Meanwhile, I rode on the overhead railway that traversed Dockland, getting to know the location of South Sandon to the many other tidal docks that stretched along the south bank of the Mersey River.

It was on the overhead railway that I first tasted alcohol. A drunken docker belligerently insisted that I take a sip of his bottle. To avoid further embarrassment, I finally weakened and took a wee sip. I little realized that I had taken a fateful step that day on the Overhead—I liked the taste!

Routine on board for we cadets seemed to consist mainly of cleaning up after the mess left by the stevedores and taking training from the naval gunlayer on how to load and unload the two Hotchkiss machine guns secured on either wing of the bridge deck. We also practised fire drill frequently, as incendiary bombing attacks, both at sea and in port, were anticipated. The need for this training became very apparent on the first of May, which ensured my final steps into manhood.

Chapter Six

The May Blitz

Merseyside had been bombed many times before, but on the first of May 1941, the Germans commenced an eight-night assault on the area with heavy bomb concentrations on Liverpool and Bootle and slightly lesser on Birkenhead and Wallasey. We on board *Mandalay* in South Sandon Dock were right in the middle of it all.

May 1 was a Thursday and I had been given shore leave, which I took in seeing the sights. Lots of shoppers around, sunny weather, very pleasant. A strange incident sticks in my mind, where a young girl followed me around Lime Street—too young to be a Maggie May clone—heaven only knows what was on her mind. I returned to *Mandalay* for supper, read for a while, then was called to action stations about 10 PM. Lots of anti-aircraft fire, followed by the dropping of hundreds of incendiaries, and then the deep thud-and-thump of high explosive bombs. I was stationed in the officers' saloon with stirrup pump at the ready and praying for the chance to man the Hotchkiss machine gun and shoot down a bomber.

It was a fairly light raid in our area, but did provide some excitement when a stick of incendiaries landed on a dockside shed across the dock from us. A Blue Star ship unloading her refrigerated meat cargo was in extreme danger, but crew members clambered onto the roof of the building and, with some effort, extinguished the flames. There was another ship in South Sandon Dock, the *Chantilly,* a Free French vessel painted light Mediterranean grey and, with the bomber moon, she stuck out like a sore thumb. In the middle of all the action, she additionally and probably inadvertently displayed lights that brought about roars of rage from *Mandalay* and the Blue Star ship. In our defence we were still suspicious of the French after their astonishing capitulation to Germany. The raid finished about 1 AM and we all settled down for a well-deserved rest.

The night of the 2nd May was a different story. It was another night of bright moonlight that the bombers used to advantage. The bombing started at about 10 PM and continued in waves until after 1 AM the following morning. It appeared to be mainly concentrated on the downtown core, but we were targeted when bombs hit the refrigeration plant and the overhead railway in our vicinity. The smell of roasting meat permeated the air for days after. Sticks of bombs landed not very far away but did not damage us. Manning of the Hotchkiss machine guns did not produce a worthwhile target, and the buckets of sand and stirrup pump were not required.

Figure 18 - Liverpool city centre destroyed, May 1941

We were getting weary with our overnight shenanigans but little knew that the ordeal was to continue for several more nights. Saturday, the 3rd May was another beautiful day but by 10 PM the dusk brought the sound of air raid warning sirens and the distant drone of aircraft, together with rumble of anti-aircraft artillery. By 10:30 PM we were being subjected to a furious bombing attack by waves of German aircraft. This continued with short intervals of quiet until about 3 AM when we were able to assess the extent of damage to the docks and the city. It was horrendous! A large part of the city centre had been destroyed—large portions of South Castle Street, Lord Street and Church Street were reduced to rubble, together with the transportation and communication systems. The Dock Road and the overhead railway were in a shambles and smoke and fire raged in the dock area.

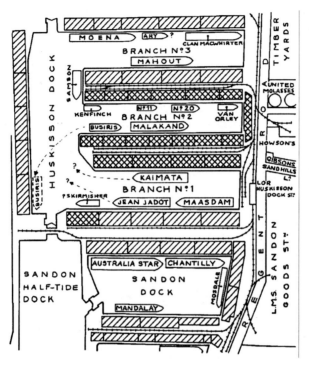

Figure 19 - Plan of vessel placement, Huskisson/Sandon docks, May 1941

It was particularly bad in Huskinson Dock just north of our berth in South Sandon. There, an accident of war had escalated into an enormous tragedy. A partly inflated barrage balloon fell on the deck of the Brockelbank ship *Malakand*, which was carrying in excess of one thousand tons of high explosive in her holds. The barrage balloon burst into flames but the fire was contained and finally extinguished by the ships crew. Meanwhile a shower of incendiaries and several high-explosive bombs had fallen on some neighbouring dock sheds and the resulting flames soon enveloped *Malakand* from stem to stern. The fight to save *Malakand* went on all during the worst of the bombing. However, the situation was desperate by the time the "all clear" air raid signal had sounded around 3 AM. Plans were then made to scuttle her by cutting a hole on her port side, but the ship blew up before the project got underway.

I vaguely recall the tremendous bang that rocked *Mandalay* and snapped some of her mooring lines—confusion reigned! We had been resting and were completely confused, as the all clear signal had signified no danger. We were shortly thereafter ordered to evacuate the ship and finally gathered with many others from other ships and dock workers about a mile away from the danger area. It was now about 5 AM and rumours flew among us while we avoided going into the square brick and concrete bomb shelters that wardens and police expected us to enter. They seemed more like dark smelly death traps to us than places of safety. Gradually, we were made aware of what had occurred and what might still happen.

Figure 20 - *Malakand*

Several additional explosions took place, but they were not of the severity of the first one, which sent steel plates from the vessel's hull soaring over two and a half miles away before crashing in the suburbs of the city. One of *Malakand's* four-ton anchors landed one hundred yards away on top of a sunken steam hopper. The whole of Huskinson Dock was demolished, with stone walls crumbled to dust. The dock overhead railway station had collapsed, together with many other dockside sheds. The loss of life was heavy. Firefighters and explosives experts dominated the scene. We were rather thirsty and hungry by the time we were allowed to return to *Mandalay*. I do remember, however, a mobile canteen arriving, manned by Women's Volunteer Services workers who dished out welcome hot tea and milk. It had been a night of unmitigated horror for many, but thanks to the selfless devotion of the whole civil defence apparatus, it was not very much worst.

Figure 21 - Destruction of *Malakand*, May 1941

That morning, May 4, brought a great change to Merseyside. The streets were blocked with tumbled masonry, covered with billions of shards of broken glass, and snakes of water hoses everywhere. The air was sharp and acrid and stung the eyes and blocked the nose. A pall of smoke and dust hung over everything. It all seemed hopeless but, by nightfall, most clearance, demolition, and salvage had been accomplished. Some fires were still burning, and the *Malakand* continued to burn white-hot with an orchestral accompaniment of occasional flashes and roars of exploding shells and bombs. On board *Mandalay,* we cleaned up as best we could and prepared for what the night would bring.

The Germans were late on the night of the 4th May, arriving just after midnight, but then keeping us on our toes until around 4 AM. It began fairly quietly, but soon wave after wave of enemy aircraft bombarded the city and docks. I even remember seeing a ship at anchor in the river hit and sent on fire. Heavy anti-aircraft shells appeared to force the waves to higher altitudes than in previous nights, preventing accurate target bombing. It was certainly a milder attack than the holocaust of Saturday night, but everyone was getting very groggy and tired, those of us who were lucky enough to survive.

Around midnight on the 5th May, the Germans arrived again and continued their punishment of Merseyside until just after 4 AM, when they headed back to their home bases, with everyone hoping that our night fighters would take a heavy toll. There was heavy damage in the city, but the docks for once were largely spared.

Another heavy attack took place on the 6th May, with the first aircraft arriving overhead shortly before midnight. By now, little work was being accomplished during the day, as all attention had to be paid to being wide awake and sharp when the horrible noise of the air raid warning sirens sounded. Little work was underway discharging our cargo as the rail lines leading to the dock sheds had been damaged and our dock shed was suffering structural damage. Harrington, West Toxteth and Brunswick Dock were extensively damaged. We did man the Hotchkiss again, but the bombers were flying too high, which was probably just as well—we were not exactly professional gunners.

The night of the 7th May was the last of the Merseyside May Blitz. It commenced again around midnight. The deterioration of the roads, communications and water supplies, together with the exhaustion of the firefighters was becoming all too obvious. Within a fairly short time, a curtain of flame encompassed Dockland from Seaforth to South Sandon. We spent some of our time extinguishing incendiaries while diving for cover when sticks of high explosives could be heard heralding their

approach with a terrifying whistle. I found myself once cowering for protection inside a coil of large hawser, then again diving
with others as large metal dock shed doors crashed onto the deck and superstructure of *Mandalay*. It was quite a night. We were extremely lucky not to have sustained any casualties, while many others died— ship's crews, firefighters, wardens and other brave souls. At 4:30 AM on the 8th May, the all clear sounded and the ordeal came to an end. Amid the smoking ruin of Dockland, we cleared up where possible and thought with a mix of fear and defiance about the night of the 8th May to come.

To everyone's great relief, the May Blitz had ended. No sirens disturbed our rest that night or any of the nights to come while *Mandalay* berthed at Merseyside. We could only add up the butcher's bill. Seventeen hundred people were killed and another twelve hundred souls seriously injured. Countless buildings destroyed, together with transportation and communication systems. Manufactured goods, foods, armaments and shipping, and many other irreplaceable items and institutions vanished forever. The wealth of a proud seaport had been plundered and its people demanded revenge. There had been some questions about the people's morale as the May Blitz wore on, some of the fear and rumour being spread by the IRA and their sympathizers. Wild stories about food riots and martial law were circulating in some circles, but the vast majority of folks just shrugged and got on with their job. My admiration for the fighting spirit of Merseysiders stems from that time and has never wavered. That spirit was clearly expressed by the shipping tonnages landed through the stricken and embattled Docklands during the May Blitz and immediately afterward:

Week ending May 3, 1941 – 145,596 tons
May 10, 1941 –   35,026 tons
June 14, 1941 – 126,936 tons.

What we did not know at the time was that Hitler was preparing for a massive attack on Russia and the bombardment of Britain would be reduced in size until he achieved his primary objective. We were thankful for a period of quiet recovery. I telegraphed my father in Greenock that all was well and was shocked and surprised to receive a reply indicating that Greenock had its own Blitz on the nights of 6th and 7th May but family was all well and accounted for.

Although not as severe as the attack on Merseyside, the Greenock Blitz was concentrated on a town and surrounding district with a population a twentieth that of Merseyside. The attacks killed about three hundred people and severely injured around the same number. The ships off the Tail of the Bank were probably targeted by the Luftwaffe, but anti-aircraft defences on either side of the river forced the planes inland so that bombing runs had to be made across the river in a north-south direction rather than following the east-west route of the river itself. This resulted in heavy damage to the town, with no ship being hit. However, the sugar refineries and distilleries were quickly set on fire and became beacons guiding wave after wave of enemy bombers. Although shipyards and drydocks were hit, the damage was comparatively light. I felt for my hometown and its people.

Chapter Seven

Birkenhead

Back in South Sandon Dock, we finally completed discharging our dates and figs and locked out into the Mersey River behind an Anglo-Saxon oil tanker bound outward to join a North Atlantic convoy. The crew on her stern had obviously been celebrating or drowning their sorrows, as bottles were consumed and thrown into the lock just in front of our bow. I wondered at what they felt awaited them out on the ocean.

Our destination, however, was not the ocean, not yet. We made our way slowly with the aid of tugs into the West Float tidal basin in Birkenhead on the Cheshire side of the Mersey River. After preparing *Mandalay* for receiving cargo, we commenced loading general cargo bound for Burma. Burma, of course, was a Paddy Henderson fiefdom, so perhaps at this point a short potted history of Paddy Henderson would be in order.

Paddy Henderson and his brothers started their shipping business in the early part of the nineteenth century, trading between Scotland, the Italian peninsula and the Levant with a few small vessels. They typically carried coal or cotton goods to the Mediterranean, returning to Scotland with marble and spices. In the 1840s, they expanded their interests to New Zealand with shiploads of Scottish immigrants to the South Island. These were larger clipper ships, always in need of a suitable return cargo, which they sought around the China Sea, the East Indies, and the Bay of Bengal. Cargoes were hard to find and it was not until the 1850s that a firm link with Burma was established.

At the same time as an opportunity for trade with Burma was presenting itself, the company became involved in the Crimean War. In 1854, the French government required transport vessels to move its troops to the Crimea. This task was accomplished with dispatch and with considerable profit to Paddy Henderson. Indeed, the French government was so pleased that they granted the company the right to fly the tricolour incorporated into their house flag.

 The link with Burma came about as a result of the British occupation of southern Burma and the establishment of the port of Rangoon. Cargoes of teak and rice became available in ever growing quantities. By 1861, Paddy Henderson was operating regular traders between Glasgow and Rangoon. This trade was even more firmly placed when the Irrawaddy Flotilla & Burmese Steam Navigation Company was formed to conduct inland river navigation within Burma. With the opening of the Suez Canal in 1871 and the demand for increased and faster passenger traffic, the company built a small fleet of steamers to supplant the clippers.

A regular service to Burma was soon operating. One of these ships was the original *Mandalay*, built in 1872 at Denny's of Dumbarton. Others were the *Amarapoora*, which was wrecked on the Maldive Islands and the *Tenasserim*, which was wrecked just south of Cape Guardafui, the most easterly point of the African continent, then looted by Somali tribesmen, before the passengers and crew were rescued by the steamer *Kwangtung*. Troubles in upper Burma affected the trade in the late 1870s. But a few years later trade was expanding again and the company added Calcutta to its ports of call by agreement with the City Line.

In 1889, the Bibby Line entered into competition with the company on the UK-Burma route. The Burma trade was certainly expanding, but would now have to be shared with an aggressive competitor. Another development in the mid-1890s was the sacking of Scottish crews and substituting lascars in their place. The decision was defended on the grounds of the difficulty of dealing with troublesome Scottish crews and of course a saving in the wage bill. The fact that the competition—Bibby, P&O, British India, etc.—were all employing lascar crews was also cited as reason for change. Looking back on things after all these years, it was probably the engine rooms, with their heat and ever-present danger, liable to explode into physical confrontation at any moment, that determined the decision. No wonder we had an aggrieved seafaring population many years later.

At the outbreak of war in 1914, the company had eleven steamers on the Burma trade. Nine vessels had passenger accommodation and two were strictly cargo ships, one of which was *Mandalay*, built in 1911 and the centrepiece of this particular part of my story. *Mandalay* and eight others of the fleet survived the Great War, with only *Pegu* and *Ava* being sunk by enemy action. One remarkable feat saved another vessel, *Bhamo*, after she was badly damaged by enemy mines. The sinking vessel was slowly steamed in high seas toward Capetown with a skeleton crew under the command of her master, Captain J. Cattanach, the same marine superintendent who interviewed me in early April 1941.

Figure 22 - *Kemmendine*, sunk in 1940 in the Indian Ocean by a German raider

Between the wars, Paddy Henderson continued the service to Burma and added to the fleet while retiring older and unsuitable vessels. Entering World War II in 1939, the fleet was composed of thirteen ships, with *Mandalay* being the oldest. Eight of the ships were semi-passenger, the remainder cargo-carrying freighters. *Pegu* was wrecked in the approaches to the Mersey early in the war. *Kemmendine* was sunk by a German raider in 1940 while seven hundred miles south of Ceylon. The survivors became prisoners of war in occupied Europe or, in some unlucky cases, in Italian Somaliland where they were badly treated. However, they were rescued when Somaliland was captured by British troops later in 1940. The only other Paddy Henderson manned ship lost prior to May 1941 was the *Empire Citizen*, a Ministry of War Transport-owned vessel—the former German ship *Wahehe*—mentioned on an earlier page. The fleet was bolstered by the addition of the newly constructed cargo ship *Kalewa* in 1940 and the *Daldorch* and *Dalhanna* purchased from Campbell & Son of Glasgow. Subtracting losses, our strength now stood at fourteen in May 1941.

The West Float was a bit of a change from South Sandon with its pall of dust, damage and clean-up activities. Parts of the East Float had received damage in an earlier bombing but our part of the West Float was relatively unscathed. The wharf was regularly used by both Paddy Henderson and the Bibby Line for the Burma trade. The stevedores were familiar with our cargo and *Mandalay's* special peculiarities—derricks, deep tanks, winches, etc. I believe the mate and the master were very pleased to be out of Liverpool and in the hands of seemingly knowledgeable fellows.

Our cargo was varied, consisting of many cases of Tennants lager, medicinal wine, nylon stockings, gas masks, clothing, military equipment, chemist's supplies, biscuits, and many other items too numerous to enumerate. Additionally, tobacco products were loaded into the deep tanks where they could be kept safely under lock and key. One of my first duties was to guard a particular hold that contained pilferable items. I soon discovered that this was a hopeless task as the dockers were all bigger and older than me and very accomplished in stealing while not above intimidating me if I was overly anxious to protect some attractive goods. A policeman I was not cut out to be. Like the other cadets, I found myself reporting some blatant thefts and winking at other less obvious ones. Such is the path of corruption!

The two most popular items of plunder for the dockers were the medicinal wine and the nylon stockings. The wine to drink down in the hold with the stockings smuggled ashore for girl friends or the black market. As the loading progressed, I got to know Birkenhead. It was of course nothing as big and sprawling as Liverpool, but it did have a certain charm, and reminded me of Greenock. I found that in uniform I was welcome in Young Men's Christian Association and Salvation

Army canteens and lounges and visited a few. However, it was a bit boring for me as they were mostly filled with army privates, just conscripted and very homesick.

Although only sixteen and below drinking age, I soon found that, in uniform, I could bluff my way into public houses and so made one further step on the road to perdition. I joined with other cadets and engineers joyously on that road, while keeping my consumption fairly low. I had no taste for beer then and drank mainly port wine, but in small quantities. Spirits I eschewed, probably mostly because of cost, my earnings being six pounds fifty shillings a month, and most of that a war bonus of five pounds. There was not much left for fun and games. The pubs, of course, were always full of girls—another drawing card. However, they were mostly older than me and certainly more experienced. Although tempted, I refrained. My fall from grace was yet to come.

There was great hilarity in our small group at these encounters in local pubs that clustered around the West Float. I suppose in part we were winding down after the bombing across the river. Some of our gang wandered off with female partners and then worried themselves sick over the possibility of becoming infected. I recall one episode on board ship after such an affair when it was decided that the mouthwash Dettol would be a suitable cleanser of exposed genitals. This decision was taken without medical advice. The resultant howls of anguish from the worried Lotharios woke up the entire midships company. The mate on watch blasted everyone in sight and we all trooped off to our bunks, chastened but hardly any wiser than before.

The visits to the locals were really few and far between. Mostly, we were occupied with keeping the brasswork around the bridge and monkey island polished and gleaming, preparing cluster lights for work in the holds, spying on the dockers, keeping watch on the gangway, etc. There was no time for learning any seamanship skills or studying texts on navigation. We did, however, ensure that the red ensign was hoisted and lowered at the appropriate times—8 AM and sunset—and tidied up the flag signal locker for use when we sailed. While working, we dressed in dungarees, but had to dress up with a dark blue patrol jacket and matching trousers for each meal appearance.

I was now more aware of our Indian crew and the duties they performed. They were all based in Rangoon, but hailed mostly from Bengal. They were largely an intelligent lot with a limited English vocabulary, although some of the senior staff had little difficulty making themselves understood. Obviously, a smattering of Hindustani or Urdu would be of great help in conversing with any of them. I regret to say that I only mastered a few phrases during my career with Paddy Henderson and some of those were scarcely printable. I soon, however, learned that the serang was the equivalent of bosun, tindal the bosun's mate, and cashab the storekeeper, with seacunny the quartermaster. The serang was a man of great authority and was the spokesman for the crew. The deck crew were mostly Moslem but the engine room crew were a mix of Hindu and Buddhist. The steward staff were Hindu and Christian. With the exception of the butler who lived midships with the cadets, the lascar crew lived on the forecastle deck, deck on one side and engine room on the other. Two separate galleys in the mast house on the foredeck served their needs. Their quarters were cramped, making ours seem palatial in comparison. The stale air and smell of unwashed bodies did not encourage exploration, although in fairness to the crew they did seem keen on personal hygiene and washed a great deal. Of course, the coal trimmers were always seeking a wash—what a rotten job they had!

My own personal washing habits were centered largely around one bucket of fresh water a day. I was still struggling with the personal laundry business, something I never had to contend with at home. No doubt a suitable laundry or dohbe wallah would have taken on my chore, but I had little money to spare and it never really entered my mind to employ someone. There were no washing or drying machines; indeed, such luxuries were very much of the future. That one galvanized steel bucket had to do for all necessary washing for the foreseeable future.

Chapter Eight

Return to the Clyde

On the 22nd May, I was entered into the ship's articles in Birkenhead by the master, Captain Kenneth Beaton, as a cadet signed on to take part in a foreign going voyage. *Mandalay* departed the West Float into the Mersey River on the 23rd May. My station was on the bridge, and I was tasked with assisting the master and third mate in communicating instructions to the 1st mate in the bow and the 2nd mate on the stern. I was really a dogsbody or gopher charged with conveying messages by phone or in person to the bow or the stern. As the phone often packed up, I did a lot of running. There was, of course, a Mersey River pilot on board, whose presence on board was signified by the letter H flag flying from the bridge halliard. The weather was brisk for late May and promised choppy seas to come.

We were only half loaded with mixed cargo and were ordered to Glasgow to complete loading for Burma. We joined a single line of vessels making their way toward Liverpool Bay, passing the sad-looking wreck of the *Pegu* on the Crosby shore. By the time we dropped the pilot in Liverpool Bay, the weather was freshening considerably and *Mandalay* went on convoy sea watches—four hours on and four off. The convoy that formed up consisted of six ships bound for Belfast and the River Clyde. By the time we rounded the Isle of Man, it was blowing a full gale and becoming decidedly uncomfortable. I felt a bit ill but managed my watches and did not disgrace myself.

One thing that sticks in my mind was the revelation that *Mandalay* was full of cockroaches. I had seen a few while we were in port, but at sea was presented with an unbelievable sight. As the ship was completely blacked out, all doors opening onto decks were fitted with electric switches that cut off the light when the door swung open and switched on when the door closed. I was ordered to the saloon pantry to make the officer of the watch's cocoa. When the door closed I was astounded to see myriads of cockroaches of all sizes and shapes crawling over the pantry hot plates, the sinks, the bulkheads, deckhead, and deck. The officer of the watch received his cocoa later than he had expected as I tried to destroy every cockroach in sight. I looked upon the saloon pantry with some suspicion from that night forward.

The weather moderated as we approached the Ailsa Craig and by late afternoon on the 24th May were through the boom defences at the Cloch and awaiting pilotage upriver to Glasgow. From the Tail of the Bank, Greenock looked at first glance relatively untouched by the bombing, but a closer scrutiny showed damaged buildings on the hills and down closer to the water's edge. I was anxious to talk to my father and brother.

Figure 23 - HMS Hood

We docked in Princes Dock, Glasgow, on the 25th May and began preparing *Mandalay* for loading cargo. I managed to get a day off and travelled down to Greenock to be with family. Dad and Gordon were well as was Mary Fernie, my mother's friend, who had volunteered to be dad's housekeeper after my mother passed away in late March. They had all been extremely lucky, as a stick of bombs had destroyed several homes

on Waverly Street and Bannockburn Street, which were very close.
I probably dominated the conversation, babbling on about *Mandalay* and
my Merseyside experiences.

Figure 24 - The river at Glasgow in the 1950s

Meanwhile, the war had continued, and to a new member of the
merchant navy it was getting close to home. On May 24, the German
battleship *Bismark* broke out into the Atlantic Ocean after totally
destroying *HMS Hood*, the Royal Navy's proudest vessel. There were only
three survivors out of a crew of sixteen hundred men. I was quite upset at
what had happened to Britain's mightiest battlecruiser as I remembered
her frequent appearances off the Tail of the Bank during the Norwegian

campaign. Luckily, honour was retrieved on the 27th May when *Bismark* was sunk by ships of the home fleet. She took more than two thousand sailors to the bottom with her.

Steaming up the River Clyde from the Tail of the Bank to Glasgow was a wonderful experience for someone who had visited Glasgow many times but always before by train or bus. The river is truly beautiful from Langbank to Dumbarton but from Oldkilpatrick on the north shore and Renfrew on the south it became a bustling, noisy, dirty, thriving centre of industrial activity.

On either side of the river stretched many shipyards and engine shops, all busily producing the maritime tools of war. The hammer of the rivet guns and the arcing of the welding torches dominated everything. Beyond this large area of bedlam, and closer to the city centre lay the Princes and Queens Docks. They were filled with ships loading and discharging various cargos. Many additional wharves lined either river bank. Downstream, opposite the River Cart, lay Rothesay Dock, which handled mainly coal, iron ore and other minerals. In the vicinity of Shieldhall on the south bank was the most modern of the docks, King George V, opened by King George V himself in 1931 in his royal yacht naturally called *King George V*.

Being headquarters for Paddy Henderson, we were besieged by various office wallahs from 95 Bothwell street. This meant mounting a special gangway watch dressed in full uniform with collar and tie and even gloves. What a pain in the derrière! When not engaged in these duties, we seemed to spend most of our time down the holds futilely attempting to prevent the Glasgow dockers from broaching cargo. What a useless job it was. These Glaswegians were much more aggressive and enterprising than their Birkenhead counterparts. Much of our cargo consisted of spirits—whisky, gin, rum, brandy—and became a prime target for these latter-day pirates. They would deliberately arrange to have a sling of cases of whisky bang against the hatch coaming, thereby ensuring a shower of good scotch whisky would drop into the hold where their comrades would be waiting with outstretched cans and bowls to recover as much of the loot for immediate consumption as possible.

It was theft on a spectacularly grand scale—wrong, but I was left with a sneaking admiration for their chutzpah. Any other pilferable items in the holds, and there were many, were considered fair game. The standards of right and wrong that I had been imbued with by parents, the kirk and school were all under attack and I was somewhat confused. Reporting any of these shenanigans to higher authority was unproductive. The mates were cynical, and my fellow cadets thought that the whole business was great fun. I joined the cynics!

The weather in early June on Clydeside was wonderful that year. It was made even better by the fact that Greenock was close by and I was able to visit fairly frequently. In addition to family, I saw something of two young ladies who just happened to have the first name of Jean—a good Scottish name. One was Jean Ritchie from my school days, the other was Jean Anderson who worked with me at Ross & Marshall. The first Jean was pretty and good company but still full of high school concerns, while I probably babbled on about *Mandalay* and all the wonderful things I was doing or was involved with. Her parents were a bit religious, and her mother belonged to some society that wanted to outlaw liquor completely. Although I was hardly at that point a drinking man, I sensed that as a seafarer I was suspect and a possible danger to her daughter. This Jean had lovely brown eyes.

The other Jean had lovely blue/grey eyes and was a tempting witch to me. We had flirted a bit in the Ross & Marshall offices, even getting into some rather heavy clinches in a back office during lunch break. She was a honey, older than me by several years, and no doubt a lot more experienced. I was like the moth to the flame. On my visit, I took her to Cragburn Pavilion to trip the light fantastic. Her sister travelled by bus with us to Gourock and kept telling Jean that I was far too young for her, but in my uniform I looked older and no doubt cut a dashing figure.

Cragburn was grand fun and we danced until closing time before getting the last bus home with Jean to Port Glasgow where she lived. We ended up in the hills above Port Glasgow clinched in passionate embrace until 3 AM or thereabouts. We swore undying love, but she was already engaged to an Australian airman, so I did not expect too much. I believe I presented her with a pair of purloined nylons and some duty-free cigarettes. I knew it could not last, but it was my first really truly passionate experience. We corresponded for some time afterward but wartime mails and other events conspired to terminate our connection.

I did hear that she married her Australian. I hope she had a very happy and fruitful life. Her nickname for me was "Young Lochinvar," rather fanciful, but I am sure quite sincere.

On another visit home, I took my cabinmate with me, Hubert Jenkins. My folks were impressed by this polished, articulate, and friendly young cadet, who was so much more sophisticated than me. My brother obviously thought I was out of my depth trying to emulate this product of the training ship *Conway*. In addition, his father was the captain of *Daldorch*, a recently acquired ship, and was also a holder of the Distinguished Service Cross for Great War exploits. Heady company indeed. Jenky was however taken with my father's paintings of the River Rhine and acquired when he served in the British Army of occupation. More about Jenky and his family later in the narrative.

We completed loading our cargo for Burma around the 10th June and moved downriver to Rothesay Dock for bunkering. This was a new experience for me and I expected to dress in dungarees preparatory to engaging in some filthy clean-up activities. However, the cadets were ordered to gangway watch as Captain Cattanach, Chief Marine Superintendent, would be paying *Mandalay* an official visit prior to our departure from the Clyde. There we were, dressed in our finest, clean white collars and full uniform as the coal cascaded from the loading platform into the bunker hatches while coal dust settled over the entire ship and most of all on to us. What a stupid experience! I began to question the wisdom of my superiors, notably our own first mate and of course Captain Cattanach. It took many soakings in laundry buckets before my white shirts and collars returned to anything like normal.

Our voyage down the river to the Tail of the Bank was uneventful, anchoring there on a grand summer evening of the 13th June. No leave was given, so I mooned around the decks gazing at Port Glasgow and visualizing my passionate amour. We practised gunnery with the DEMS Royal Navy ratings on board and started to learn gun drill on our four-inch gun. The gun was positioned on a turret above *Mandalay's* counter stern. It was an ancient weapon manufactured in 1910, older than our ancient ship. Shell and cordite cartridge were separate, making the loading procedure slow and a bit more hazardous.

Other preparations for sea continued with shining brass still to the fore. On the 16th June, the other ships destined for our North Atlantic convoy had assembled and one by one we wended our way down the firth past the Cumbrae and Ailsa Craig to the North Channel where we formed up in eight lines, each containing seven vessels of various shapes and sizes. Our anti-submarine escort consisted of several converted trawlers, two elderly destroyers and a more modern one housing the escort commander. Convoys were sometimes protected against enemy raiders by the presence of an armed merchant cruiser, usually a converted pre-war passenger liner.

The weather was freshening; I was feeling uncomfortable as a great adventure lay ahead.

Chapter Nine

To Burma via the Cape

I wish that I could remember all that happened on the next few days after the convoy assembled and maneouvered itself into eight columns roughly three cables apart with each column containing seven ships in line ahead roughly two cables apart. I kept my watch, four hours on, four off, mostly as a lookout on the wing of the bridge, charged with looking for aircraft and submarines and any other suspicious looking object. To enable me to carry out my duties, I was equipped with a small pair of binoculars.

Additionally, I was charged with supplying the other watchkeeping officers with hot cocoa and with calling our reliefs to duty. All of this in heavy seas and howling winds and while suffering from what seemed like an incurable bout of mal de mer. I threw up on the bridge, in the saloon and in the toilet, but no mercy was shown. Then suddenly I recovered and re-entered the land of the living. The weather was still rough but somehow or other more benign.

I began to take some interest in flag signals again and learned that two ships had been torpedoed and lost, and that our escort had expended a fair number of depth charges while hunting the submarines. I also got some practice on the Aldis lamp under the eagle eye of the watchkeeping mate. There were several more submarine alerts highlighted by depthcharging, which sometimes echoed strongly through our hull. Otherwise, it was a routine convoy passage.

We were south of Greenland when we were advised by radio that Germany had launched a massive attack on the Soviet Union—the date was 22nd June. The war was becoming ever larger. A few days later, being beyond the range of German aircraft, the main part of the convoy continued toward the coast of North America, while *Mandalay* and other vessels bound for more southern waters departed unescorted toward their various destinations. The weather had moderated considerably, and *Mandalay* returned to regular fours hours on eight off watchkeeping. For the watchkeeping cadets, add on two hours deck work every day. Nevertheless, it was heaven after the North Atlantic.

Perhaps now is a suitable time to describe the members of the ship's company that I recall. The master was Kenneth Beaton from the island of Skye, a good seaman but rather bad-tempered at times. He was probably fair-minded but was apt to jump to conclusions and did play favourites among the mates and cadets. The first mate was called Campbell, a nice enough appearing man, but not as fair-minded as he ought to have been. Beaton was in his fifties, Campbell in his forties, and obviously hungry for promotion to captain. The second mate is a blank in my mind.

The third mate, whom I spent much time working with, was from Inverness and just a short time before had been a cadet on *Mandalay* before getting his second mate's certificate. He was fair-minded and competent. The engineers are also just a blur with the exception of the *Empire Citizen* survivor and his buddy during the Liverpool May Blitz. The chippy was a Greenock man, a hopeless lush around port, but away from demon drink a thoroughly capable and likeable man.

We had three radio operators, but none registers on my recall button. Additionally, there were three Royal Navy gunners assigned to our protection. The senior was a leading seaman known to all and sundry as Guns. He was in his forties, a bit overweight, been in the navy from a boy seaman, boastful but a bit of a character. His two companions were hostilities only ratings and proud of it. One came from the London area, the other from Leicester. They were competent and agreeable men. There were four cadets on *Mandalay*— Hubert Jenkins and myself and two more experienced cadets. Jenkins and I were cabinmates so we saw a great deal of one another; the other two older cadets kept much more to themselves.

On that long lonely voyage southward to the Cape of Good Hope, my circle of conversational friends was restricted largely to the other cadets, chippy, the gunners and the butler who lived in the midships accommodation. The captain lived in solitary splendour beneath the bridge deck, the mates underneath one side of the boat deck together with the chief sparks, the engineers underneath the other side of the boat deck. The two additional sparks lived on the boat deck next door to the radio shack. The mates, engineers, sparks and cadets all messed in the officers' saloon—with separate tables for each designated group. What a display of class distinction, as the groups seldom joined in cross-tables discussions. Heaven only know where chippy, the gunners and the butler convened for a meal.

It was also soon impressed upon me that fresh water was a scarce commodity on board *Mandalay* on a long sea voyage. Salt-water showers and baths were available but fresh water was restricted to one bucket a day per crew member for personal hygiene and laundering of clothes. Once a day in the tropics, a glass of cold fresh water was made available to each of us by the butler who guarded the keys of the tank ferociously.

We had access to short wave radio broadcasts and while interested mainly in news about the war, we were fascinated by the many broadcasts from the USA that we picked up daily. It was a totally different world to ours, full of music, commercial endorsements, and chaps droning on about subjects that were no doubt vital to them but totally incomprehensible to our ears. The music was mostly swing, featuring characters I had scarcely heard of such as Benny Goodman, Artie Shaw and others. Jenky was much more sophisticated than me and soon initiated me into the mystique of the big bands. He also had a wind-up gramophone and a small number of records that he played at every opportunity. Around this time, he and I had a serious disagreement about something long-since forgotten, which ended up in a bout of fisticuffs in the steering flat. The deck of the steering flat was greasy and the ship was rolling about a bit so few damaging blows were struck. I believe I lost on points but honour was satisfied.

I learned to rig the ship's log successfully on this long haul down the Atlantic Ocean, but failed miserably when attempting to operate the deep-sea wire-sounding machine. What a mess of twisted wire! I desperately needed instruction, but all I received were curses from the mate. The unfairness of life was all too present. Mind you, some of the chastizing I thoroughly deserved. In the tropics at night in perfect weather I had a hard job keeping awake while on watch, and on a few occasions nodded off while carrying out my duties. A loud shout in my ear awakened me to the scorn of an irate mate. I was ashamed and vowed not to be found wanting in the future.

Sometimes, I was kept awake by watching the dolphin trails in the water at night. Sometimes they spooked me by rushing in a group toward the ship's side looking just as I imagined a spread of German torpedos would look. Other times, watching stars on the horizon, which could have been the lights of ships slowly move upward in the sky as the night wore on. It was a clammy sticky passage and nights seemed worst of all. We had, however, some entertainment most evenings, when Captain Beaton would march up and down his deck playing many a bagpipe tune, much to the dismay of the older cadets whose cabin ventilator stuck up in the path of the master's solitary march. They often shouted rude remarks up the ventilator when he was playing but learned to be quiet and listen when he would attempt to eavesdrop. It all was no doubt very childish but at the time seemed hilarious.

As we steamed southward, the weather gradually changed, becoming windier and cooler. We found ourselves being escorted by several huge winged birds, our first albatross. It was a delight to watch them soar and swoop among the waves, no doubt attracted by the dumping overboard of our garbage. By this time, I had experimented a number of times with washing my heavier working gear by towing them from the stern. One day I lost the wash and part of the line, and forever blamed the albatross, which may have mistaken my gear for the usual garbage. That was my last over-the-stern attempt at washing.

We had seen very few other vessels since departing the convoy, but now, as we approached the Cape, several vessels appeared on the horizon heading toward Capetown or heading out into the southern Atlantic. We kept a close watch on these craft and tried to avoid close contact. The possibility of enemy surface raiders was uppermost in our minds. Then one glorious day we sighted Table Mountain in the distance, partially cloud-covered but still very recognizable. We were halfway through our long voyage to Burma.

After passing the guard vessel, we anchored off Robbin Island to await the harbour pilot. The smell of land was carried on the wind and everyone looked forward to setting foot on South Africa. We had to wait until the following morning, when we were boarded by an Afrikaner pilot who was accompanied by a large oceangoing tug to ease our passage into the docking area. All went well until, in the narrow entrance to the dock, the tug's hawser that was fastened to our starboard towing bollard beneath the forecastle head parted under the strain and sent a large part of the panama lead casting high into the air before landing on the number one hatch. I had just left the forecastle with a message for the bridge when the accident occurred and could only have been a few feet away. Bags of panic for a few seconds before order was restored and a new hawser made fast. Eventually, we docked safely and gazed up at the mighty Table Mountain in awe.

Figure 25 - Capetown and Table Mountain

Mandalay did not have much cargo to discharge, but one item I particularly recall—several very large glass wireless valves bound for the Falkland Islands' admiralty wireless station. I hope another ship managed to pass them on safely to the Falklands as we had exhibited much care in conveying them to Capetown. Being junior, I drew the short straw for the gangway duty that night, and had to listen to the others boasts of conquests ashore when they returned. Their stories were all no doubt inflated, but they did create great envy in my soul and made me determined to explore Capetown the following day.

Meanwhile, I soon discovered that the vast majority of dock workers were Cape Coloureds, supervised by relatively few white supervisors. They appeared to be a fairly happy bunch of people as I found later when exploring ashore. The main street was Adderley, named after some British luminary, a wide thoroughfare with lots of shops and public houses. The customers were mostly white, and in the shops predominately female. I had admired the pretty Cape Coloured girls, but here in the centre of the city was a cornucopia of lovely white women who all seemed to bestow welcoming smiles on one uniformed cadet.

The shops overflowed with all the things that were in very short supply in the British Isles. Fruit of all kinds—oranges, apples, pears, plums, pineapples, melons, lemons, limes—and many more varieties of tropical and semi-tropical fruits. There were sweet biscuits, chocolate and ice-cream, tobacco, wines and spirits—and all in limitless supply. Coming from the Blitz and severe rations, it was overwhelming. Clothing was available in every shape and size and in any quantities, and the pubs were doing a brisk business. I found the railway station to be the focal point for action and joined my shipmates there. Lots of girls passed through the station, and some would stop and chat, but even if they passed on their way without comment, the scene was ever changing and well worth the effort. I did not make contact that night, ending up in a pub by the station where I indulged in port wine again and managed to be spotted by the old man who was passing through the station. Nothing was said, but I had an uneasy feeling that I and the other cadets would pay for our indiscretion.

Sure enough, the following day we prepared for sea and, as we sailed out of the dock into Table Bay, I was ordered to the foremast crosstrees to dismantle the cluster lights and lower them to the deck for proper stowage. Why this order was not given earlier while still tied up alongside I could never fathom. Anyhow, there I was up on the foremast crosstrees, clinging on for dear life as *Mandalay* pitched and rolled her way out of Table Bay. Eventually, the job was accomplished in the face of great difficulty while suffering from a horrendous port wine induced hangover. When I reported back for duty on the bridge, Captain Beaton said that he hoped I had learned a lesson. That was my farewell to the beautiful Western Cape.

We set off along the dangerous coastline of Cape Province making for Port Elizabeth in the Eastern Cape. We were now in the Indian Ocean and the weather felt a bit warmer, even if it was still winter in the southern hemisphere. It was slightly more than a day's steaming from Capetown. We docked in the early morning and commenced discharging cargo immediately. The docks and cranes were modern and were well laid out. The dockers were black fellows from the Transkei supervised as usual by white South Africans. This was an interesting area as it was in the interior of the Eastern Cape region that the Bantu hordes from the north clashed with the waves of European settlers moving from the Western Cape to exploit the arable land between the many rivers of the Eastern Cape. After much fighting in the early part of the nineteenth century, a peace of sorts was hammered out with the rough boundary line on the eastern edge of the Transkei. There was a tension in the air even after a hundred years had passed, a big change from the air of tranquillity that seemed to describe Capetown and its environs.

We were sailing that evening, so I saw very little of Port Elizabeth but did manage to enjoy some ice cream and chocolate at a café just outside the dock gates. Our passage from Port Elizabeth to Durban was uneventful, except that *Mandalay* rolled around considerably to the discomfort of all. The bluff that protects Durban from the south soon appeared in its protective coating of bright green foliage. After being hailed by a South African navy examination vessel, our pilot boarded and took us into Durban harbour where we docked at the bunkering wharves on the west side of the bluff. Before continuing our Durban saga, a short report on the events of the major episode of our times—the war!

It was now late July 1941, and many things had occurred since we left the River Clyde. The war had not gone well in the Mediterranean and Middle East. After victories against the Italians in the western desert, Churchill had sent thirty thousand fighting troops to Greece to assist the Greeks in their battles against the combined German and Italian invading forces. The gesture, while no doubt appreciated by the Greeks, was in vain. In a few short weeks, Greece and Crete had fallen to the enemy. A Paddy Henderson troop ship, *Salween*, took part in the evacuation, successfully taking a thousand New Zealand and British troops to safety in Egypt. More on this later.

The soldiers diverted to Greece were badly missed in the western desert, when the Germans under Rommel joined the Italians in sweeping the remaining Allied army back out of Libya to the Egyptian border.

Meanwhile, the German onslaught against the Soviet Union had met with nothing but success. By mid-July, the Germans were in Smolensk and everywhere advancing rapidly. It was a grim picture indeed. The Mediterranean, which used to be controlled by the Royal Navy, was now an extremely hazardous route for Allied shipping. We held Gibraltar at the western end and Alexandria at the eastern end, with Malta holding out against all odds in the middle. Even heavily protected convoys suffered great losses. But here we were on *Mandalay* in Natal, South Africa—in Durban—in an oasis of peace.

Figure 26 - The entrance to Durban Harbour

The bunkering of *Mandalay* at the Durban bluff went on apace. The workers again were black, this time of the Zulu tribe. I gazed at them with some interest. After all, these were the descendants of the Zulu impis who terrorized much of southern Africa, defeated the British Army at Islandawana before being defeated by the British in the Zulu wars of the early eighteen eighties. They were all big, well built men, but some of them were convict labour, very closely guarded and fettered when not working. That caused me some thought, but I was assured by the guards that these were very dangerous individuals.

There was a pub on the bluff docks that we used to wet our thirst, first of all making sure that the old man was not in the vicinity. I found South African beer a refreshing drink and learned to know the brand names, Castle and Lion as well as our Scottish equivalents, Tennants and MacEwans. This pub was largely frequented by seamen and white South African workers. I noted however that blacks were served their brew through a small opening at the rear of the building, my first dawning appreciation of what segregation was about. Coal dust lay over the ship and invaded every nook and cranny. Cleaning up was quite a chore, but at least we were not required to man the gangway in full dress uniform.

Eventually, we had an opportunity to explore Durban, and what a wonderful place it turned out to be. A ferry from the bluff took one to the point where many of the cargo wharves were located. From there, buses and tramcars ran into the city proper and were very frequent. Additionally, there were lots of taxis. Surprisingly, all the drivers were white, as were the passengers. Indeed, when we went shopping, we found that we were served by whites.

The centre of the city was delightful with lots of small hotels and picture houses, parks, bowling greens and office blocks mixed in with large and small shops selling a variety of goods. Everywhere were shops selling fresh produce. It was so very different to the United Kingdom where rationing was tight and choice was very limited. Palm trees were on every main thoroughfare and the air temperature a balmy seventy-five degrees Fahrenheit. After all, we were only twenty-eight degrees south of the equator. The centre of Durban lay just south of the harbour, but the pièce de résistance lay to the north and east, where a magnificent beach stretched northward from the point docks fronting onto the Indian Ocean. Many hotels and apartments stretched along the beach road, while tennis courts, bowling greens and swimming pools dotted the foreshore.

We headed for the ocean in rickshaws pulled by colourful Zulus and were soon swimming in the waves. There was a strong undertow, but that did not bother us too much. A wrecked merchant ship lay three hundred yards or so offshore and it became our target for exploration and diving efforts. It was also known as a gathering point for sharks. However, we were lucky!

We also met a number of white South Africans of British background who befriended us and insisted on entertaining us. Some of them had lovely young daughters, which was an added plus. Actually, Durban seemed to be full of well-endowed young women—or perhaps we were just suffering from seagoing deprivation. No, it was not a hallucination.

It was also notable that there were many Indians on the streets of Durban. They were largely the descendants of Indians brought to Natal to grow and harvest the sugar crop. Their status was slightly above the Zulu, but definitely below the white. In many ways, to a seafarer this was a semi-tropical paradise, but the racial mix and segregation raised questions that never quite disappeared from sight. We departed Durban with some sadness, sailing out from the bluff into a blustery northeaster.

The weather moderated somewhat on our way northward and became pleasant but hot when abeam of Mozambique. It continued thusly as we passed through the Mozambique Channel between Madagascar and the mainland, before threading through the Comoros Islands and heading further out into the Indian Ocean. We were well aware that we were approaching an area where German surface raiders were active, and therefore operated with heightened tension and strengthened lookouts. It was a time when the old hands on board regaled the newcomers with tales of disaster and escape.

The story of the sinking of *Kemmendine* south of the Maldive Islands was rehashed. In July 1940, she became the first Paddy Henderson ship to be sunk by enemy action. The crew of one hundred and seven and the forty passengers all survived the sinking, but some were later drowned when a captured ship taking them to Germany was sunk off the French coast, probably by a British submarine. The remaining crew members lived on board the German raider for three months before being transferred to another captured ship and then landed in Italian Somaliland. They were treated very badly before being liberated by British troops in early 1941. The Italians latterly were running short of medical supplies and one Paddy Henderson cadet was operated on without anaesthetics. He was never quite the same afterwards.

Then followed a tale about *Salween* evading a German raider south of Ceylon and of course the old hands on *Mandalay* loved telling the story of how, in February 1941, while bound from Aden to Mombasa, a suspected German raider had followed them for some time. As it was overtaking *Mandalay,* night fell and *Mandalay* was able to make her escape. With all these tales of derring-do and the very real threat of being sunk ourselves, we travelled across the Indian Ocean toward the Bay of Bengal in a heightened sense of tension.

In reality, it was an uneventful voyage, hot and sticky at times, but very pleasant most of the time. I realized how lucky I was to be on deck or on the bridge in the tropics, when looking at our coal trimmers and firemen taking a well-earned break on deck from the hell below. That view, coupled with the noise from the engine room, made me very glad not to be a member of the black gang.

Finally, in late August we approached the Burmese coast and rendezvoused with the Rangoon river pilot. It was early morning, with monsoon clouds drifting around, the land distant and flat. A slight wind brought the smell of land to us, tropical, scented with various perfumes, dung smoke, and spices, stronger smells too but muted, altogether the indefinable but unmistakable smell of the Orient. In honour of our impending arrival in Rangoon, the old man ordered canvas awnings to be erected from bow to stern. At this moment, the pilot vessel dispatched the pilot cutter to come alongside *Mandalay.*

What a performance it was. The pilot, a stout Scot, was followed by his assistant, a half-caste chap, then two helmsmen and, last but not least, a tea wallah carrying an expensive silver tea service and all the fittings. It was very impressive to a young green cadet, a symbol of empire, as it were. The pilot and his entourage were then escorted to the bridge, to be greeted professionally by Captain Beaton. Shortly thereafter, we were underway and slowly entered the river. It was several miles wide at the entrance but gradually narrowed, giving one a good view of both sides of the river.

The land was low-lying but green and fertile, with rice paddies predominating and, scattered among them, small golden pagodas gleamed in the sun that condescended to peak through the monsoon clouds. In the river approaches were many sailing fishing vessels and, in the river itself, a constant procession of small craft such as motor launches, powered barges, and every type of sampan imaginable. It was simply unforgettable. Halfway up the river to Rangoon, the butler served a wonderfully cold shandy to the watchkeepers, including the cadets. The old man was not pleased to see the butler serving the lowly cadets and made his displeasure known. He spoiled what was a memorable occasion, the silly old Skye donkey.

MAP OF BURMA

Figure 27 - Burma

By mid-afternoon, we were approaching the port, the monsoon clouds thickening and heavy rain sweeping the river. With much shouting and puffing of the tugs now fastened to our bow and stern, we secured alongside the riverside wharf and heaved sighs of relief which were short-lived as we were immediately invaded by swarms of Indian and Burman dockers intent on stripping off our hatch covers and discharging our cargo. They were accompanied by the usual tribe of officials high and low and all sorts of hangers-on. Customs and immigration authorities were appeased, old acquaintances welcomed, and plans laid for a well-deserved run ashore. Not, however, for the junior cadet who found himself on gangway watch once more. This night duty was highlighted for me by the sight of huge rats departing *Mandalay*, in several cases using the gangway itself as their transportation corridor. I had mentioned the cockroaches earlier but had not realized that *Mandalay* was also a home to a large colony of rats.

My shipmates, when they returned on board, regaled me with stories of their exploits—real and imagined. I could hardly wait to see the sights for myself. So the following day I took a walking tour of the city highlights that were closest to the docks. I visited the Sule Pagoda, which was not too far from the dock gates. It was a marvellous oasis of peace and quiet, with many impressive shrines and stupas, with large statues of Buddha in every posture imaginable. The bustle and noise of the streets I soaked up before ending up in the Mayo Marine Club, a very elegant mansion with high ceilings and slowly rotating punkahs—just the spot for a weary and dry sailor. Outside in the gardens surrounding the Mayo Marine Club, souvenir salesmen peddled their wares, occasionally venturing onto the verandah to whisper "Sahib-souvenir—teak elephant?" I no doubt was finally persuaded to purchase an elephant with my few remaining rupees and annas, leaving just enough to hire a rickshaw wallah for the trip back to the *Mandalay*.

I found that I could easily get lost in Rangoon. Once, after getting to a picture house in the city and seeing the latest Hollywood extravaganza in cool air conditioning comfort, I came out on to the street in late afternoon and did not have a clue as to my directions back to the ship. People milled around, Indians, Burmans, mixed races, and I was the only white person in sight. After a few panic-stricken moments and failing miserably to communicate my concerns to anyone while fending off pedlars of various goods that I did not want, I spotted a white police sergeant sorting out a traffic jam. He was busy and bad-tempered but did find me a rickshaw to send me on my way home to the familiar sight of *Mandalay*. Before letting me go, he warned me that I was in a bad part of town and that racial violence between Burmans and Indians was a regular event. I was more careful in my roamings and exploring from then onward.

That episode with the sergeant brought home to me the tiny white presence in Rangoon among these teeming hundreds of thousands of coloured people of every description. I also noted the undercurrent of racial tension on board ship between the stevedores, where holds one, three and five were manned by Indians and urged on by their half-caste foreman, and holds two and four where Burmans held sway under the tight control of another half-caste foreman. There were things about Burma that I had yet to understand.

Rangoon was a bustling busy port in 1941, serving not only the usual trade with Britain but also the growing importance of the Burma Road into China. The Japanese had made great strides in invading and occupying much of China, including the coastal zone, thereby denying supplies to the Chinese government forces holding out in the interior. The Burma Road was an attempt by Britain and the United States to keep the Japanese at bay.

Tied up just ahead of *Mandalay* at the wharf was an American vessel named *Shickshinny* from somewhere in Alabama. She was discharging lorries and armoured vehicles and other war materials bound for Chiang Kai Chek's forces. These ships and their supply route made for quite a small American colony in the Rangoon area. They were bolstered by the arrival of batches of American fighter pilots from the American volunteer group known as the Flying Tigers and fighting against the Japanese in southwestern China. They were a rambunctious gang, as could be expected, and they made their short leaves in Rangoon memorable ones. A local nightclub known as the Silver Slipper was their favourite haunt. Typical Yanks, they threw their money around like it was water, driving up prices not only of liquor but also and probably more importantly put the attendant ladies of the night out of the reach of their British military counterparts. I hasten to add that these matters were largely reported to me second hand, although I did manage to visit the Silver Slipper once and sipped an expensive drink while listening to the dance orchestra play "Ramona."

The Burma Road also heightened tensions between Japan and the British, Dutch and American possessions in Southeast Asia. That tension was reflected in Burma by some anxiety about the future, as the Japanese were already putting considerable pressure on Thailand to allow access for its troops. Japanese undercover agents were already believed to be working in Burma with dissident Burmese groups ready to foment trouble. On prominent Japanese dentist was pointed out to me as being under surveillance, all in all a bit scary for all those Europeans and Americans who had to face the expected onslaught.

Figure 28 - Rangoon Harbour and the Sule Pagoda

We completed discharging cargo at the wharf in early September and moved out into the river to moor preparatory to loading for the United Kingdom. Once again, we had the competition between the Burmans and the Indians, now wrestling with bags of rice, logs of teak and animal hides. The noise, the sense of fierce activity, the occasional small accident, all combined to make life difficult for all on board, and this on a twenty-four-hour working day. When off duty, it was all-important to slip ashore for a few precious hours. I managed to visit the awe-inspiring

Shwedagon Pagoda outside the city proper, truly a magnificent sight—the golden stupas glittering in the sun and everywhere devotees of Buddhism worshipping at their favourite shrine—then a pleasant visit to the Anglican lake mission for lemonade and relaxing company.

A memorable event for me was an initiation into a small part of Burmese life. The butler, a friendly fellow, decided that he would show me that Rangoon nightlife was not confined to the Silver Slipper or the Strand Hotel. He was, of course, a non-European, and as such apparently of lower standing than the white staff on board ship, even we lowly and much-despised cadets. However, we struck up a bond of friendship on the voyage, and the initiation was his way of saying thank you.

He took me to various restaurants and teahouses, visiting friends, and then to some of their homes where we drank copious amounts of tea and polished off lots of sweet biscuits and cake. The ladies in these modest homes were very interested in me, how old I was, my parents, et cetera, while plying me with goodies. Most of them had fairly serviceable English, but lots of Burmese and Indian was used also. My burra sahib's Hindustani did not help me translate anything that was said. However, it was all very interesting but somewhat like an Oriental version of a Presbyterian church social. Early in the evening, the butler, a male friend of his and I departed to seek some slightly different company. We were out among the lakes north of the city, where a number of houseboats moored. One of these houseboats was our destination, where we were welcomed by a beautiful woman garbed in a gorgeous sari. The houseboat was elegant but comfortable, and soon we were drinking beer and being introduced to several attractive young girls, all Burmese with white powdered cheeks. One very shy girl apparently took a fancy to me and I to her. It was a very pleasant ending to a perfect evening. I have been forever grateful to the butler for that unique evening, and forever fascinated by the Orient.

A very different episode occurred one night on board *Mandalay* while at anchor. While sleeping off-duty in the tropical heat, naked to catch any movement of air, I found myself being accosted by our gunlayer. The temptation had been too much for old guns brought up in the navy tradition of rum, bum and baccy. I was shocked wide-awake and so was the gunlayer at my reaction. He was all apologies, but I felt that I had no choice but to report him to the first mate. It was most unfortunate and did cause some bad feeling, but such uninvited approaches must be dealt with quickly and harshly. He was eventually reduced in rank from leading seaman to able seaman. I do not believe that I am homophobic, but early experience led me to beware of pedophiles and indeed of predatory homosexuals. Let them keep themselves to themselves.

The last social event that I attended in Rangoon was a very select dinner party ashore put on by a family connected with the Dallo Dockyard Company. It was very nice of them to invite some of the officers and a couple of overawed cadets to this sumptuous feast. It took place in a mansion located in a monied suburb of Rangoon. The house and gardens were spacious and well cared for by a large corps of servants. The family did their very best to make us feel at home, but I found the evening dragged on, and felt intimidated by the vast array of utensils placed before me. I also pondered over what to do with a crystal bowl of water filled with perfumed flowers. I eventually made a choice and committed the social sin of drinking the finger bowl. Later in the war, that family was travelling on *Salween* as refugees from the debacle in Burma, and I was able to have a chuckle about the finger bowl with the young daughter of our dinner party hosts.

The passage from the anchorage to shore was an experience itself, sometimes by motor launch, but mostly by motor-powered sampan. The river traffic was always heavy and there was always a lot to see. If the journey from ship to shore was a set fee—a couple of annas—returning to *Mandalay* was beset with some hard bargaining, especially at night. It paid to be sober. No lifejackets, minimal freeboard and the fast flowing river were all hazards that we dismissed with the supreme confidence of youth.

One last description of a Rangoon landmark before we prepared for sea. Fairly close to the docks was the best hotel in the city, the Strand. It was very elegant, with strong connotations of late Victorian/Edwardian times. It really was a hotel resplendent with its celebration of the days of the British Raj. I could never afford to dine there but did manage a lemonade while watching the waiters twist the dining room napkins into the shape of swans and various other birds and waited for my made-to-order poplin shirts to be completed at minimal cost.

Our loading was conducted in meticulous fashion, with huge teak logs in the lower holds, the rice, well ventilated, was stowed in the tween decks with packages of animal hides. Finally, packages of partially processed teak wood were secured on deck. So, on a monsoon dull day in September, we departed Rangoon bound for home via the Cape of Good Hope. Although aware of the impending threat of Japanese invasion, I never thought that it would be another fifty-six years before I saw Burma again. What changes had swept across the world in the interim!

Chapter Ten

Burma to Home

As we depart Rangoon and head down into the Bay of Bengal, I would like to highlight the Irrawaddy Flotilla, the backbone of the Burma trade and an essential part of the Paddy Henderson empire. The name "Mandalay" itself is synonymous with the Irrawaddy River and the flotilla that sailed upon its waters. Forgive me, while I quote Kipling to make the point.

> *By the old Moulmein Pagoda, lookin' lazy at the sea*
> *There's a Burma girl a sittin', and I know she thinks of me*
> *For the wind is in the palm trees, and the temple bells they say*
> *"Come you back, you British soldier, come you back to Mandalay.*
> *Come you back to Mandalay where the old flotilla lay.*
> *Can't you 'ear their paddles chunkin' from Rangoon to Mandalay?*
> *On the road to Mandalay where the flying fishes play*
> *An' the dawn comes up like thunder outer China 'crost the bay."*

The Irrawaddy Flotilla Company had a modest beginning. Few countries are as dependent on water transport as Burma, with its great water systems of the Irrawaddy and Chindwin, together with the Salween and the Sittang. The navigable portion of the Irrawaddy alone ran over one thousand miles from Rangoon to Bhamo close to the border with China.

British connection with river transportation began in 1852 to support the military in the second Anglo-Burmese war. Trade with Burma was potentially very rich indeed, but upper Burma remained under the control of King Mindon who was reluctant to give up any trading privileges to the colonial power. However, in 1878 King Mindon died. He was succeeded by King Thibaw after much slaughter of royal contenders to the throne. The new Burmese government signed a commercial treaty with the French, causing great consternation in Burma and India.

The government of India issued an ultimatum to King Thibaw to live up to his obligations. The Irrawaddy Flotilla was employed on evacuation of civilians and in support of military operations. The Expeditionary Force attacked in November 1885. It was all over in two weeks, with the British in full control of Burma and the royal family in exile in India.

In a united Burma, the Irrawaddy Flotilla Company quickly expanded into one of the largest and most efficient inland water services in the world. Its fleet of steamers, floats, barges and eventually motor boats were all built at Denny's shipyard on the Clyde at Dumbarton, then dismantled for shipment to Burma before being reassembled at the Dallo Dockyard in Rangoon. In 1941, the Irrawaddy Flotilla Company was deploying more than six hundred and fifty vessels of all kinds. Passenger traffic and trade of all sorts, including the staples of teak wood, rice and animal hides, made the river systems of Burma a virtual hive of activity.

Homeward bound, *Mandalay* seemed to pick up speed as we headed out of the Bay of Bengal into the Indian Ocean. All an illusion, of course, but we were heading south and it felt as if we were going downhill. It was mainly hot and sticky, with little to interrupt the daily routine. A new chore had been added to keep us on our toes. Frequent inspections of the temperature of the rice cargo became the order of the day with the thermometers being secured inside the cargo ventilators for easy access. Sometimes, the rice would sweat and the hatches would be opened at the corners to provide cooling air while good sea going weather prevailed on deck.

We had one German raider scare north of Madagascar when a suspicious-looking ship suddenly materialized out of a rain squall and appeared to be following us. It was sufficiently scary that several of our lascar crew began placing their belongings on the forward hatches preparatory to abandoning ship. According to our first mate, the following ship looked like a pre-war German merchant ship he remembered. However, we never had to test his memory as *Mandalay* ducked into another rain squall and then proceeded to take evasive action. The raider, if it was a raider, was not seen again and the crew restowed their gear in their berths.

Durban was a welcome sight, all lit up at night. With pilot on board, we awaited daylight before docking once more at the bluff for bunkers.

There was A Blue Funnel ship ahead of us at the coaling wharf, bound for Hong Kong. We were now into October and the news from Southeast Asia was anything but reassuring. I met some of her officers and passengers, among whom were several serving army officers who were on their way to join their regiments. They were cheerful fellows, but it was easy to tell that they had some doubts about the situation. I often wonder what happened to them in Hong Kong and if any of them survived the war in the Orient.

There was not enough time for a proper run ashore so, after completing coaling and cleaning up the dust and debris, we departed the Bluff bound for Capetown. The weather had deteriorated and grew steadily into a full gale. By the time *Mandalay* was abeam East London, the ship was taking quite a battering from the confused seas whipped up by the storm and the southward flowing Agulhas Current. Some of our deck cargo shifted and required resecuring, while we sustained damage to one of our port lifeboats. We were not unhappy to see Table Mountain ahead and to dock in the harbour safely.

While repairs were carried out and some additional cargo loaded together with fresh fruit and, most importantly, fresh water, shore leave was granted to some of us and I won the lucky straw. It was a fine day, if windy, and I enjoyed the afternoon exploring downtown Capetown. In early evening, I joined some of my shipmates in a celebratory drink, which became two and then several. By this time we were in the Del Monica, a popular drinking spot with a ceiling painted to look like a tropical night sky with numerous stars and even a waxing moon. There was a lot of female talent around, which is probably the main reason we were there. However, I imbibed too much and was in no shape to return to *Mandalay*, knowing that Captain Beaton would be somewhat displeased. One of the gunners, the chap from London, took pity on me and insisted that I eat breast of chicken sandwiches washed down with gallons of hot black coffee. I was therefore able to climb up *Mandalay's* gangway in reasonable shape and avoid the old man's censure. I wish that I could say that a lesson had been learned and that I would henceforth behave myself.

While in Rangoon, I had purchased a package of Burmese cigars as a gift for my father. Before leaving Capetown, I hid the package in the starboard deep tank to avoid paying duties in Britain. There they lay as we headed up the Atlantic, a constant nag on my conscience and my Presbyterian soul.

We departed Capetown in late October bound for Freetown in West Africa, which was a convoy assembly port. The weather was fresh but not uncomfortable, and we made good time until we ran out of the trade winds. Once again, we were escorted by a number of albatross who entertained us with their aerial acrobatics.

We had seen few other ships, but as we got within a thousand miles of Freetown we encountered a number of vessels, and Sparks, our wireless operator, made us aware of many other ships in the vicinity, all apparently heading for Freetown. *Mandalay* adopted a predetermined zigzag course, and watchkeepers went on wartime four hours on four hours off watchkeeping cycle. The tropical heat was intense and tension was in the air as we received radio messages of submarine attacks on nearby vessels. Finally, on the night before arrival in Freetown harbour, we witnessed the aftermath of a torpedo attack on a British tanker. She was on fire on the horizon, but we were instructed to continue toward Freetown as other rescue ships would soon arrive. She was eventually salvaged, as damage was mainly limited to the engine room with some loss of life.

Mandalay anchored off Freetown, joining many other merchant ships awaiting a convoy to Britain. The harbour was protected by a boom defence and Royal Air Force coastal command flew patrols of the area. Seagoing escorts seemed to consist of elderly converted trawlers and some newer looking corvettes. In pride of place lay the *Edinburgh Castle*, an ex-Union Castle liner converted into naval headquarters for the region.

Bumboats of various types thronged the harbour, selling everything known and unknown to man. One particular boat shilled its wares by displaying a partially clad young female who kept advising her shipboard audience that she was "all same Queen Victoria—pink inside." Others peddled liquor, beer, fruit, clothing and toiletries, and medications of every kind. Only the master was allowed ashore, so the rest of us had to make do with the floating entertainment. We could pick up American broadcasts at night and were once more entertained by the big bands and also heard Kate Smith sing "God Bless America" for the first time.

After one week in Freetown, *Mandalay* joined thirty-odd merchant ships escorted by the naval trawlers and corvettes and departed Freetown bound for the North Channel. Sunderland flying boats patrolled the seas ahead of us and on either flank. Our course took us northwestward of the Cape Verde Islands before we started heading north up the Atlantic. The Sunderlands disappeared and we were left with our small anti-submarine escort. The weather was pleasant enough, but there was some tension in the air as we crept toward the vicinity of the Canary Islands which were controlled by Spain and used by the Germans as a base to attack Allied convoys. Our track northward lay about five hundred miles west of the Canaries but was still well within range as our escort indicated by the frequent laying down of depth charges.

We were also joined by additional escorts from Gibraltar as we moved ever further north. Two merchant ships were sunk over the next few days, while the convoy tightened up and took occasional evasive action. North of the latitude of the Canary Islands and west of Madeira the weather worsened and the threat of a U-boat attack was somewhat diminished. However, German long-range aircraft did make an appearance, dropped a few bombs ineffectively and then departed never to be seen again.

Then one day, we found ourselves approaching the North Channel between Scotland and Ireland, where we were ordered out of the convoy to proceed independently to an anchorage off Oban in the Inner Hebrides. This was a surprise to all, as we had run a pool on our port of entry and Oban was not on the list. It was very nice nevertheless to be safely anchored off Tobermoray in the Sound of Mull, even if the rain came down in buckets and we could scarcely see the shore. Captain Beaton was delighted, as he was very close to his home on the island of Skye. The rest of us relaxed thankfully in the less tiring watchkeeping mode of four on eight off.

Two days later, we were boarded by the convoy commodore and his staff, preparatory to *Mandalay* leading a small convoy around the north of Scotland to the port of Methil, where we were to bunker. The captain was beside himself with *Mandalay* being the commodore vessel and charged around the bridge supervising everyone in sight including the commodore and the yeoman of signals on his staff. They of course paid little attention to his bombast, so he then directed his wrath at the mate on watch and even more so on the lowly cadets. I got told off for being late to report a sighting on the horizon when everyone else on the bridge had clearly heard me report the sighting some considerable time before.

It was that sort of a passage up through the Minches and then eastward through the Pentland Firth. One small escort followed by eight vessels of varying size in double column and lead by *Mandalay*. Apparently, it was *Mandalay's* first chance to play commodore vessel since being in the eastern Mediterranean earlier in the year, and Kenny Beaton was making the most of it. One good thing came out of this experience. We were bullied so much regarding identification of flag hoists and the assembling of correct and prompt replies that we were ready for whatever was required. I swear Kenny had tears in his eyes as we steamed past the island of Skye.

The remainder of the voyage to Methil proceeded without incident. However, the Methil pilot managed to have *Mandalay* strike the pier heavily while approaching, shaking us all up and damaging the hull about ten feet above the water line. Temporary repairs were made with a cement box, the ship completed bunkering, and we set off to join an east coast convoy bound for the Thames.

We were no longer commodore ship, which no doubt displeased the captain, but took our place about halfway down the inner column of a twin column convoy of coasters and deep-sea vessels bound from the Firth of Forth to various ports on the east coast of England. We were travelling on a clearly demarked route that took us inside the extensive minefields of the North Sea and a few miles off the coast, except when crossing the shallow approaches to the Wash. The enemies to watch for were German E-boats—fast armoured torpedo boats—and of course German aircraft.

The early part of the voyage was mostly uneventful with vessels departing or leaving the convoy off the Tyne, the Wear, the Tees and the Humber, and hailing and passing northbound convoys that all reported encountering E-boats operating in the vicinity of the Wash and Lowestoft and Yarmouth. We were to shortly experience our E-boat baptism of fire.

The convoy route across the Wash and southward to the approaches to the River Thames was then known as E-boat alley. The German E-boats were based in Ostend and other Belgian ports and made a fast run across the southern North Sea to attack Allied convoys servicing East Anglia and the port of London. They ranged as far north as the mouth of the Humber River and as far south as the Foulness lightship in the approaches to the River Thames. They preyed on the convoys by attacking under cover of darkness, sometimes tying up to large navigation buoys to escape detection by convoy escorts, or racing up between the convoy columns and thereby making it very difficult for ships to defend themselves as they were all too aware of the danger of hitting another ship in the adjoining column.

Just south of the Wash off Lowestoft, we encountered the E-boats. They had just attacked successfully a northbound convoy to the south of us, leaving one coaster sunk and a large tanker ablaze from stem to stern. The night sky was filled with tracer fire and the air resounded with the noise of high explosives and the hammering noise of automatic weapons. In the middle of all this display, a German E-boat shot down between our columns hotly pursued by one of our destroyer escorts. Intense excitement and sheer terror reigned for a few moments and then relative peace and tranquillity was restored while our southbound convoy steamed slowly past the battered remains of the northbound ships illuminated by the flames from the tanker. It was quite a night. We had been very lucky, many of our comrades had not been.

At daylight, we were boarded by the river pilot off Foulness and proceeded slowly up the River Thames to the Royal Docks. At high tide, *Mandalay* was towed and warped into Royal Victoria where we immediately prepared for discharging. It was a welcome relief to know that we had safely completed a long and sometimes arduous voyage from Britain, via the Cape of Good Hope, to far distant Burma, and returned safely. No one else seemed to care. The war was going badly for Britain, with huge merchant ship losses. There had been some recovery in North Africa, with the Italians defeated in Ethiopia and the Germans and Italians held in Libya, but the Germans were making great strides into Russia. Leningrad was besieged, Kiev had fallen months ago and the German army was approaching the outskirts of Moscow. Things did not look too good.

Chapter Eleven

Leave and Diphtheria

A quick look at the Dockland showed the great damage incurred on the city since the summer of 1940. Huge areas of former factories and homes had been levelled, and sunken ships still blocked some berths. People were weary but defiant, and very happy to be spared any heavy raids since the Germans attacked Russia in June 1941. Some pubs were still standing, and cheerful music escaped from the doors even at night. Vera Lynn singing "Yours" was a particular favourite. The cockney spirit was still very much alive.

I paid off *Mandalay* on St. Andrew's day, the 30th November, and was given a few days' leave. I left Euston Station late that night and arrived home on the Clyde early the following morning. The train was packed with soldiers, sailors, and airmen squeezed into every nook and cranny of the train, including the toilets and the luggage racks. It was conducive to a friendly if not restful journey.

Dad was there to meet me at the Greenock West station and I was soon in the company of my brother Gordon and Aunt Mary. I was able to present the smuggled cigars to my father, together with small presents for Gordon and my aunt. They were all well and wanted to know about *Mandalay's* voyage. I, in turn wanted to know more about the Greenock Blitz, and was taken to nearby bombing sites and supplied with more information than I could usefully absorb about the horrible events of May 6th and 7th 1941. We walked along the Cut and admired the view of the Mountains of Arran, and strolled along the esplanade to view the Tail of the Bank and the remains of the French destroyer *Maille Breze*, that awful reminder of the Norwegian campaign. She and her crew had been active in the war before the torpedo tragedy, escorting the battleship *Bretagne* and the cruiser *Algérie*, carrying French gold reserves to Canada in 1940. She also took part in actions against German forces invading Norway, and had just returned from Namsos, where she protected the landing of French forces. She was a sad loss, and linked very much with my hometown. After a short few more days visiting friends and contacting girl friends, it was time to return to *Mandalay*.

The day I rejoined my ship was the day that ensured our final victory. The Japanese attacked Pearl Harbour and, although a defeat for the Americans, it meant that we were no longer alone. *Mandalay* moved into drydock for repairs and the installation of additional gunnery. Our cargo had been landed safely and we were now engulfed with the noise, dirt and mayhem associated with any ship in the hands of a dockyard crew. Gun turrets arose on either side of the bridge deck and boat deck. They were constructed of steel and bitumastic slabs. Heavier machine guns were to be mounted in these turrets, and additional protection was to be mounted around our four-inch howitzer in the stern.

Shore leave was spasmodic, as some cadets were on leave or being posted to other vessels. However, I did manage to journey to the West End, where I enjoyed a performance of "The Merry Widow." I also visited Trafalgar Square, Piccadilly Circus, and Leicester Square. I even visited the Paddy Henderson offices near Fleet Street. After sampling the pubs, I found ballroom dancing emporiums in the vicinity of Tottenham Court and in Hammersmith, which provided me with the opportunity to not only trip the light fantastic but also to strike up an acquaintance with some of the prettier ones. I do remember two sisters from Pembrokeshire in South West Wales. They looked like twins and dressed in similar fashion, angora wool sweaters and tight skirts. They worked in London and lived close to Paddington Station. I thought they were great fun, but Hubert Jenkins, man of experience and Welshman himself, surmised that they were probably ladies of considerable experience.

I never got a chance to confirm his views, as I became quite ill in the taxi coming back to the ship. The taxi driver was not pleased and blamed it on drink, as I did myself, but it turned out that I had contracted diphtheria and was running a high temperature. The next morning, I was shuffled off to Plaistow General Hospital to an isolation ward, where I remained over Christmas and until early in January 1942. I felt humiliated. Surely diphtheria was a child's infection, and I was a grown-up survivor of a dangerous at times voyage to the Far East. There I lay in a private room just off the children's ward. It was too much to bear!

The nurses were pleasant in the main, although prone to wake one up at the ungodliest of hours. I was obviously looked upon as a most unusual specimen and subjected to much questioning. After all, I was nearly seventeen, reasonably handsome, opinionated, probably obnoxious, a Scot, and a seafarer to boot. The ward sister was a bit of a tyrant, who nevertheless spent some time with me, discussing and arguing about the progress of the war. My views on the poor management of the war clashed with her passionate defence of our every action. I am sure we both enjoyed these verbal clashes of opinion. Christmas was, however, a dull and sad affair, being away from both family and my shipmates. I felt abandoned.

Then salvation appeared in the guise of my Great Uncle Duncan. I had met him before the war when he and his housekeeper visited with us in Greenock. Dad had advised him of my whereabouts and he determined to ride to the rescue. He was a tall man, but very large, and dominated any assembly by his very presence. Somehow or other, he persuaded the hospital authorities and more importantly the ward sister that I was fit enough to be released into his care. So shortly thereafter, he took me in a taxi to Romford in Essex where he lived. There, I was warmly welcomed by Mrs. Luckman, his housekeeper of many years. It was wonderful to be spoiled, and I was thoroughly for several weeks before Great Uncle Duncan decided that I had recuperated completely.

My Great Uncle Duncan McCulloch was then in his eighties, with a lengthy and illustrious career behind him. He had been a seafarer like me, but on the engineering side. He joined the Peninsula and Oriental Steamship Company in the early eighteen eighties and by the early nineteen hundreds was Engineering Superintendent with the company. He then moved to Babcock & Wilcox in a similar capacity and was employed on special projects relating to aircraft design during the First World War. His wife Sarah died and he retired in the early nineteen twenties. Mrs. Luckman had been with him since that time. Her husband had been one of the fallen in Flanders. His home was located in Rush Green on the outskirts of Romford, a quiet neighbourhood of bungalows and gardens. He had been a keen gardener but his constitution was no longer able to cope, so he employed a part-time helper. He still pottered in his greenhouse. I can still see him sitting there with his skullcap on to protect him from the sun, while he shelled some peas.

I gradually became more mobile and soon was venturing forth to explore the city of Romford. I found newsagents where I could purchase copies of the skimpy newspapers that were the rule in wartime Britain. I was avid for news of the war and most of all for news about the war at sea. The BBC radio news was reliable but without information in depth. I read everything I could get my hands on and concluded that the war was still not going right. Hong Kong had fallen, the Japanese had swept into Malaya, Burma and the Philippines. Their navy and air force were winning every battle. The Russians had however held the German advance before Moscow and were reported as counterattacking. The war at sea was heating up with expanded submarine attacks on convoys in the mid-Atlantic. I could hardly wait to become more closely involved.

On one of my visits to Romford and the local cinema, I got to know an attractive young lady. We found each other's company mutually agreeable and dated several times. She was older than me, and better off financially. She owned and operated a small taxicab company. The romance heated up and everything was going swimmingly when Mrs. Luckman apprised Great Uncle Duncan of the affair. Before I could realize properly what was happening, my father had been informed of events and I was being transported north to Scotland. I had been deemed fit to resume my seagoing career—my rehab had been terminated. If I was well enough to get into a sexual entanglement, I was well enough for anything. I was forever grateful to my great uncle for a great interlude in my life. I was now seventeen years old and ready for a posting to sea.

I renewed ties with family and friends, writing to both Jeans—the blue eyes and the brown—hoping that I did not get them mixed up. The news from Malaya was appalling, with the sinking of the battleship *Prince of Wales* and the battlecruiser *Repulse*. No air cover—someone should have been shot! My father and I were travelling on the train to Glasgow when the news broke. I was very angry, but he reminded me that worse days had overhung Britain in the Great War and that we had eventually been victorious. It was somewhat comforting, but not entirely.

The summons came in mid-February 1942. Report at once to *Kindat* lying in the West Float, Birkenhead. I had purchased some new gear more suitable to the seagoing environment than that which my father had generously provided prior to joining *Mandalay*. The outfitter in Greenock who sold my father the uniforms should have been charged with dereliction of duty and the supplying of inferior goods. A packed train from Glasgow to Liverpool took me uneventfully back to Merseyside.

Chapter Twelve

Kindat

Kindat was lying in the West Float, the old stamping ground for *Mandalay* in 1941. She was loading mixed cargo for the Far East—port of discharge unknown—as the war situation deteriorated rapidly in Southeast Asia. War materials predominated, but there was lots of room for luxury items such as women's clothing, biscuits and the ubiquitous Hall's Medicinal Wine. I figured that last item and other liquors kept the empire going. The ship displaced about six thousand tons gross and was a single deck vessel in contrast to the *Mandalay*. However, she did have a raised forecastle, which provided accommodation for the lascar crew. Two holds forward with the third hold located abaft the bridge and holds four and five abaft the midships.

Figure 29 - *SS Kindat*, 1942

She was fitted with the usual derricks and heavy lift gear. Her decks were constructed of teak wood similar to *Mandalay* and even in port gleamed from daily holystoning. *Kindat* was listed as being capable of ten knots steady steaming. The total crew consisted of forty Indians and twenty Europeans. I found myself joining three other cadets, only one of whom had any previous experience. He was a lad called Carslow from Rhu in the Gareloch. The other cadets were from Glasgow and Edinburgh. The Glasgow cadet was named MacDonald, the Edinburgh man's name I have forgotten. Anyhow, he left us later in Glasgow to join the fleet air arm. He was a product of Fettes College and thought himself superior to the rest of us.

Our work in port consisted of the usual brass polishing, watchkeeping in the cargo holds against pilfering (to little avail), and a new task for me—greasing bottlescrews. Our mate had a thing about bottlescrews (turnbuckles for you North Americans). Another change was taking part in a proper training scheme to bring us up to snuff on combatting enemy air attacks. In addition to the classroom, where we were exposed to some very realistic dive bombing sequences projected on the inside of a dome. We were bused out to the coast at Formby and directed to shoot at targets towed by fairly slow moving aircraft. The weapons we were trained to load and fire were machine guns similar to the ones on board *Kindat*. It was not the complete answer to a German aircraft attack, but the training did give us a greater awareness of what we could expect and how we should respond.

I suppose I frequented the dockside pubs as usual, but it must have been restricted to short visits because I cannot recall the events. However, I was able to see a bit more of Birkenhead and its surroundings and attended a dance at the Kingsland Ballroom where I met a lovely girl who impressed me enormously. Her name was Doreen and she was petite with smiling medium brown eyes and dark brown hair. We appeared to hit it off, but she would not go to the nearest pub with me, settling for a milk shake instead. I then escorted her home, by bus and walking, where we exchanged a chaste kiss and agreed upon a date on the following Saturday. I little realized that her sister and boyfriend were on the same bus to keep an eye on me, the proverbial sailor. The Saturday date never transpired as *Kindat* joined a convoy outside the Mersey that same day bound for Glasgow to complete loading. I was disappointed, but immediately wrote to her expressing my desire to see her again. I had the address correct but the name I had recorded was quite incorrect. I re-sent it several times during the voyage and finally, after six months or so, we re-established contact. I was smitten!

The voyage north to the Clyde was stormy but otherwise uneventful. The Glasgow dockers exceeded their previous behaviour when loading *Mandalay* and smashed case afer case of whisky against the hatch coaming, while half-drunk stevedores in the holds rushed with every sort of container to catch the golden flow from above. It was not an edifying sight.

I managed a couple of short visits to home, and went to see Jean of the brown eyes. She was a nice person, but there was no spark between us. I would have loved to see Jean of the blue eyes, but it was too complicated with our age difference and her forthcoming marriage. Perhaps Young Lochinvar did not have the courage of his convictions.

There was of course lots of possible action in Glasgow that could be explored. One night, several of us picked up three sisters at a dance and went home with them, thinking we were on to a good thing. They were Highland girls and two of them were quite young. The Edinburgh cadet was most condescending to these Highland lassies and was prepared to take advantage of their youth, but the older sister would have none of it and made us all feel thoroughly ashamed of ourselves. She was Highland Scot and Christian and defended her sisters with devastating wit and derision. It was quite a performance. We snuck out of there with the remainder of our booze and sadly returned to *Kindat*.

We sailed from the Clyde in convoy in early March 1942. This time, I was able to navigate the North Channel without disgracing myself. The weather was not too bad, but the threat of submarine attack was prevalent. Lots of depth charges were deployed and our hull rang at times with the explosions. One ship was lost in an outer column. She sank very rapidly, but some crew were saved by our convoy rescue ship. South of Greenland, our section of the convoy dispersed, but not before being warned of heavy concentrations of U-boats to the west of us and in particular along the eastern seaboard of North America. The battle of the Atlantic had shifted focus as the Germans took full advantage of the American Navy's refusal to adopt the British convoy system.

Kindat zigged and zagged her way south seeing very few other vessels and being apprehensive about each and every one of them. As we moved into tropical waters, we were fascinated by waterspouts on the horizon and the antics of giant stingrays that threw themselves out of the water with great abandon. Four on four off watchkeeping was terminated and we resumed normal watchkeeping duties plus two hours deck work every day except Sunday, when we were subjected to cabin inspection by the captain and first mate. MacDonald and I shared a cabin, and once got in terrible trouble during inspection when MacDonald disposed of a filled ashtray out the open porthole onto the outside alleyway right in the path of the official inspection team. Our cabin itself was spotless, brass shining, bulkheads gleaming, bunks firm and inviting, basin sweet smelling, but our attempt to dispose of the tobacco ash brought us several hours of extra duty and a rocket of a reprimand from the captain.

The captain was another Highlander with little sense of humour. The first mate was a younger man and much more relaxed. It was a pleasure to be on his watch. I do not remember very much about the second and third mate, nor any of the other Europeans on board. But I do recall the butler whose cabin was next to ours, midships below the starboard boat deck. He was a well-spoken Indian who looked after the culinary needs of *Kindat* satisfactorily. He liked an occasional dram while at sea, but was always careful not to overdo it. We teased him at times and once bombarded him with raw potatoes dropped down a ventilator over his head as he sat on the throne in the toilet. However, he did make sure that we cadets got a few extra titbits. He had a secret hobby that he once unbent to display to me. He had a small horde of precious stones, which he had hidden in his cabin. There were diamonds, emeralds, rubies and others which he showed and described to me while illustrating ways of determining the authenticity of each stone. I wish I had paid more attention at the time—I could have perhaps become an expert myself. No doubt he traded these precious jewels from time to time and to some purpose that was never revealed to me.

Kindat made good time down the South Atlantic and soon there on the horizon was Table Mountain. We docked in Capetown to discharge a small quantity of cargo while taking on fresh produce and water. Capetown was once again a welcoming spot and we were treated well. One change had been implemented, partial blackout restrictions to reflect the Japanese menace in the Indian Ocean. That did not spoil our fun, but very shortly we were on our way into the Indian Ocean and bound for Durban. Once again, our destination was the bunkering wharves at the bluff. It was wonderful to get away from the ship and the pall of coal dust hanging over the bluff. After travelling on the ferry to the point, we decided to employ Zulu rickshaw drivers to take us to the beach. It was an exciting race and very shortly we were able to plunge into the Indian Ocean. The surf was strong and pulled us off our feet with ease, but further out the swimming was easy. It was simply grand. All too soon we had to return to the heat and dust of the bluff.

The following day, we departed from Durban. I had been experimenting with tobacco and, not really liking cigarettes or cheroots, I decided to try the pipe. After all, my dad smoked his pipe, so why should I not? So there I was, relaxing and taking tentative draws on my pipe as *Kindat* cleared the Bluff and headed out into a choppy Indian Ocean. I persisted with the pipe for a while, but gradually lost interest as my stomach advised me to desist. According to my shipmates, I then turned green in colour and deposited the contents of my stomach over the side. So much for my experiment with smoking a pipe. I never ever tackled the tobacco weed again.

It was now April 1942, and before leaving Durban we had been advised that the situation in the Indian Ocean and the Bay of Bengal was bad. Ostensibly, we were now bound for Ceylon but with almost daily announcements of evacuations and abandonment of ports in Southeast Asia, who knew where we would end up? As we proceeded north of Madagascar, the news became even grimmer. A Japanese fleet had penetrated the Bay of Bengal and attacked Ceylon with its carrier-based aircraft. Inside a few hours, they sunk the British carrier *Hermes* and several cruisers and destroyers off Ceylon, and pulverized the naval base at Trincomalee where the Paddy Henderson ship *Sagaing* was one of the early casualties. In the air, the Royal Air Force lost forty-seven aircraft to losses of only fifteen aircraft to the Japanese. The remaining British fleet had retreated to the Arabian Sea and indeed its battleships had removed themselves to the safety of Mombasa on the east coast of Africa. Our orders were changed to head for Bombay. We no longer had to worry just about German raiders; our new concern was the whereabouts of the Japanese fleet. Tense days followed, but we were cheered by the sighting of a number of British cruisers steaming toward the Maldive Islands. It appeared that we had not yet lost Ceylon.

Figure 30 - Paddy Henderson vessel *Sagaing* after Japanese attack on Trincomalee Harbour, 1942

One morning at dawn, we were off the approaches to Bombay harbour and saw a remarkable sight. Hundreds of ships of all shapes and sizes cluttered up the bay. There were warships, troop ships, tankers, freighters, Dutch coasters and even coasting steamers from the China coast. We anchored a long way from the port and awaited our orders. We were not too far from a British warship that entertained us with naval ceremony. From the raising of the white ensign at eight o'clock in the morning to the sunset ceremony, the noise of bugles and bosun's whistles kept us agog. Of particular interest to us was the constant coming and going of naval launches containing high-ranking naval officers. We wondered what was being plotted. Probably only a sampling of pink gins!

It was several days before the captain decided to visit the port authorities and, when he did, he insisted on the cadets manning one of the lifeboats and sailing from our anchorage to Ballard Pier, the naval control centre. What a performance! We were youthful and keen but without experience, and our shortcomings were all too obvious to not just our master but also to the viewers on the decks of the many ships that were assembled. After much trial and error, we tied up to the floats at Ballard Pier. Here he abandoned us and stalked off to find someone in higher authority. India was at hand with all its allure and mystery while we were besieged by mobs of Indians plying us with glass stoppered bottles of fizzy drinks, cigarettes, cigars and sweetmeats of infinite variety, meanwhile trying to avoid the projectiles of red betel juice being showered in every direction.

We were definitely in the Far East, but it felt different from Rangoon. Burma was exotic, India, as represented by Bombay, was more of a mix of Indian and European cultures, recognizable even if different. The outer side of Ballard Pier was lined with large troopships, all now painted the familiar wartime grey. They were all discharging their troop cargoes onto the pier prior to deployment inland in India. Most of the soldiers appeared to be British, and were making a fearful noise. Eventually, we received a message from our captain ordering us to return to *Kindat* forthwith. He would be returned in style on the ship's agent's motor launch. He evidently did not trust us to sail him safely back to his own ship. It was late in the day before we, weary but undaunted cadets, completed our sail back to *Kindat*.

However, now that we had made contact with the shore, regular trips with the motor launch could be arranged, and we managed to see a bit of Bombay. Money was short, however, and a tarpaulin muster had to be arranged before each trip ashore. Our funds were divided up thusly: so many rupees for the ghari to the cinema, so many rupees to buy us ice cream and other necessities, so many rupees to buy us each one alcoholic drink and if anything was left, a ghari ride back to the floats where the motor launch would be patiently waiting.

The cinemas in Bombay were quite modern and thank goodness were air-conditioned. As the monsoon was close to breaking and the heat was at times almost unbearable, visits to the cinema were greatly valued. The films were quite modern, usually produced in the United States. There were other cinemas where films produced in India were shown. These films were often about great events in India's past with Urdu or Hindi being the chosen language. Although often exotic and sometimes even erotic, no kissing or caressing could be shown on the screen.

Figure 31 - The Gateway of India, Bombay

We visited the Gateway of India on the waterfront, a huge stone monument to British power in India. Close by stood the exotic looking Hotel Taj Mahal, named after the beautiful shimmering tomb built by a Mogul emperor for his adored wife. We gave the Hotel Taj Mahal a quick inspection, concluding that the price of drinks was way beyond our means. Another visit that had to be made was to the red light district. Forrest Road and Grant Road were at the centre of this sprawling district. Establishments available ranged from the cages where girls were displayed for sale to the expensive plush-lined mansions of high-class madams, where decorum was expected, civilized conversation a must, selection by mutual consent and drinks served as a matter of course. The cages we found unacceptable, and the mansions were out of our price range.

After almost three weeks at anchor, *Kindat* moved into the Victoria Dock to discharge cargo. Much to my surprise, on the 13th May I was transferred to the *Salween*, another Paddy Henderson vessel, to relieve another cadet who was returning to the UK to sit for his second mate's foreign going certificate. I had enjoyed the three months I had spent on *Kindat*, but had not made any close friendships. I was quite ready to start anew on *Salween*.

Chapter Thirteen

Salween—1942

The *Salween* displaced about seven thousand tons and was driven with turbine engines that could propel her through the water at fifteen knots, much faster than *Mandalay* or *Kindat*. She was the last Henderson passenger liner built at Denny's of Dumbarton in 1938. *Salween* was in Bombay undergoing refit. She had been converted to trooping earlier in

Figure 32 - *SS Salween*, with Liver Building in the background

the war and was capable of carrying up to eighteen hundred bodies plus much of their equipment. I reported on board and was assigned to my cabin on the starboard side of the shade deck. My cabin mate was a Glasgow cadet called Jimmy Paterson. The two other cadets, like Jimmy, were hoping for relief shortly as they all were fast approaching eligibility to sit for their second mate's certificate. The ship was spacious compared with *Kindat* and it did not take me too long to find my way around.

Salween had a fairly uneventful war until late in 1940, when she was converted into a troop carrier. Her first voyage as trooper was from the Clyde to South Africa in early 1941 with seventeen hundred very seasick British soldiers on board. She then transported African soldiers to Suez. From there she proceeded up the Suez Canal to Port Said and Alexandria, where she joined a convoy of eight troop ships escorted by the cruiser *Carlyle* and the destroyers *Kingston* and *Kandahar*. Their destination was Greece and their purpose was to evacuate our troops who were in danger of destruction by the German army and air force. *Salween* was ordered to Port Raphtis with instructions to enter the port at midnight and be clear of the port by three AM. En route, they were subjected to three separate dive-bomber attacks, while the escorts maintained effective anti-aircraft fire and no ships were hit. The fast-running tide made the evacuation difficult with the lifeboats pressed into service. Several boats were damaged and at least one had to be abandoned. Finally, eight hundred and forty-five Australians and New Zealanders were successfully embarked on *Salween* and she joined the convoy preparing to return to Alexandria.

The convoy was subjected to three heavy air attacks. There were a number of near misses and the *Slamat* and *Costa Rica* were missing and presumed sunk. *Salween* reached Alexandria on the 29th April 1941, and from there proceeded to Australia via Colombo. She bunkered in Fremantle and discharged her homesick cargo in Adelaide. From there *Salween* returned to Mombasa and resumed her troop-carrying duties between East Africa and Suez, African troops north and Italian and German prisoners south, known locally in these politically incorrect days as the wog and wop ferry. *Salween* was presently undergoing refit in Bombay, preparatory to transporting Indian troops to the Persian Gulf.

The captain and chief officer of *Salween* were each awarded the Distinguished Service Cross and the chief engineer the Order of the British Empire for their contribution to the success of the Greece evacuation. Well deserved, but no doubt others deserved praise. Captain Wilson was still on board *Salween*, but chief officer Marsh had taken the place of chief officer Willis. The second mate was a chap called Hogg, the third mate's name was Trevaelian (he was a Frenchman from Brittany), and the fourth mate was formerly with Hogarth's. The chief radio operator was known as Marks the Sparks. In addition to Chippy, the ship's carpenter, there was quite a number of European staff on board, including storesmen. There was also a corps of medical staff manning a well-equipped hospital, with doctors, nursing sisters and support staff. *Salween* also had six engineering officers and twelve naval ratings to supervise and man the considerably enhanced armaments that were being added during her refit. Four Highland quartermasters ensured that the ship was in good seamanlike hands. Last but not least came the Indian crew who numbered about sixty souls and who did all the dirty work on board. They were mainly Moslem on deck, Hindu in the engine room and Goan Christian in the steward department. There were many more people to interface with than on *Mandalay* or *Kindat*.

Figure 33 - A coal bunkering operation

I saw a great deal of Bombay during this refit period, and found it to be a much larger and more complex city than Rangoon. There was much to see and explore in both the westernized sections of the city and in the crowded marketplaces and slums of which there were many. There was some tension in the air, mainly around the railway and bus stations, where banners displaying the words "Quit India" were prominent. However, it was perfectly safe for a European to go just about anywhere without fear of trouble. Surprisingly, there were few signs of a police or military presence, although there were lots of military personnel on leave in the streets.

I explored Colaba Point and its barracks and churchyard. It represented the establishment of British power in the Maharati States, and was very interesting to a young history buff. Then on to Apollo Bundar and the naval dockyard, and another look at Victoria and Princes Docks. Transportation was plentiful, whether by ghari, bus or train. I continued to explore and found the Malabar Hills and the Parsi Towers of Silence where Parsi dead are laid out in the towers to be eaten by kite hawks. I was told by someone that Parsi women looked for suitable young white men to mate with to keep the race light skinned. If true, it was not my luck to be so accosted!

Further up the Arabian Sea coast lay Beach Kandy, a mecca for many of us. It was an open air bathing pool situated right on the beach, big enough for swimmers and yet comfortable for the inexperienced, a wonderful place to be in the scorching heat of pre-monsoon Bombay. I also roamed around Cumballa Hill inland from Beach Kandy, and visited the Walkeshwar Temple on Malabar Point and walked the marine lines where small apartment blocks fronted onto the Arabian Sea. To add to the feeling that we were absorbing British Indian culture, *Salween* was challenged by Indian teams to football and cricket matches and was thoroughly beaten. We were just about ready to go back to sea. The teeming bazaars with their exotic colours, the smells of the Orient—pungent and intoxicating—the racial mix of Pathan to Madrasi to Chi Chi was all very well, but we were growing too soft. We said goodbye to the Dutchmen on their coasters and warships who had fled their East Indian empire and all the other seamen we had met, and lay at anchor awaiting orders as the monsoon broke over the Bombay anchorage. The rain came down in buckets and there was a marvellous cooling breeze sweeping *Salween's* decks.

Figure 34 - Bombay and the west coast of India

In early June 1942, we tied up to Ballard Pier and embarked two battalions of Indian soldiers bound for Basra in the Persian Gulf. These men were well-drilled fighting soldiers and were most impressive in every way. Unfortunately, three of them became sick on the voyage and were buried at sea with full military pomp and circumstance. The voyage in convoy was otherwise straightforward and we discharged our Indian troops in Basra. It was very hot in the Persian Gulf. Added to that fact was the tense atmosphere in the Middle East as the Germans threatened the area from their latest capture of much of the Russian Caucasus and their threat to Egypt from their recent victories in the western desert.

No shore leave was granted in Basra, and we proceeded to Bandur Shapur in Persia. This was a small port that was mainly employed in forwarding war materials to Russia. Our cargo was a sad-looking gang of Poles, mostly women and children, who had fled eastern Poland into Russia in 1940 and had made their way without much help from anyone to the Persian Gulf. We were to transport them to East Africa, where it was expected that they could join a small community of Poles already there. The real victims of the war were right in front of our eyes.

Salween joined several other troopships in convoy and made her way out of the Persian Gulf, then southeast to the coast of East Africa. Our port of discharge was Tanga, just north of Dar Es Salaam. Tanga had been the site of a battle in the First World War, when Tanganyika was German East Africa. An invasion force of British Indian army troops landed by sea on the beaches at Tanga and were slaughtered by the better prepared German African forces. I hoped this was not a bad omen for our poor Poles. Many years later in Canada I met one of the Poles, so they did survive after all.

I liked the pleasant climate of the East African coast and was delighted when we were ordered to Zanzibar to bunker. Zanzibar was ruled by a sultan but was under British jurisdiction. The city was small, with very narrow winding streets and white stone buildings. Minarets rose everywhere and the Moslem call to prayer could be clearly heard five times daily. The smell of cloves permeated the air. Zanzibar and the adjoining island of Pemba were renowned for the cultivation of cloves and their export to the world. Swimming off the harbour was a glorious experience and we cadets took advantage of every opportunity to practice our sailing skills with one of *Salween's* lifeboats while exploring the many islets that sheltered the harbour entrance.

There were many Arab dhows plying their trade around Zanzibar, continuing a practice of many centuries. On our passage from the Persian Gulf across the Arabian Sea, we had seen numerous large seagoing dhows en route to Zanzibar or returning to Arabia. It was exciting to contemplate this unique traffic. Up until the late nineteenth century, Zanzibar was the centre of the slave trade from the heart of Africa to Oman and the Gulf. It was a Scottish missionary explorer who finally managed to put an end to this terrible trade—David Livingstone. The old slave market was still preserved in the city centre. The city was dominated by the Sultan's Istana, an attractive white domed structure. Needless to say, we did not receive an invitation to visit.

The shops in the back alleys were interesting, and hard to find items for gifts were readily available. Our bunkering was completed in similar fashion to Bombay, with long lines of coolies, both male and female, carrying small loads of coal on their heads from barges to our bunker facility. It must have been backbreaking work, particularly in the heat of the day.

We reluctantly departed from the enchanted island of Zanzibar bound for Mombasa in Kenya. Mombasa had become a very busy strategic port since the main elements of the British fleet had fled Trincomalee in Ceylon. Its protected harbour at Kilindini was large enough to hold several fleets with lots of room left over. When we arrived from Zanzibar, the harbour was dominated by three elderly battleships of the Revenge class and several light cruisers of the Capetown class. Additionally, there was a flotilla of destroyers and supply ships of various kinds. Among the supply vessels was *Burma*, an older Paddy Henderson liner. It was good to see another ship of the company and to make contact with her crew. She had been trooping earlier in the war, but in the late summer of 1942 she seemed to be mainly employed as a supply and storage vessel. We cadets from *Salween* challenged *Burma's* cadets to sailing and rowing races. I believe that *Burma* won both events, which we put down to having more practice and less sea time.

There was not much to see ashore at Kilindini, with the exception of a long modern wharf well fitted with cranes for loading and discharge. Mombasa itself lay a mile or so inland and was a typical outpost of empire with its well laid out centre with streets of shops and businesses. Churches and offices of government administration were also much in evidence. The prevailing décor was white or beige, with open verandas running along either side of the streets. There were lots of whites and many blacks who lived in separate areas outside the city centre. There were some nice hotels where a cool lager could be drunk in plush cool comfort. There were of course some less salubrious but livelier places where I was once entertained by two drunken naval seamen dancing on a table while singing and going through the motions of "I've got a lovely bunch of coconuts, there they are standing in a row, big ones, small ones, some as big as your head," etc. I hope the two of them survived the war, they had the right spirit!

North of Mombasa, in its own small harbour, nestled Fort Jesus. Fort Jesus was the site of the original Portuguese settlement in the sixteenth century. My sense of history was captured as I envisaged the events that must have occurred here. With Christianity came empire and slavery. In the early years, Fort Jesus and Zanzibar must have been in competition for both empire and slaves. What a thought!

We eventually proceeded alongside at Kilindini and loaded our African troops bound for Egypt. They were pioneer corps, destined for road building and other heavy construction tasks in the western desert. Most of them looked as if they had come straight out of the jungle, with little experience of the white man's ways. I learned later that they were recruited through their local chief and had little say in the matter. The majority of them were strong and fit, but even so, six of them died at sea and were buried with due ceremony before we reached Suez.

We had an otherwise uneventful voyage from Mombasa to Port Tewfik, in a small convoy to off Aden and then on our own up the Red Sea. It was hot and the smell from the oil refineries at Suez funnelled down the gulf so that it was in your nostrils from more than a day's run away. The African troops were unloaded onto barges and we prepared for Italian prisoners of war. They arrived alongside, behaving more like holidaymakers than captured soldiers, carrying assorted coloured bags and occasionally bursting into song. The war was obviously over for them and they were so glad. To guard them, we had a number of East African Askaris carrying ancient Lee Enfield rifles. What a joke!

The Italians lived up to their billing and were perfectly behaved all the way to Mombasa. However, they livened things up a bit by substituting for some African sentries that they found asleep on watch, taking over their rifles and completing the watch themselves. Thank goodness we were not carrying Germans!

After clearing the straits of Bab el Mandep at the southern entrance to the Red Sea, we were ordered to Aden for bunkers. Much has been written about Aden and it is all true. The barren rocks of Aden are a hellhole at any time, but notably in the late summer. The heat comes off the land in waves and inhibits all movement. How on earth the Arabs carrying coal on their heads survived the heat is a mystery. Choking clouds of coal dust everywhere helped to make life on board absolute torture. No shore leave was given, and none requested. It was with great joy that we departed Aden and headed around Cape Guardafui for Mombasa. The weather in the Arabian Sea was brisk and *Salween* was tossed around quite a bit, but after Aden it was a mere pinprick. Within a few short days, we were saying farewell to those reluctant warriors, the Italians.

In Mombasa, we were delighted to receive orders to proceed to Durban forthwith to complete refit and then load British troops bound for the fighting in the western desert. We had a number of civilian passengers

Figure 35 - A happy cadet on *Salween*

on board, including several Frenchwomen from Madagascar who had been captured by our forces when we attacked the Vichy French in Diego Suarez. They stood out from among the others, probably because they were attractive and had that indefinable Gallic presence. This reminded me of my high school exchange teacher. Without a doubt they cut a merry swath among the ship's company. Affairs were noted, some more passionate than others, but cadets were not in the winners' circle and suffered in envy. We reached Durban in a state of barely suppressed sexual torment and descended on the available female population in dire need of solace.

I had become quite close to Guns, the naval gunner petty officer on board, and he and I went looking for female company. We struck lucky on the beach and spent a great deal of time at the Coogee Beach Hotel where the girls were staying. They were on holiday from Johannesburg, of Scottish stock and lots of fun. Guns was a Welshman named Morgan who did not mind the Scottish connection and in fact revelled in it. All in all, it was a good time.

He told me about an episode that occurred when *Salween* visited Colombo en route to Australia with Australian soldiers from the Middle East on board. Apparently, shore leave in Colombo was restricted by the commanding officer to officers only, which infuriated other ranks. They rioted on board and broke into the spirits locker. Several of them had trained under Guns as spare gun crews for the four point seven anti-submarine gun on *Salween's* stern. They loaded the gun with shell and cordite charge and trained it on the Galle Face Hotel where their officers were relaxing. They then realized that they needed percussion tubes to detonate the cordite. Guns had the percussion tubes in his cabin under lock and key. They pounded on the door to persuade him to hand them over. He had a loaded rifle and threatened to shoot whoever broke down the door. After more drinking and more threats, they finally gave up and unloaded the four point seven.

What a mess that could have been! Guns, as befits a Welshman, had a fine voice, which he used to accompany his recordings of famous opera singers. Through him I learned of Miliza Kordus, Elizabeth Schumann (Hitler's favourite) and many others. It was quite a change from that other Welshman Jenkins on *Mandalay* and his love of Benny Goodman and all the other American bandleaders of swing.

All of us knew that our chances of seeing Durban again were small and that we were probably fated to plow the waters of the Indian Ocean and

Red Sea for some time to come. We therefore made the most of our stay. The dim-out at night to confuse enemy ships and submarines did nothing to dampen our enthusiasm. People were very friendly, everything was in plentiful supply, what more could we ask for. Refit was carried out in the dockyard with additions to our vessel's armament being the main item of business, together with some improvements to the troop deck living quarters. I remember carrying a fire extinguisher down the long steep wooden ladder to number two troop deck, slipping on the wet step and catapulting down twenty feet or so to land on the deck with the fire extinguisher still clutched in my hands. There was no sympathy or concern expressed. Indeed, I was chastized loudly and descriptively by the first mate Marsh.

The dockyard was located in a tough part of town and care had to be taken when passing through the area. There had been several murders and cases of robbery with violence. The attractiveness of the city centre, the beach and the better suburbs masked an underlying tension. In addition, the antics of the Afrikaaner Broederbond and other pro-German groups cast a bit of a pall over things. Most of the Afrikaners were supporters of Jan Smuts and on our side, but a worrisome number were prepared to sabotage the war effort. The memory of the Boer War died hard.

We moved to the Bluff for bunkering before going to the Maydon Wharf to embark troops. *Salween* took on board roughly seventeen hundred British soldiers. There were part of an infantry battalion and a large contingent of the Royal Artillery. At dockside were several other troop carriers, all loading British troops bound for the western desert. Bands played, flags waved, and a lady with a truly magnificent singing voice serenaded us with "Tipperary" and all the old favourites. It was a grand farewell to Durban, our home away from home for a wonderful two weeks or so. Among the ships in the fast convoy assembled were the three-funnel British India liner, *Takliwa*, and a Blue Funnel liner that took part with us in the wog-wop exercise. (I ran across both vessels on other occasions, the Blue Funnel liner as a mine casualty of the Normandy landings in 1944, and *Takliwa* en route to Mombasa in 1946.)

The convoy was escorted by the armed merchant cruiser *Mooltan* and a C-Class light cruiser. We headed up between Madagascar and Portuguese

East Africa, then straight up the Indian Ocean to Cape Guardafui before turning into the Gulf of Aden. At this point, we were shadowed by aircraft of the Royal Air Force until we entered the Red Sea, when each ship proceeded on its own toward Suez. Our troops had not been idle on the voyage. Drilling on deck for other ranks and plane surveying tactics for the artillery officers using a miniature model of the western desert set up abaft the bridge on the boat deck. I got a good view of this daily exercise as I was employed on repairing anti-aircraft kites close by.

These young officers were keen and anxious to get to the battle zone as soon as possible. At this time, the Germans and Italians under Rommel had been stopped at the first battle of El Alamein, only ninety miles from Alexandria. There was much talk and speculation about a new British offensive, and our troops would be part of that effort.

Just south of the Gulf of Suez, we had a bit of excitement when three soldier prisoners broke out of the brig above the chain locker and launched two small emergency rafts over the side. Two prisoners were recovered but one got clean away. What a hazardous undertaking in such shark-infested waters. They must have been desperate or deluded. We learned later that the one who got clean away was later found on a small reef. I never did find out why they were in the brig but knew that severe punishment probably awaited them in Egypt.

The war elsewhere was a mixed bag of news. The battle of the Atlantic was largely a disaster area with appalling losses of Allied shipping, but small groups of hunter frigates and escort aircraft carriers were beginning to have some positive effect. However, in Russia the Germans had advanced deep into the Caucasus to the vicinity of Grozny, but were being held at Stalingrad on the Volga. In the Pacific, the Americans had won a great victory at Midway by destroying a large part of the Japanese carrier fleet. When this battle was first reported, many of us dismissed its success as overblown American bravado. But it was a genuine victory that had opened the way to eventually defeat the Japanese. In Burma, the last of the British forces had withdrawn into India to regroup and hopefully fight another day.

Salween discharged her British Army charges in Suez wishing them every success. We then took on board several hundred Greeks, mostly women and children, who had fled from various Aegean islands to the safety of

British-controlled Egypt. They were a poor unhappy looking lot and appeared to be looking forward to being temporarily relocated in East Africa. Several nursing sisters joined *Salween*, primarily to look after these weakened women and children. Additionally, we had a number of passengers, mostly British Army officers, on board. One of them, a medical officer, shot himself with his own revolver when we were passing through the Straits of Bab el Mandep. He must have intended to fall clear of the ship into the sea, thereby causing little trouble. However, unfortunately, he fell into one of the outer lifeboats. Poor fellow, it was a messy affair. I hope his family did not suffer.

We bunkered again in Aden, and were convoyed to the vicinity of Socotra by a destroyer —a new innovation. The Greeks were unloaded in Dar Es Salaam, a beautiful little harbour in Tanganyika, and the capital city of that territory. It had formerly been part of German East Africa, but was being administered by Britain under a League of Nations charter. The entrance was partially blocked by a German ship scuttled there at the outbreak of World War II, making navigation tricky. We visited the Gymkanna Club for relaxation. There seemed to be little or no nightlife.

Once more, without undue delay, we sailed to Mombasa and loaded more African service troops bound for Egypt. It was getting a bit monotonous. However, our next port of call was Massawa in the Red Sea. the former Italian port for Eritrea. It was a hot sticky spot with not much to commend it. As in Dar Es Salaam, the harbour entrance was partially blocked by a scuttled vessel; in this case she was Italian. We were to pick up some Italian prisoners of war, who also happened to be entertainers, and convey them to Berbera in Somaliland. They were a wild exotic gang, theatrical in their mannerisms, but very talented. They could not be persuaded to go down into the sweltering troop decks and camped out on deck from where they gave continual impromptu performances. I learned much about Italian opera on that voyage and appreciated those glorious voices raised in song. A British Army officer was in charge of this colourful group. I am sure that he had his hands full.

One sour note spoiled this happy interlude. A Royal Air Force pilot on board who had tangled with the Italians in Eritrea was most incensed at the antics of this group and wanted them all locked up. His experience had embittered him, but he should have been able to appreciate the beautiful music of Verdi and Puccini accompanied by these incredible voices.

While in Massawa, I visited the local hotel and at midnight swam in the open-air salt-water pool to attempt to cool off. The water was so warm that I felt quite sick. I also joined a line-up of soldiers in front of a darkened building. Rumour said that a shipment of cold beer had arrived. It turned out to be an army-controlled brothel where six Italian women of indeterminate age did a brisk business. An experience better forgotten. The last night in Massawa was New Year's Eve, and I celebrated it in true Scottish style by getting pie-eyed and attempting a reel while poised on a table in the petty officers' mess on board. Good-bye to 1942, what would 1943 bring?

Chapter Fourteen

*Salween—*1943

As we sailed out through the restricted harbour entrance, we hit an Arab dhow and carried him on our bow for some distance from shore. I hope the fellow received adequate compensation. Not a good start to a new year. The Italian entertainers were deposited without undue incident in Berbera, a desolate looking little port on the Gulf of Aden. We discharged cargo there with the help of a wild looking bunch of Somalis. The cargo consisted mainly of packaged goods, most of which were in short supply. I found myself keeping watch over these scallywags, but eventually fell to temptation myself. One case of Van Der Hum liquor brandy received damage and I purloined a bottle for my own consumption. I had remembered its unique flavour from visits to Durban. Naturally, it was shared with my shipmates.

From Berbera, we headed again to Tanga where we loaded several hundred Italian women and children, previously captured in Ethiopia. The women had been without their men for a long time and were a handful. They were to be part of an exchange of civilian prisoners of war between Italy and Britain. The British prisoners were to be taken to Sweden for onward traffic home, while the Italian prisoners in East Africa were to be taken to Berbera where we would meet the Italian passenger ships *Vulcania* and *Saturnia*, which would transport them around the Cape back to Italy. All of this was to be done under terms of the Geneva Convention and under the banner of the Red Cross. Our volatile group refused to go down to the troop decks—sweltering heat once again—and set up sleeping quarters for themselves on the shade deck and on top of all our deck hatches. They clamoured for ice water (always in short supply), and used their squalling brats to play upon our sympathies. As some of them were quite shapely and attractive, that was easily taken care of. So we set off northward for Berbera accompanied by our British India and Blue Funnel friends and other transports to keep the unprecedented rendez-vous with the enemy.

These women were convinced that Italy would win the war, and supported Mussolini with fascist fervour. They believed that the British victory at El Alamein in November 1942 and the subsequent push into Libya and beyond were just British propaganda. They made known these views to us on every opportunity. Many of them had acquired a considerable English vocabulary during their period of captivity. Probably as a result of close relationships with their stated enemy. Even so, a watchkeeping inspection of the shade deck at night resulted in whispered invitations and even forceful grabs at legs and arms. Talk about the hazards of war!

The night before *Salween* reached Berbera we could clearly see the Red Cross lights of *Vulcania* and *Saturnia* on the horizon. As daylight came and the Italians could see their own ships, they burst into a series of patriotic fascist songs culminating in a spirited rendition of "Il Duce." Shortly thereafter, we entered the harbour anchorage at Berbera and, after the proper formalities had been observed, the great exchange commenced. Our prisoners left us singing in defiance but when they boarded *Vulcania*, to their indignant dismay, they were consigned to the deepest bowels of the vessel. It had been an interesting and thought-provoking interlude.

We returned to Mombasa to load more African troops for Suez. Then one more load of Italian service personnel from Suez back to East Africa. With the emphasis on Egypt as a war zone receding, our efforts were to turn to the Indian Ocean and the war against the Japanese.

However, *Salween* carried one more shipload of African Pioneer Corps north to Suez before loading Indian soldiers from the North African war and returning them to India. During our stay in Suez, we changed captains, some officers, and two cadets. The new captain was Duncan, formerly of the sunken *Sagaing*, the first mate was Campbell, formerly of *Mandalay*, and the two cadets were products of Glasgow Tech. I had been fairly happy under Captain Wilson and his regime, but with Duncan and the others on board, I began to long for a change of venue. I thought Duncan was overbearing, Campbell played favourites, and one of the new cadets was a schemer with little sense of loyalty to me who now found myself acting as senior cadet. No doubt time passed quickly, but for me it was not a happy time.

Two incidents occurred worthy of comment while we were alongside in Port Tewfik. A large United States train ferry loaded with tanks and other armoured vehicles and with an Egyptian pilot on board entered the port at excessive speed and even the dropping of both anchors failed to stop her progress. She just missed *Salween's* bow but careened onward and hit a Port Line reefer vessel amidships but above the waterline. The resulting gouge on her side opened up the insulation material, which poured down into the harbour. There appeared to be little damage to the American vessel. This Port Line vessel had been undergoing repairs to her stern after an accidental explosion of her stern gun shell during a normal gun drill at sea. It was a solemn warning to our own gun crew to be extra careful.

Just before sailing from Port Tewfik, I had to see a dentist about an infected tooth. It was a harrowing experience that coloured my feelings about dentists and Egyptians for a long time to come. Mind you, thank goodness at that time, the British were the imperial power in Egypt. There were two sets of authority on the dock gates—Egyptian and British. I remember once being delegated by my shipmates to smuggle a bottle of Scotch whisky ashore, and it slipping from my clothing and smashing to smithereens in front of the authorities. The Egyptians wanted to jail me on the spot but a kindly British corporal overruled them and I went free to get up to all sorts of mischief ashore. This tight British control stemmed from the events of mid-1942, with the Germans at El Alamein and close to the heartland of Egypt. King Farouk planned an insurrection before departing the Abdin Palace for shelter with the fascists. The British Army was deployed around the palace and the king stayed put while the British kept a very close eye on all Egyptian institutions. With the Allied successes in North Africa, the defeat of the Afrika Corps in Libya, coupled with Allied invasions of Morocco and Algeria, leaving only Tunisia to be subdued, the tight rein on Egypt was being eased somewhat.

Salween conveyed her Indian warriors home quickly, stopping only at Aden for bunkers on the way. The troops were disembarked at Ballard Pier in Bombay to a hero's welcome. After tidying up and conducting essential repairs, we sailed for Colombo to another rendez-vous with returning heroes. This time, we were part of a troop convoy scheduled to depart Colombo with several thousand King's African Rifles infantry returning from a year's fighting against the Japanese in Burma. They had conducted themselves well in Burma and were ready for home leave.

It was a long haul across the Indian Ocean in the company of an armed merchant cruiser escort. The AMC was refuelled about halfway on the voyage by a royal fleet auxiliary tanker from Diego Garcia in the Maldives. It is strange to have Diego Garcia hit the front page of newspapers again in the early twenty-first century.

Salween was a bit top heavy with all her rocket and gunnery emplacements built above the boat deck. Even all the ballast provided close to the keel could not compensate when we encountered a large swell. As a result, we waddled our way across a large part of the Indian Ocean, the only relief coming when we zigged or zagged course out of the main effect of the swell. It became so violent at times that our steam turbines had to be nursed carefully or we would lose power. The violent roll at times seemed to upset many things on board including the sudden appearance of a few rats—an ominous sign. Considering the fact that a thorough gas fumigation of *Salween* had taken place roughly every six months, and that huge sackfuls of dead rats and cockroaches were collected after each fumigation, it was incredible that they still managed to survive.

The excessive rolling and the rats did not keep us from our destination, and in due time we steamed into Dar Es Salaam harbour to the cheers of a big crowd assembled to meet us. Our battalions were led off the ship by a fine African pipe band that could be heard in the distance as they marched through the centre of the city.

Salween departed for Mombasa to bunker and prepare for another voyage to Suez with more African troops. As usual, we enjoyed the sailing and swimming and short visits to Mombasa itself. When we tied up to the main wharves in preparation for loading, we found ourselves inboard *HMS Capetown*, a C-Class cruiser that we had been in convoy with earlier in the war. As her crew had to cross our deck to reach *Capetown*, we were provided with a spectacle each evening. Sober sailors had no difficulty navigating the companionways, but inebriated matelots faced a major trial in trying to successfully pass inspection of the watch. If they could stand erect and salute the quarterdeck they were home free, but a number failed and were charged. Thank goodness, we were not subject to such discipline.

It was on *Capetown* that I watched a very elegantly dressed senior officer address a large body of seamen on the hazards of venereal disease. His punch line was "some of you men would put your penis where I wouldn't put the end of my walking stick," meanwhile twirling his walking stick for emphasis.

The last unusual event was when one of our gang, after a few drinks, borrowed an army lorry parked on the dockside, and drove it around the wharves. He was arrested, charged with all sorts of offences, and spent a night in custody before being released into the tender care of our captain.

Salween departed Mombasa in late July 1943. I did not realize at the time that it would be a number of years before I would see East Africa again, or that my relief was awaiting me in Suez. But so it was to be, while safely discharging our latest load of African troops, relief cadets for Hughes and myself stepped on board. Although I had wanted to leave *Salween*, it was nevertheless a bit of a shock to lose one's home after a period of sixteen months or so. When my gear was deposited on the dock, I touched *Salween's* hull for the last time. What would lie ahead until home was reached safely?

Chapter Fifteen

Egypt and Homeward Bound

Hughes and I were deposited at a large private home in Port Tewfik owned by an Irishman, formerly a Suez Canal pilot. He and his wife ran the place as a sort of boarding house. Every nook and cranny was filled with military or seagoing personnel en route to somewhere else. As I recall, there were Australian air force officers, Royal Naval officers and others, but the most interesting group to us was the survivors from *Yoma*, another Paddy Henderson ship that had recently been sunk in the Mediterranean off Derna. She had been carrying a large number of troops, of whom many were lost. The captain and chief engineer and twenty-nine crew members also perished. The survivors were picked up by naval minesweepers. There were six of these survivors staying at the Irishman's establishment. There was the first mate and three cadets—one called Ritchie, another called Woodcock but known to all as "Timber," the third one's name is lost to me. The others were I believe radio officers.

We soon established rapport with the *Yoma* gang and spent much time in their company. They had been in Port Tewfik for several weeks, awaiting a passage home around the Cape, but were on a waiting list. That did not augur well for we recent arrivals. They had some harrowing tales to tell of their rescue and journey by lorry from Derna to the Egyptian-Libyan border and then by freight train to the Egyptian delta. They were more than ready to go home or break out or do something wild. In their company, we saw the sights of Port Tewfik and Suez, the open-air cinema, the illicit drinking establishments, the French Club—where we ogled the young wives of the Suez Canal officials and generally made a nuisance of ourselves. The first mate was an alcoholic, which inhibited our actions somewhat, as we had to keep watch on him.

Then one fine day we were given a special assignment—to take a brand-new small tug from Suez to Alexandria and deliver it there to the appropriate Royal Engineers dock operating company. It felt like deliverance, and our thoughts went to the possibility that we might have a better chance at a ship bound home from Alexandria or Port Said. We said good-bye to the others remaining and to our Irish host, and assembled in the naval dockyard to board our tug. She was small, about fifty feet in length, built in Canada and transported to Egypt in a heavy lift ship. Our first mate, known as Cap, was in ostensible command but, with his problem, command responsibilities really lay with Ritchie, the senior *Yoma* cadet.

Our crew therefore consisted of Cap, Ritchie, Woodcock and myself, plus that essential ingredient—a Maltese engineer. We had a trial run around the harbour, then set off up the Suez Canal. There was a small fridge, but little other storage space. We planned to stop in Port Said for anti-mine degaussing before entering the Mediterranean, where we would also refuel and take on stores. We stopped off Ismailia in the Bitter Lakes while awaiting a northbound convoy. There, the very competent engineer carried out some necessary adjustments to the engines and we proceeded north to Port Said without further incident. After contacting the authorities, we were degaussed and prepared for tests the following day.

That evening, we went off to see the nightlife in Port Said. In the bar at one hotel an Egyptian businessman took a fancy to Woodcock, who led him a merry dance while he and I were plied with drinks. We then went off in a ghari to view the red light district, which was a dreadful place. Without further ado, we returned to our tug. The following day we carried out our degaussing exercises and then went ashore for a farewell drink in Port Said. It must have been quite a party because, when I awoke the following morning, I felt like the proverbial wrath of God. If I was comforted at all, it was to know that my companions were in a similar state. Only our Maltese engineer was bright and sober, thank goodness.

We headed out into the Mediterranean, past the statue to Ferdinand de Lesseps, builder of the Suez Canal in eighteen sixty-seven, between the twin piers that mark the harbour approaches to Port Said. There was a steady swell sweeping down the piers that started bouncing us around and, when we altered course to proceed westward, our tug began rolling about in a most uncomfortable manner. In the wheelhouse, we had to lash ourselves into place to avoid being thrown about and injured. We also had to tie buckets in place on either side of the wheel to take care of our excessive vomit. This weather continued all night long. By dawn, we were exhausted and had not got a clue where we were. There were no lights or shapes visible along the shoreline of the delta. If we were heading west that should be safe enough, but if we were heading northwest, then we were on our way to Crete, which was not where we wanted to be at all.

Luckily for us, poor navigators that we were, we spotted a felucca fishing vessel in the distance, which laughingly pointed to us the course to Alexandria. It was yet another illustration of the incompatibility of liquor and common sense.

Before describing our arrival in Alexandria in late August 1943, a brief review of the war situation in the Mediterranean theatre is called for. The Mediterranean had been virtually closed to the Allies since the fall of France in June 1940. Malta had held out valiantly against almost continuous aerial attacks and provided a platform for Royal Air Force sorties against Italian convoys to Libya that were supplying Axis forces in the western desert. Additionally, Royal Navy submarines based on Malta added to the toll on Axis shipping. By 1942, the position of Malta was becoming desperate, with everything from food to defences in short supply.

Allied rescue convoys were mounted from both the eastern and western ends of the Mediterranean. These convoys were protected by enormous fleets of warships, but nevertheless largely failed in their attempts to relieve Malta. Fighter planes were flown off aircraft carriers to join the garrison, but even that effort failed to stem the tide. However, a large convoy from the east having turned back after running out of anti-aircraft ammunition, a convoy from the west managed to get four ships safely into Valletta harbour after fighting off sustained enemy air attacks and by Italian motor torpedo boats. Allied losses were heavy, ten merchant vessels, the aircraft carrier *Eagle* and several destroyers. This relief took place in August 1942. Malta was able to hold on until November 1942 when Allied landings in North West Africa and the

British Eighth Army's sweep westward from El Alamein to Tripoli narrowed Axis options in the Mediterranean.

The Allied landings in North Africa were a combined British-American operation aimed at Morocco and Algeria. Most of the huge convoy sailed from the Clyde anchorage at the Tail of the Bank, with the Paddy Henderson vessel *Dalhanna* in their midst. The French did not oppose the landings, but the Germans mounted strong aerial attacks from Tunisia on the ships discharging at Oran, Bône and Algiers. Many ships were sunk, but the landings were successful. The Germans, however, had been given time to regroup in Tunisia and it was not until May 1943 that Tunis fell to the Allies and the Mediterranean partially opened up for the transit of Allied shipping. In July 1943, the Allied invasion of Sicily followed and on the seventeenth of August all of Sicily was in Allied hands.

Such was the situation as we approached the harbour of Alexandria in our tiny tug. We eventually made contact with the proper port authorities and tied up feeling that we had accomplished something, even if our navigational skills had not been up to snuff.

Alexandria has a magnificent harbour and an imposing shoreline. It is, of course, steeped in history. The ancient civilization of the builders of the pyramids, Alexander the Great, Cleopatra, the Roman conquest and more recent events, all combine to enhance a feeling of being in a special place. The ruins of Cleopatra's palaces lay just below the waters of the inner harbour. Eastward, on the shore of the delta, at Aboukir Bay, lay the remains of the French fleet destroyed by Horatio Nelson in the Napoleonic Wars. In the city itself were countless monuments to past glory. But in 1943 we were initially more interested in the signs of the present conflict. These were highlighted by the sight of half a dozen French warships at anchor and the vast armada of Royal Navy vessels tied up to wharves or at anchor. The French warships had been in Alexandria since the fall of France with their weaponry disabled and their engines decommissioned, thus rendering them no threat to the Royal Navy.

Two Royal Navy battleships took pride of place in the centre of the harbour. They were *Queen Elizabeth*, the flagship, and *Valiant*, another elderly vessel. Every day, these ships hoisted their colours at eight AM and lowered them at sunset. They had been doing this since December 1941 when they were mined by a daring group of Italian divers. The divers were captured and, with no information about the success of the attack leaking out to the enemy, the vessels were allowed to sink a few feet into the muddy bottom and persuade the population of Alexandria that the Royal Navy Mediterranean fleet was still very much a threat to the Italian fleet. What a bluff!

We departed our tug and the Maltese engineer with some regret, and found ourselves assigned to a boarding house in the city, but not too far from the docks. Across the road from our new home was a factory that manufactured handbags and other leather goods. The factory windows were always open and usually filled with girls who took great interest in we newcomers to the boarding house. They were Christian Copts, as we could tell from their open attitude and lack of veils or other coverings on the head or around the face. We exchanged waves and other gestures but were unable to progress any further as they were shepherded out of the factory by male guardians. It was frustrating and getting more so by the day.

Once, when out seeing the sights of the city we found the Sporting Club where one could meet young ladies while swimming or playing tennis. Woodcock and I managed to strike up a conversation with two lovely girls. They were of Greek background, and on our stroll in the gardens were heavily chaperoned. As we were not prepared to offer marriage, the relationships went no further.

All over Alexandria were wonderful pâtisseries that served great sweet cakes of many varieties. There one could ogle the young ladies who came to buy and no doubt to ogle back. There was much to see in Alexandria besides the girls. I am only sorry that we were not there long enough to see all that was worth seeing, but I did visit Pompey's pillar, a granite pillar over eighty feet high. Apparently it was actually built to honour the Roman emperor Diocletian and not poor old Pompey. Also visited the site of the Pharos of Alexandria, the lighthouse that was one of the seven wonders of the ancient world. It was located on the entrance to the great harbour (eastern harbour), and must have been quite an awe-inspiring sight. There are virtual layers of cities built on top of one another since its founding by Alexander the Great in 331 BC. In fact, the city can trace its beginnings to Homer, who mentioned the good harbour in the Odyssey. However, it was Alexander's vision that made the city great. He never saw the finished city.

Figure 36 - The Pillar of Pompey, Alexandria, Egypt

The first city could be called the Ptolemaic city that lasted from Alexander's death until 30 BC when Cleopatra lost the battle of Actium to the Romans. The Ptolemies were all descended from Ptolemy the first, a Macedonian general. Under the Ptolemies' rule, Alexandria became one of the largest metropolises in the world. Their legacy includes the Pharos lighthouse, the great library, the Heptastadion Dyke and many other great buildings. However, the later Ptolemies created great economic hardship for their citizens and indulged in great family scandals that undermined their reign.

The Ptolemaic city was followed by the Roman city from 30 BC to 641 AD. The early years of Roman rule saw the birth of Christianity. The new religion was introduced into Alexandria by St. Mark, who was martyred in 62 AD. Many others died as persecution raged during the era of the martyrs around 284 AD. However, in 312 AD, the Roman emperor Constantine made Christianity the official religion of the empire and Alexandria flourished. During the next two centuries, the spiritual power of the Coptic Church grew. Then, in 642 AD, the Roman city fell to the Arabs.

The Arabs greatly admired Alexandria, but it was a city located on water and they were largely a people of the land. They were happier with Cairo and let Alexandria gradually decay away over the next thousand years. The city population declined drastically and corruption reached peak levels.

On July 1, 1798, Napoleon Bonaparte and the French army entered Alexandria and a new era for the city began. Although the French expedition eventually failed in 1799 due the defeat of the French fleet by the Royal Navy at Aboukir Bay just east of Alexandria, its influence on Egyptian history was dramatic. Ottoman isolation and Mameluk corruption was also faced with the imperial power of Britain, which now recognized the strategic importance of Egypt to its supply lines to India. A new political figure arose in Egypt. He was an Albanian officer named Mohamed Ali, who eventually became Khedive of Egypt, with Egypt an autonomous state under Ottoman sovereignty. Alexandria's role as a modern city was about to begin.

He was a controversial man who nevertheless revived Alexandria by building new canals and prepared the western harbour to become Egypt's main port. He is honoured in Alexandria by the naming of the main square after him. In 1943, it was the centre of the world of the theatre and of an evening, always packed with servicemen and their companions.

To continue the story of the modern city of Alexandria: the British influence in Egypt became all-pervasive in 1882 when the Khedive of the day called upon the British to help put down a revolt. The ensuing naval bombardment of Alexandria by the Royal Navy destroyed part of the city but brought the revolt to an end. The city recovered quickly and expanded its trade to Europe through the Mediterranean and to the Orient through the Suez Canal, which had been completed in 1867. The city continued to prosper until 1940, when Italy declared war on Britain and the land battles began in the western desert. These battles and the closing of the Mediterranean to through traffic inhibited its normal growth. Now, with the beating of the Axis at El Alamein and all across North Africa, Alexandria was ready to flourish once more.

I really liked the city and its history, and soaked up as much of its culture as was possible in such a short visit. The local YMCA even had musical appreciation sessions where one could listen to the classics and take part in discussions on the music and the composers conducted by experts who just happened to find themselves in the British Army in Egypt. There were, of course, establishments that catered to the more basic urges of the vast male population. We did not visit these dens of iniquity, having little money and a healthy fear of contacting venereal disease. However, we did hear of an up-market bordello, which restricted its clientele to upper class senior officers in the British services. It was called "Mary's House" and was located in an exclusive enclave of the city. It was hit during a bombing raid in 1942, and many people were killed or wounded. According to the story, a list of those killed was promulgated that designated the dead as "killed in action," rather than the anticipated "killed on active service." So the next time you see a report listing the war dead with reference to Colonel Snapdragon, Grenadier Guards, "killed in action," you will be forgiven if the unfortunate episode at "Mary's House" comes into your mind.

One final lighter note on the city: it boasts a very mixed population base of Syrians, Greeks, Albanians, Turks, French, British and, of course, Egyptians. Out of this polyglot group springs a considerable group of street entertainers. They can be found in action anywhere the crowds are likely to be large and generous. Impromptu performances of jugglers, tumblers, acrobats, high-wire artists, mimes and singers enliven every street scene. It was another wonderful memory to treasure.

During our sojourn in Alexandria, we had haunted the military movement offices trying to get us on to the next troopship bound for home. All to no avail, with rumour suggesting that we would probably have to backtrack to Suez for a long journey around the Cape. We consoled ourselves by continuing to enjoy life. Then suddenly we were ordered to proceed posthaste to Suez to join the troopship *Stratheden*. Our leader, Cap, was in hospital rehab for treatment and unable to travel, so we had to leave him behind. The rest of us arranged train transport to Cairo, which turned out to be comfortable, and a pleasant way of seeing the delta countryside.

On arrival in Cairo, we soon discovered that no one seemed to know anything about us. However, a British Army officer known to the *Yoma* gang and also bound for Suez advised us to hop aboard an army lorry bound out of Cairo to a railway depot where a troop train would be leaving that night for Suez. Accordingly, we piled on to a lorry and were duly deposited at the rail depot. It was located out of Cairo and close to the Giza plateau. It was surrounded by a very high brick wall topped by barbed wire. It became dark just after we arrived and the reason for the wall became quite apparent. A howling mob of Egyptians gathered on the other side and commenced hurling stones and other items, including dead animals, over the wall. We were obviously very popular!

The train consisted of two carriages and about forty closed wagons. We soon discovered that the army had designated the carriages for their officers only, and that we merchant navy types were to join the other ranks in the wagons. Or we could go back to Cairo and perhaps miss the ship bound for home. We were upset at the rigidity of the system, but determined to carry on. So we boarded our wagon and, after getting past the maniacs outside the depot, made our way south to Suez. It was a miserable journey; the desert cold permeated everything, and the wagon was filthy. We attempted to rest by lying on our suitcases or sleeping bags on top of the steel floor, but the train continually changed speed and sent us sliding from one end of the wagon to the other. In my innermost soul I cursed the army, the Egyptians, and Paddy Henderson for inflicting such indignity upon me. Eventually, however, dawn broke and found the train stopped on a high plateau with the Gulf of Suez appearing in the far distance.

The stop continued, and we grew more anxious by the minute. But fairly close to us was a highway, which with daylight appeared to be very busy.

In fact, streams of army lorries were passing in both directions. Without further discussion, we abandoned our miserable chariot and set out for the road. Inside a very short time we had hitched a ride into Suez courtesy of the army. The harbour was filled with ships but we could clearly see our vessel. Enquiries established the fact that *Stratheden* was not ready to receive us that day, so we returned to the tender care of our Irishman. He welcomed us warmly and had huge breakfasts put in front of us, with as many eggs as we wished to eat. One thing that was never in short supply in Egypt was eggs—there must have been special production facilities out there in the desert. As we had not eaten since breakfast the previous day in Alexandria, we really needed to fill up.

The following day, we boarded our troopship and were assigned a small cabin, which I shared with Hughes from the *Salween*. Some of our petty officers from both *Yoma* and *Salween* fared much worse and found themselves down in the troop decks. Without delay, we entered the Suez Canal and, after the usual wait in the Bitter Lakes for the southbound convoy to pass, proceeded to Port Said. There we took on additional passengers, including members of the Dagenham Girls Pipe Band who had been survivors of the torpedoed *Yoma*. They were a lively bunch, considering all that they had been through. Their piping, though, was not impressive.

There were also quite a number of soldiers in rehab who had been severely wounded. Finally, the biggest surprise was the presence of a number of young Turkish students on their way to British universities. We must have been winning the war at last.

We sailed in convoy from Port Said to Algiers without incident. Although we went alongside in Algiers, no shore leave was granted, which was a pity as it appeared to be a very attractive city. We consoled ourselves as best we could and thought about the aerial attacks on the merchant fleet supporting the Allied landings in Algeria. Our own Paddy Henderson vessel *Dalhanna* was nearly lost at Bône in January 1943, and several P&O troopers were sunk or damaged off Algiers and Oran. We never did discover why no shore leave was granted in Algiers, but unrest in the local population was probably the determining factor. After almost a week in Algiers, we sailed for the UK in the company of a large troopship convoy containing at least twenty large troopships, among them the *Ile de France, Orangei, Niew Amsterdam, Aquitania* and of course ourselves.

The voyage home was not unpleasant. Lots of female company as there were many ATS women returning home together with nursing sisters and of course the Dagenham Girls Pipe Band. Time passed quickly while I must have marched around the boat deck and shade deck a thousand times. The weather was cool after our sojourn in the Middle East, but the seas were moderate, the food was passable, and being treated like an officer in the dining room and lounges was not to be sneezed at.

I spent some of my spare time thinking about my life at sea. I knew that I enjoyed most of it, but felt undertrained for the profession of seafaring. I had worked fairly hard on board various ships but had received little instruction in the intricacies of navigation. We were not even encouraged to spend time examining the navigational chart in use at the time. I knew all about the theory of the sextant but never received any practical training. Considering that I had received hands-on training in chartwork and much on the theory of celestial navigation while at James Watt Nautical College it all seemed to be a waste of time. There was a correspondence course run by Glasgow Tech, but in wartime conditions the material was received and dispatched spasmodically with no real continuity. A waste of time.

I thanked the Highland quartermasters who taught me some seamanship, but had found Paddy Henderson masters and mates sadly lacking, with a very few honourable exceptions. Mind you, I knew I could be difficult at times, but even so I believed that Paddy Henderson were benefiting from cheap labour from its cadets and giving little in return. My bolshie instincts were aroused.

All of that ire was put on hold when we entered the North Channel and saw the green hills of Ulster on one side and the equally green hills of the Mull of Kintyre on the other. I truly understood what was meant by channel fever, particularly when I discovered that we were bound for the Mersey where lay the young lady I had briefly met in February 1942 and with whom I had maintained sporadic contact via air letters whenever possible. Eventually we arrived in the river Mersey to be greeted with the whistles of other ships and lots of flag bunting as we pulled alongside the landing stage adjacent to the Liverpool pierhead dominated by the mythical birds on the top of the Liver Building. We all accepted the warm welcome but knew that it was mainly aimed at the rehab wounded warriors from the western desert.

It was good to be back in Britain, but it was a long drawn-out process of security check, customs, immigration, military travel authorization, etc. before we finally stepped on to land. I had been away for almost twenty months, and many things had changed in my absence. There was no longer the nightly threat of air raids, although the city was better prepared for attack with waterpipe connections to the river running up the sides of all the main streets. All the rubble from the bomb damage had disappeared, but great gaps could be seen between buildings in the city centre and of course in Dockland. All transportation had been fully restored and the railway stations were open for business.

In accordance with my travel orders, I boarded the night train to Glasgow. Trains were still packed to overflowing and most uncomfortable, but I was home in Greenock by noon the following day. It was good to see everyone. My brother Gordon had grown up enormously and was obviously cutting a swath through the female population. Dad seemed to me to be the same as ever, and Aunt Mary was making sure they were well fed and kept in order. Dad paraded me in front of friends and colleagues, showing me off. I felt that I was being portrayed as a hero returned when I knew I did not really deserve the adulation. Dad, however, was so truly pleased to have me home that I just smiled modestly and soaked up the praising comments. When I thought of the dead and the severely wounded that I had seen, I felt a bit ashamed. I was a member of the merchant navy where casualty figures were running at thirty five per cent of our pre-war total, but I had tremendous admiration for the really sharp end warriors, those in the fighting ships of the navy, the air force aircraft crews, the poor bloody infantry. I was doubtful that I would measure up to their standards of bravery and was quite glad to be where I was.

I was determined to contact the young lady that I had met briefly in early 1942. So I set off for Liverpool once more. I tracked down her home telephone and talked to her mother who advised me that she was out dancing at the Hulme Hall in Port Sunlight, and gave me directions. I spotted her fairly easily, asked her for a dance, then let her slowly realize who I was. When the dance ended I escorted her home while chaperoned by a giggling girl who turned out to be a close family friend. The air raid sirens went off en route and we sheltered under a railway bridge. We arranged to meet the following day, and so we got to know one another. I met her family and friends and generally enjoyed myself. However, I overindulged in alcohol one evening and ended up in the doghouse. She forgave me before I headed for home to complete my leave.

Upon returning to Greenock, I was posted to *Amarapoora*, a Henderson line passenger vessel converted to a hospital ship for the duration. She was tied up in the Queens Dock, Glasgow, for repairs and alterations. She had seen an interesting war, being sent to Scapa Floe as hospital tender to the North Atlantic fleet in 1939. In 1942, *Amarapoora* was deployed as hospital ship with the allied fleet taking part in the North African landings. When the Allies landed in Sicily and began the long slow push up the Italian peninsula *Amarapoora* was in support of these activities.

Figure 37 - *SS Amarapoora* before World War II

She was steaming slowly off Salerno in September 1943 in the company of two other hospital ships, at night, with clearly illuminated Red Cross markings, when they were attacked by German bombers. One of the other ships was hit and set on fire but *Amarapoora* was able to proceed to the beaches and take her precious cargo of wounded on board safely. She returned directly to Britain with her wounded where she was pronounced in need of an extensive refit and well-deserved leave for her crew.

Most of the regular crew were on leave when I boarded her, and I felt a bit like an usurper as I prowled around her decks. My main job seemed to be checking the lifeboats and life rafts for missing supplies, and restocking where required. The pemmican tablets and chocolate were a big improvement on the dry old biscuits that we had on *Mandalay* back in 1941. The casks containing fresh water were constructed of tin, which was much better than the old wooden barrels, which got quite scummy after a spell. My hands and wrists got quite roughened and torn from screwing open containers, which I complained about to a girl I picked up at a dance. She was not impressed and said emphatically that my hands were not the hands of a real working lad. Humiliated, I hurriedly changed the subject.

There was an American troopship tied up astern of *Amarapoora* that was also undergoing refit. Ashore in the local pub, I met the chief steward of the vessel and we became friends. He even presented me with a large lemon cream pie from his own bakery after I had complained about the dearth of sweet desserts on *Amarapoora*.

After two weeks on board, I was suddenly required to proceed to Merseyside to join the *Ocean Viceroy* in the West Float, Birkenhead. I was overjoyed to be returning to my true love.

Chapter Sixteen

Convoy to Murmansk

Ocean Viceroy was a Ministry of War transport vessel operated by Henderson's. She had been built in the United States to British specifications, seven thousand one hundred and seventy-four gross tons. The ship was of flush deck construction with the usual two holds forward of the bridge deck, a midships hatch forward of the boat deck, then two additional holds forward of the after housing. There was no accommodation in the bow; the captain was located just below the bridge with officers and cadets on the deck immediately below. Abaft number three hold were the cabins for the engineers and other officers. One tier above were the radio shack and additional cabins for petty officers and gunners, of which we had a very large contingent.

Back aft was the crew's accommodation and additional space for our gunners. All in all, the ship's complete complement included the following: one master, three mates, three cadets, five engineers, three radio operators, three quartermasters, one bosun, one carpenter, one donkeyman, ten deckhands, ten oilers, one chief steward, five stewards, and twenty-four Gunners, Royal Naval and British Army, a total of seventy-one souls. We were obviously bound for a hotspot. However, it turned out that we were loading for Murmansk, a definite cold spot. Our cargo was certainly war-like, no whisky or frilly clothes, just armaments of every kind and description. The ship was equipped with heavy lift derricks that were deployed usefully when loading tanks and other heavy equipment. *Ocean Viceroy* appeared to be a virtual hive of activity, but there were signs that not everyone was pulling their weight in the war effort. Repair work being carried out in the steering flat and other parts of the ship were often packed with workers playing cards or lazing about waiting for some part to arrive. The cost plus system was in full effect. As we were part of the sharp end of the war effort, it was upsetting to me to see our support so badly managed.

Ocean Viceroy was not new to the war scene. She was delivered in 1942 and had been badly damaged in March 1943 when hit by an acoustic torpedo that wrecked her steering gear and flooded the shaft tunnel. An emergency steering gear was rigged in the heavy seas and *Ocean Viceroy* set off under her own steam to haven in the port of Belfast. Captain MacFadyen and chief engineer Kennedy were awarded the Order of the British Empire, while second engineer Lochtie and third engineer McCutcheon were awarded the MBE. It was a great demonstration of seamanship under duress. Captain MacFadyen was to be our master on the voyage to Murmansk.

My social life was going well. Doreen seemed to like me as much as I liked her. However, she pressed me hard about my age, as she felt that she attracted too many boys quite a bit younger than herself. I was eighteen and she was twenty-one, so I lied about my age. However, I had a friend of mine, Jimmy Paterson, who was standby mate on *Ocean Viceroy*, formerly a cadet with me on *Salween*. To him I spilled out the story of my passion for this woman. He mentions this to Doreen when he meets her while indicating to her that he thought that I had something to confess to her. She thought that I was about to confess some terrible misdeed, even perhaps a marriage, that she forgave me my youth. All was well on the love front.

On the eighth of December 1943, we sailed from Birkenhead in convoy to Loch Ewe, the gathering point for the convoy to North Russia. The weather was horrible, with strong winds and seas sweeping the Minches. Even in the shelter of Loch Ewe, it was quite miserable on deck. At this point in time occurred a small event that perhaps changed my life. It was a Saturday afternoon, and I was relaxing off duty when I was ordered to the deck to trim ventilators as the wind had veered somewhat in the last hour or so. There were seamen and quartermasters available for such jobs, but the mate figured that they would have to be paid overtime, so let's get a cadet up on deck in the howling December gale—he doesn't cost anything. I completed the miserable task but vowed never to be taken advantage of again. Perhaps I had been spoiled by too long in the tropics, but there an Indian crew would have carried out the task. On board *Ocean Viceroy* we had an all-white crew who were treated like fine porcelain by the officers who wanted no trouble. The cadets were easy targets.

My cabin mate on the ship was a small chap called Angus Paterson. I had met him briefly before when he was serving on board *Burma* in Kilindini harbour. After leaving *Burma* to return to Britain, he was a passenger on the *Empress of Canada* when she was torpedoed off the West African coast. There was heavy loss of life, mainly caused by shark attacks. Angus said he survived by being small and finally managing to get on a small raft. He had joined *Ocean Viceroy* in June 1943 for a voyage to Buenos Aires. When the convoy broke up, another Henderson ship, *Henzada*, was sunk but *Ocean Viceroy* made it safely to South America and returned to the Mersey. He had a good sense of humour and was a fine shipmate. Once, we had a discussion about family crests or coats of arms. He told us, with a perfectly straight face, that the Paterson family coat of arms was depicted as a flaming penis on a field of monkeys' fundamentals. After that description, the rest of us were speechless with admiration.

The mate was Charlie Weir, a longtime employee of Paddy Henderson and rumoured to have considerable shares in the company. He certainly behaved like an owner at times, threatening severe punishment for losing or damaging any deck equipment. He was a Chi Chi of Anglo-Burmese stock, which was most unusual on board Henderson ships. The master was known to us as MacFadyen the bad yin, although he got that appellation more from a naturally rhyming sense rather than anything specific. The chief steward was from Leith and was a jolly soul who kept us cadets well fed and supplied with chocolate bars. We got to know the gunners early on in the voyage as we practised on the twin Oerlikons on the bridge and boat decks and the twelve-pounder located on the bow. All the other vessels in Loch Ewe were similarly armed, with Bofors guns prominently displayed. It was indeed an armed merchant ship fleet that was being dispatched to North Russia.

Our convoy departed Loch Ewe on the 21st December 1943, accompanied by a number of escorting frigates. It was blustery out in the Minch as we formed up in two columns. Just north of Cape Wrath, we were joined by another convoy that had sailed directly from North America. We then commenced regrouping ourselves into six lanes of merchant ships with five vessels in each lane. While all of this manoeuvring was going on, a drifting mine was spotted just ahead of *Ocean Viceroy*. While attempting to avoid the mine, our helmsman managed to get the spokes of the wheel caught up in his life jacket. I was on watch at the time and helped bring the panic stations scenario under control. Several of our gunners took pot shots at the mine as it drifted closely by, and an escort finally sunk it. Shortly after this event, the enlarged convoy was joined by a large number of tribal class destroyers from Scapa Floe as we proceeded north and west of the Orkney Islands.

The weather was moderate, with good visibility, but getting colder by the hour. There were many air attack alarms, as German aircraft shadowed the convoy from the horizon. Additionally, U-boats were reported in the vicinity, and the thump of depth charge explosions could be heard from time to time. The convoy did a fair amount of zigging and zagging as we awaited the arrival of our heavy outer escort of cruisers led by the battleship *Duke of York*. While the weather remained moderate, every ship took advantage of the few hours of daylight to practice gunnery. In the middle of one exercise, two German aircraft decided to have a go at the convoy and its close escorts. It was as if one had upset a wasp nest, with the sky partially blotted out with myriads of tracer shells. The German attack was unsuccessful, but had made sure that everyone was on their toes and ready for anything.

Figure 38 - Convoy to Murmansk under attack - 1943

We slept fully clothed close to our battle stations when off duty and were frequently called to stations by the noisy alarm located on the deckhead. The weather deteriorated badly and we spent much time in the stormy darkness securing cases of aircraft parts that were part of our deck cargo. It was miserable work, but very necessary. There were U-boat attacks on the convoy at this time, and two merchant ships were reported sunk. Christmas Day went by with little time for celebration as the weather worsened still further. The convoy was now sixty miles or so north of the north cape of Norway. We would soon be making the turn eastward into the Arctic Ocean before heading south toward the Russian port of Murmansk.

Boxing Day 1943 was another dreadful weather day, with only about one hour of daylight. The convoy had altered course in response to the presence of the German battlecruiser *Scharnhorst* to the north of us. At around suppertime on Boxing Day, the flashes of heavy gunfire could be seen on the horizon and the convoy prepared to scatter. Our outer escort was engaging the enemy about ten miles away. *Scharnhorst* made her way to within six miles of the convoy before being halted and sunk. The British cruiser *Belfast,* supporting *Duke of York*, finished off *Scharnhorst* at about 1930 hours on that day. In the wild weather there were few survivors, with more than two thousand Germans perishing. Today the media would make a big play of such a "chilling" event. At the time, we were just thankful that we had escaped disaster. The use of the word "chilling" was all too appropriate in these circumstances as the survival time overboard was about two minutes maximum.

Figure 39 - German battlecruiser *Scharnhorst* in Norwegian fjord - 1943

The following day, in the brief daylight period and in moderate weather, the convoy deployed in two columns as we approached the entrance to Kola Inlet. Russian coastal escorts and aircraft provided a welcoming committee. However, the most cheering sight of all was the appearance of *HMS Belfast*, with shell holes in her funnel and upper works, as she steamed past the convoy to great applause from all assembled on deck. We arrived off Murmansk in the early evening and went alongside our designated berth immediately. Lights were rigged preparatory to unloading, and numerous workers, all in heavy parka-type winter clothing swarmed aboard. They were not regular stevedores, but had been conscripted from their factory to do this work for which they were completely untrained. Consequently, a number of small accidents occurred within a short period of time. The workers were both male and female, although it was rather difficult to tell them apart in their identical clothing.

Shortly thereafter, the air raid sirens sounded and the lights were turned off as waves of German bombers from Petsamo in Finland flew over Murmansk. We had not realized it before, but the finger wharf we were secured to was a nest of anti-aircraft weapons that erupted in thunderous fire. As some of the weapons were very close to *Ocean Viceroy* we felt obliged to join in and manned our guns with glee. Whether we hit the enemy or not, it was a grand experience, which was repeated most nights we remained tied up alongside. Meanwhile we got to know the Russians, at least as much as they allowed.

Naturally, some of our crew made contact with the female workers in the holds and cigarettes, nylons and other tradable items were bartered for nookie. A close watch was kept on all the workers by Russian guards, and such transgressions could and did lead to punishment. Shore leave was permitted, but quite restricted. Identity cards were scrutinized carefully by guards at the dock gates who often could not read or write. Murmansk itself was a mess, being heavily damaged from almost continuous bombing since 1941. There were really only two places to go—the International Club and the Red Army Club—both well supplied with good-looking Russian hostesses who were bilingual and spouted the communist party line while smiling provocatively at the same time. Officially, two glasses of vodka were the limit but more could be obtained by a little bit of bribery. The Russian girls tried hard to convert us, but for the most part were wasting their time.

Some of the exchanges of conversation were worthy of record, if only a good tape recorder had been available. Even the implicit offering of sexual pleasure failed to shake the Allied seamen in their own beliefs. The vodka could cause problems, as our own lads could attest to. Fights broke out on the dock and on our deck as seamen, firemen and gunners grappled with one another after consuming the illicit firewater. It was a no-holds-barred affair, stripped to the waist, thumping, gouging and kicking, before being forcibly restrained. All of this in the ice and snow, while a Russian crowd of workers watched in obvious enjoyment.

These Russians did not have much else to enjoy, living in hovels and ruined tenement blocks, practically on starvation diets. On top of that, they had to put up with nightly bombing and the tight police and political control of their lives. Their soldiers and sailors were brave in fighting the enemy. One could only salute them and join them in achieving victory. We got to know the Russian gunners on the wharf quite well and shared many a drink and cigarette together.

An eyeopener to us was the arrival alongside of a Russian heavy lift ship that was manned completely by women. It was compelling to watch them grapple and lift armoured vehicles from our holds without problem or seeming effort. Was this the wave of the future? Shortly after this event, Ocean Viceroy moved out into Kola Inlet anchorage to clean up and prepare the holds for another cargo. It was now 1944 and very soon I would have my nineteenth birthday. A time for reflection on my personal life and also on what was happening in the worldwide war.

My personal reflections were enhanced by my medical condition. We had all been issued with winter clothing before departing Birkenhead. The clothing was not all new but in some cases had been worn previously. However, we were assured that they had all been dry-cleaned before reissue, and were clean. In some cases it was not so, and I was among a number who contracted what turned out to be ringworm. The parasite spread around my testicles in particular and by the time we anchored out in the inlet, it was causing a great deal of discomfort. The chief steward was our paramedical and prescribed iodine applications to the affected area followed by precipitant ointment.

The treatment eventually worked, but the patient underwent an agonizing period of pain and discomfort. It was only relieved by the joking companionship of my shipmates, the occasional illicit can of beer, and the nightly air raids which allowed us to get rid of our frustrations by firing off our Oerlikons. We cadets also found ourselves employed by the mate in breaking up ice that formed daily on the forecastle head and in the shrouds. Once again, this was a task not asked of the seamen. The mate enjoyed this sort of physical labour himself and was oblivious to our resentment. If the ship had been in danger it would have been different, but it was a make-work project for the lowest of the low, the cadets. My reflections hardened into a desire to get out of Paddy Henderson when I qualified to sit for my second mate's foreign going certificate.

The war picture had changed greatly since the summer of 1943. The battle of the Atlantic had turned in our favour, and many German submarines were being sunk by Allied warships and aircraft. Waves of Allied bombers were pounding Germany and the occupied countries in preparation for the anticipated landings in France. In Italy the Allies were battling for Anzio while attempting to outflank the German army at Cassino and Ortono. The Italians were out of the war, supposedly now on our side. The Russians had retaken Kiev and were pressing the Germans ever westward. In the Pacific, the Americans had retaken the Gilbert Islands and had landed on New Britain, while in Burma Allied forces had held off a Japanese attack on the Arakan. With the exception of Burma, the war seemed to be turning in our favour. For the first time in years, people began to think about a future without war.

In late January 1944, we proceeded alongside to load nitrates for the UK. The two thousand tons we loaded was only sufficient for ballast, which we needed for our voyage home. It was then farewell to Murmansk as we departed in convoy, escorted by our tribal class destroyers. The weather was not too horrible, and except for the usual Fokke Wulf shadowing, the convoy was uneventful. Our port of discharge was West Hartlepool, which *Ocean Viceroy* reached safely in early February.

West Hartlepool was a friendly town, and we were made very welcome, so much so that I nearly drowned, and entirely my own fault. The pub that we had ended up our drinking session at threw us out at closing time and I found myself with two girls who decided that I had enough to drink and had better be escorted back to my ship. One girl was very friendly, the other more cautious. Anyhow, they did escort me to the dock gate where I merrily waved them on their way and staggered toward *Ocean Viceroy*.

Unfortunately, I missed the gangway and found myself in the harbour, fully dressed and weighed down by my Great Coat. There was no one around and I sobered up quickly as I swam toward the only light I could see. It was from a nightwatchman's brazier and was a welcome sight. I made it to a slipway and dragged my waterlogged carcass toward the light. An old fellow appeared and made me very welcome, as I sat close to his fire and drank his proffered tea. He did not seem at all curious about my curious arrival and wished me well when I departed half wet and half dry. I made my way out of the small shipyard back to the wharf where *Ocean Viceroy* was tied up and slunk toward my cabin in the predawn quiet. By noon, I had my uniform dried and pressed and headed off on leave. I should mention that West Hartlepool was famous or infamous for an event during the Napoleonic Wars when the authorities were supposed to have hung a monkey as a French spy.

Before going home to Greenock, I travelled to Merseyside to see Doreen. She was pleased to see me but did not approve of my recent bathing activities. However, her mother was more sympathetic and I was soon made a welcome guest. Our courtship did not go smoothly, however, as my boorish ways came in for criticism. As one example, I had to exit a tramcar prior to arrival at our destination. A full bladder was my legitimate excuse, which she ignored by remaining on the tram. Luckily, I got on another tram shortly afterwards and followed her home. I was smitten!

From Merseyside, I travelled home to see family and friends. I even managed to date an old flame but my heart was still in Higher Bebington.

When I rejoined *Ocean Viceroy,* she had moved to Leith to load war materials bound for Australia and the Pacific theatre. That was a bit of a surprise as I had anticipated another reasonably short voyage. The Pacific would mean a voyage of at least eight months and probably twelve, which would not be helpful to my plans to sit for my second mate's certificate by August 1944 at the latest. Because of wartime losses of qualified mates, the four-year qualifying period had been shortened to three and I was ready to take advantage of it. While carrying out my usual duties and partaking of the joys of Leith and Edinburgh, I mulled over my options. I liked my ship and my shipmates well enough, but the rules were irksome and I was not learning anything new or being given the opportunity to learn anything new. However, I felt some loyalty to Paddy Henderson who had made me a cadet. I therefore requested an interview with Captain Cattanach who was visiting our ship. At the interview, which was very short, I respectfully asked for a transfer to another vessel to meet my career plans. He was abrupt and said no in a rather threatening manner, which automatically caused me to resign immediately. My days with Paddy Henderson were over.

When leaving *Ocean Viceroy*, I was saddened to be leaving my only home for several months. A number of my shipmates wished me the best of luck and the first mate, Charlie Weir, made my day by setting up a bogus search of my bags for shackles, bottlescrews and other deck gear. The event caused great hilarity, as Charlie watched deck gear with a very proprietary manner. I was sorry also to be leaving Leith and Edinburgh which were fun cities for a seafarer, with dance halls and pub crawls the order of the day. I then set off to Greenock to explain my action to my father. He was surprised but took it well, although he was somewhat disappointed.

Chapter Seventeen

El Ciervo, D-Day, the Certificate

I set out the following day to register myself at the Merchant Navy Pool in Greenock, fully expecting to be sent to join another vessel, but this time as seaman instead of cadet. Nothing happened for a spell, then one day I was ordered to report to the Pool. Much to my delight, I was to report on board the tanker *El Ciervo* as third mate. I had fallen on my feet, thank goodness. The ship was anchored off the Tail of the Bank.

El Ciervo displaced about eight thousand tons and was fifteen years old. She was owned and operated by C.T. Bowring and pre-war had been on the Ecuador–UK run. She carried mainly bunker fuel, with diesel fuel in the deep tanks. Her officers were younger than their counterparts at Paddy Henderson. The captain was only twenty-seven—a dynamic, cheerful man who taught me a lot about navigation in the three and a half months I spent on board. The crew were of course British, most of them good fellows, but we did get the occasional rogue. Shortly after signing on, I found myself confronting such a character who refused to obey legitimate orders. I took him before the captain who backed me up and had the man sent ashore. He was abusive and dangerous, being sent to sea by some idiot of a magistrate who only wanted him out of his jurisdiction.

El Ciervo had recently returned from the United States, but now found herself acting as a fuel tender to other vessels in the Clyde anchorage and on the River Foyle in Northern Ireland. We refuelled the newly arrived troopship *Queen Mary* and were rewarded by a bombardment of cigarette packages hurled by many of the fifteen thousand American soldiers on board. It was pleasant but ironic, as *El Ciervo* had crossed the same Atlantic Ocean only one week earlier.

Figure 40 - *SS El Ciervo*, C.T. Bowring & Co.

Our base temporarily became the oil depot of old Kilpatrick on the River Clyde. From there, we supplied Allied naval vessels at the Tail of the Bank and up the Gareloch and Loch Long. Our next venture was to Lisahally on the River Foyle in Ulster, where we refuelled United States escorts from Allied convoys. It was a lovely area and a trip up river to Londonderry was a highlight. It was, however, thought-provoking to look across the river and look at a neutral Republic of Ireland. Knowing that the bright lights of Dublin had assisted the Germans to navigate and attack Liverpool in 1941, it coloured my thinking more than somewhat.

On the voyage back to the Clyde, we got a bit of a scare in the North Channel when a submarine suddenly surfaced ahead of us. Much to our relief, it turned out to be a British submarine on exercise. When we returned to the Tail of the Bank, all members of the crew were required to sign a special agreement relating to the anticipated invasion of France. It was an indication of a forthcoming change of venue for *El Ciervo*. Within a few days, we departed Clydeside and headed south down the Irish Sea to Milford Haven at the entrance to the Bristol Channel. Milford Haven was filled with LSTs (landing ship tanks) and other vessels clearly earmarked for the landings. We left there after topping up with bunker fuel, in a small convoy bound for Falmouth in Cornwall.

Falmouth was an ancient naval port having served the Royal Navy well against the Spanish Armada and in all the wars with the French in the eighteenth century and early nineteenth century. When we arrived, it was packed with American landing craft and Allied escorts and minesweepers. Ashore were thousands of American troops milling around and drinking the pubs dry. It was a real drought, with very limited pub opening hours and only beer and cider

of thirsty servicemen queuing up for hours to await the opening of a licensed outlet. I got the distinct impression that the population of Falmouth was not exactly enthralled by the presence of so many Yanks.

While here, I had a chance to review my personal affairs. On my last visit to Merseyside, I had asked Doreen to marry me. As I was only nineteen, I felt that I needed the support of my father. Doreen had not refused me but wanted to ensure that I had that support. My father was taken aback by my news and pointed out all the pitfalls. I am sure that he was influenced by Doreen's family name of Petcovich (certainly not English) and the Catholicism of her family. For a staunch Presbyterian, that was particularly hard to take. Without advising me beforehand, he and a family friend headed off to Merseyside to meet these foreign folks. As far as I was aware, Doreen's people were most pleasant to my dad. He praised his son and they praised their daughter, which lead to some sort of unspoken agreement that there would be no marriage for the present. As a result of this major meeting of our families, and in view of my perceived youth, Doreen and I agreed to go our separate ways. I was footloose and fancy free, but not exactly enjoying it.

It was now May of 1944 and the entire south coast of England was astir with the sights and sounds of war. We moved from Falmouth to Weymouth Bay under the protection of Portland Bill. Once again, the anchorage was crowded with landing craft of every kind. Additionally, there were floating drydocks and many destroyers together with a peculiar floating metal contraption, which we eventually found out was called Mulberry and would be assembled in the approaches to the beaches as temporary harbours. I went ashore with the captain for orders and additional charts, and we found ourselves facing armed Yanks everywhere who demanded identification or else. One could not help but wonder if we still owned our own country. However, misunderstandings were overcome and we got our orders and navigation charts.

Every night, German aircraft flew over the harbour seeking information on Allied preparations for the landings. They were usually fairly high up and flying singly above the inevitable bursts of anti-aircraft shells. However, as D-Day approached, they changed their tactics and came swooping in over the sea to drop bombs and mines in Weymouth harbour. The bombs, of course, exploded on contact with the water, but the mines lay hidden on the bottom until some unsuspecting harbour craft set them off. Such was the case when I was awakened at dawn by an enormous bang as a small landing craft set off the acoustic trigger on a mine and blew itself up. Several others exploded before our minesweepers got underway to defuse the menace. When these low-flying aircraft appeared, the sky was filled with tracer as every ship in the harbour took a pot shot at the raiders. At least two of them were shot down, but were claimed by destroyers deployed beyond the confines of the anchorage. An LSD (landing ship drydock) anchored close to *El Ciervo* was hit by a bomb during one attack and we assisted in the firefighting.

By now it was the third of June, and countless landing craft were waiting their turn to beach and load their cargoes of men and materials. We had fully expected to sail with them to France but instead were assigned to refuel the smaller vessels as necessary. Not knowing of the horrors that lay ahead for many of those in the landing craft that fuelled up from our tanks, I was gung-ho to go with them but was told that I did not have the training that was required. One of the American junior officers borrowed a set of our binoculars and promised faithfully to return them after the operation was successfully completed. All of these craft were bound for Omaha landing beach in Normandy, with an inland goal of reaching a place called Ste-Mère-Eglise.

The convoy departed Portland Bill late on the evening of the fourth of June in rapidly deteriorating weather. The various convoys from Falmouth, Plymouth, Weymouth, Portsmouth and other ports were scheduled to hit the beaches of Normandy on the morning of the fifth of June. However, the unsuitable weather caused a twenty-four hour delay, so that many smaller landing craft had to return to port for refuelling and to provide a short respite for seasick soldiers. However, everything was underway again on the evening of the fifth of June, with clearing weather, and that same evening, just before dark, we were treated to an awe-inspiring sight—hundreds of low-flying Dakotas towing gliders on their way to drop paratroopers on French soil.

At 0630 hours on the sixth of June 1944, Allied troops commenced landing on the beaches of Normandy and the retaking of northwestern Europe was underway. On four of the beaches, the landings went according to timetable, but on Omaha, the beach that our Americans left for, the outcome was in considerable trouble. The German resistance was fierce and the Americans were subjected to withering fire in attempting to land and clear the beaches. Our Americans in their LCTs never even made the beaches, being sunk by shellfire in the shallows. However, eventually the battle was won and the Americans flooded inland. Months later, the binoculars were returned with thanks, so some of our Americans must have survived.

From the sixth of June onward, *El Ciervo* kept busy day and night refuelling American destroyers, Canadian minesweepers, British gunboats and every other variety of warship. We worked very hard, long hours, only too happy to serve these men who had been at the sharp end. By the middle of June, the bustle was abating, so I decided that as I now had sufficient sea time in hand to sit for my second mate's foreigngoing certificate, I should depart *El Ciervo* and return to Scotland to study. After a short leave in London where I saw the sights of the West End, I registered at the James Watt Nautical College in Greenock for revisory instruction.

It was a pleasant relaxing change from the previous years, as I caught up with all the things I should have already absorbed while at sea. Captain Davidson was the principal instructor, as he had been when I was at the college in the winter of 1940/1941. Thanks to him, I became reasonably well prepared for the exams. Meanwhile, there was lots of fun with old school pals and girlfriends to keep me entertained. Cragburn Pavilion was a magnet for Auxiliary Territorial Services girls from the anti-aircraft batteries in the hills behind Gourock, which added to our choice of dancing partners. For a change of pace, there was Green's Playhouse or Barrowland in Glasgow. Naturally, the pubs did well on these occasions.

On a slightly more serious note, I did renew acquaintance with Jean Ritchie. She was as pretty as ever, but as a university girl her interests were very different from mine. She was, however, very good company, and I once more met her family. They were nice people, but stern upholders of the anti-liquor brigade. I liked a drink but felt that I could easily do without; nevertheless total prohibition was beyond me. The romance was not going anywhere.

My dad was good company, but I saw little of my brother who was working on a farm in the neighbourhood. In late August, I felt that I was ready to take my exams and passed my written exams without too much trouble. My oral skills were however found wanting, and I had to return two weeks later to persuade the examiner that I knew what I was talking about. In early September, he gave me a pass, and I became the holder of a Second Mate's Foreigngoing Certificate. Immediately afterward, I reported on board the *MV Benedick* lying in Cammel Lairds shipyard in Birkenhead.

Chapter Eighteen

Benedick **and** *Cape Breton*

Benedick was another C.T. Bowring tanker of about eight thousand tons gross displacement. She was, however, a motor vessel and fitted out to carry light oil in her tanks. The shipyard was engaged in major refit activities and so life on board was far from normal. The shipyard was enormous, with many ships, naval and merchant, under construction. In addition, there were many other vessels under repairs like us. In one drydock I noticed a Blue Funnel Line ship with a huge hole in her bow. This was the ship that had partnered *Salween* on the infamous wog and wop run from East Africa to Suez and return. She had encountered a mine in the English Channel during the D-Day operations and sustained damage and loss of life.

Figure 41 - *MV Benedick*, C.T. Bowring & Co.

There was a fine pub just outside the shipyard gates with which I became well acquainted. It was patronized mainly by shipyard bosses in bowler hats and ships' officers like myself each lunchtime. At night, it was as dead as the proverbial doornail when one had to move further afield for convivial company. I was a regular lunchtime guest at the fine pub and, after a period of several weeks, graduated to a much-prized pewter mug to contain my beer. I felt that Queenie, the pub manager had bestowed upon me a well-deserved honour. It was a small gesture indeed, but it did boost my fragile ego.

The other pubs close to the shipyard and beyond had a livelier atmosphere and of an evening were filled with females looking for males. It was a time of wild parties for me, most of which have become blurred in my mind. Once, I had to sneak out of a house in the early hours of the morning pursued by a very angry mother. What did stick in my mind was how hungry all these girls were—their barter price was a good late supper in some black market café. I had forgotten how well fed we were on board ship compared to the miserable rations available to the civilian population. My conscience was only aroused later in life.

Then I met a lovely happy lady and became respectable once more. Her name was Wyn Murphy and she was employed in the C.T. Bowring office in Liverpool. I gave a number of the girls in the office typing pool a tour of *Benedick* and decided that she was my favourite. She was engaged to an Air Force chap who was undergoing training somewhere in North America. She was lonely, but cautious, and I enjoyed her company. We went to the theatre, to dinner and to other events and it slowly blossomed into a low-key romance. She was still engaged and committed to her boyfriend beyond the seas, and I guess I was content to leave it at that.

Just as I was settling into this relationship, *Benedick* completed her refit and I was promoted to second mate and sent to join *Cape Breton*, which was discharging iron ore in Irlam on the Manchester ship canal. The *Cape Breton* was a cargo ship, mainly engaged in the bulk cargo trade. She was C.T. Bowring's only cargo vessel, every other ship being oil carriers. *Cape Breton* displaced about six thousand tons, and was a steamship with regular reciprocating engines capable of a maximum speed of ten and a half knots. While I learned about the ship and her crew, I was still able to find and frequent the local pub. It was well patronized by servicemen from nearby airfields who seemed to be mostly Canadians. I found myself in the company of a large but attractive lady who told me that her name was Tessie O'Shea. She did look like the popular entertainer of that name. However, she rapidly became intoxicated and staggering, so I had to help her find a cab. An odd event!

Figure 42 - *SS Cape Breton*, C.T. Bowring & Co.

The captain was from the south of England and been with Bowring during the depression years when many ships were laid up for years. That experience coloured his thinking about many things and the other mates were products of the same era. It was a bit of a letdown to one of my normally cheerful disposition. The radio officers were friendlier and the two cadets were filled with youthful enthusiasm. The engineers were a mixed bunch—the chief had·been production manager in an aircraft production factory and his second was a thoroughly obnoxious hard core communist from the River Tyne. Thank goodness, the crew were by and large a decent bunch—the deck crew were from Merseyside and the engine room squad from Cardiff, mostly of Arabic background. I knew that I was in for interesting times. From Irlam, we sailed up the Manchester ship canal to Salford, the port of Manchester. There we commenced loading cargo for the next voyage.

Salford was a typical seaman's town with lots of noisy pubs close to the docks. However, the city of Manchester was within easy travelling distance and had much more to offer. It was too bad that our visit was so short. In mid-December, we were on our way down the ship canal, then out into the Mersey before joining a North America-bound convoy.

It was the day that the Germans launched an offensive in the Ardennes that caught the Americans napping. Christmas Day was celebrated in style on board *Cape Breton* in mid-Atlantic with no interference of our convoy from enemy submarines or aircraft. A far cry from Christmas 1943 when we rounded North Cape and faced *Scharnhorst*.

Our destination was Newport News, Virginia. The highlight of our stay centered around a silly episode featuring some of our crew purloining an American flag from the local legion hall flagstaff. It was a drunken prank, but the legionnaires took it very seriously and wanted the police to charge our fellows with desecration of their flag and insulting the United States of America. After much haggling, our crew were released and confined on board for the remainder of our stay. Not much of a sense of humour!

We then sailed for the nearby port of Norfolk, a huge bustling naval base, but also a major coal port. It was in Norfolk that I realized that the colour bar was alive and well in the United States. As the ship's unqualified medical officer, I was required to escort a crew member to the local hospital. Upon completing his admission, I left the hospital looking for transport back to the ship. I sought the assistance of several locals, all black females, who walked away from me and refused to answer. They were frightened to be seen consorting with a white man. In bars, the reaction was similar. Compared with South Africa's racial divide, the one in Virginia was much more rigid, with a tinge of fear in the air. I also found myself in a bar one day that turned out to be a hangout for homosexuals. They were by and large a jolly group, but when I found myself being propositioned by a charming sailor from Kansas, I decided to quit the scene and return to the heterosexual world with which I was more familiar.

We loaded a full cargo of coal for North Africa, and moved to Hampton Roads to await our convoy. While there, we learned that the German offensive, known by the Americans as the Battle of the Bulge, had been defeated and the Allied armies were once more advancing toward Germany. It was now early 1945 and the future seemed to be a bit more secure. This was my first visit to the United States and I was much impressed by most of what I had seen. The busy shipyards in Newport News, the display of naval strength in Hampton Roads and in Norfolk itself, and last but not least the friendliness of ordinary individuals, together with the cornucopia of goods and foods in the shops. It was all quite remarkable. I learned also what a short arm inspection entailed, parading before the port medical officer.

We sailed in a large convoy, well protected by surface escorts and aircraft, even a blimp. However, it was designated as a ten-knot convoy and we were finding it hard to keep up. A combination of inexperienced firemen and trimmers and poor quality bunker coal continued to put us in the doghouse with the escort commander. Additionally, we were making far too much smoke, which could draw unwelcome attention to the convoy. As anticipated, we found ourselves almost out of sight of the other ships and were ordered to proceed on our own to the Azores and await further orders.

We set course for the island of Pico, which we found hiding behind an extensive cloud bank in the hour just before dawn. Pico was mountainous, with cultivation reaching well up the hillsides, which were perused through the binoculars as we ran a course westward toward the smaller island of Horta and its port of Fayal. We anchored off, as the port was not large enough to accommodate *Cape Breton* and a couple of liberty ships that had tagged along behind us when we left the convoy. The captain and the third mate went ashore in the jolly boat seeking orders, but managed also to snag the outboard engine on a wire hawser and lose it into the shallow waters of Fayal harbour. It was eventually salvaged after much effort and expense. We took on some fresh supplies and a few bottles of brandy and wine for the master's consumption before sailing in a small convoy heading toward Casablanca.

The voyage to Casablanca was uneventful and we went alongside to discharge our coal cargo after a couple of days at anchor. The port was operating largely as an Allied military affair, but the French influence was much in evidence in the city of Casablanca itself. The local Berber and Arab population were numerous but not in power. Food was rationed, but as always in northern Africa, eggs were plentiful. The French cuisine in the few open cafés was excellent, with a slight Moroccan flavour. Some bars were open, but the wine served was Algerian plonk, a dreadful concoction. The weather was pleasant and we made friends with a few French civilians who were working in the dock area. Thanks to one of our radio officers who was fluent in the French language, we were able to get a picture of events just before the Allied invasion of Morocco and at present. They all seemed to be supporters of the Free French government now back in Paris, and very glad to get rid of the Germans. What their feelings were about the Vichy French in Morocco prior to the Allied invasion was more difficult to ascertain. Upon completion of cargo discharge and clean up, *Cape Breton* departed for Pepil in Sierra Leone without convoy.

The weather was fine and the only unusual happening was encountering a very large swarm of butterflies off Dakar in Senegal. The harbour at Freetown was much quieter than on my previous visit on *Mandalay*. Shore leave was granted, but it was not exactly a pleasant place to take a walk, with pickpockets everywhere and a threat of violence in the air. A young pickpocket managed to get his hands on my expensive fountain pen purchased a short time before in Norfolk, Virginia. After surviving many foreign ports, I had finally allowed myself to be jostled and robbed by an enterprising thief in his early teens. It was most annoying, but I knew that it was my pride that was hurting most of all.

A river pilot came on board and navigated us up the river to Pepil where we loaded iron ore. Pepil did not have much to commend itself to our crew. I nearly broke my foot trying to stop a runaway hawser when berthing, but otherwise the visit was uneventful. We departed Freetown bound for Middlesborough in late February 1945. We passed west of the Canary Islands and made our solitary way north to the English Channel. While heading eastward up the English Channel at night, we were overflown by an armada of Allied bombers on their way to bomb Germany. Suddenly, there was a huge explosion in the sky above us as two Allied bombers collided. Our lookout on the forecastle head came running up to the bridge in a very agitated state. He had been a survivor of *Fort Stikine*, a vessel that had blown up in Bombay harbour in 1943 with large loss of life. Poor fellow. I kept him on the bridge for the remainder of the watch. *Cape Breton* arrived at Middlesborough without further incident.

The "boro" was a friendly port with friendly people. We were all made most welcome. I took some leave, visiting both home and Liverpool. Everyone was well at home and I visited with my Aunt Bessie in

Glasgow. My low-key romance with Wyn continued, while I sowed my oats among the willing ladies of Middlesborough.

All too soon, we completed discharging and sailed in ballast for Quebec City via the Pentland Firth in a large convoy showing a relaxed attitude to normal convoy discipline. Merchant ships were scattered over many miles of ocean in dubious formation. Even the escorts seemed relaxed, as the defeat of Germany appeared imminent. *Cape Breton* left the convoy off Newfoundland and sailed up the Gulf and River St. Lawrence to collect a pilot at Father Point. This was all new territory for me. I found the combination of fog, cool weather, and the many coastal villages along the Gaspé Peninsula a thorough change of scene. The fog was a nuisance, but was usually burned away later in the day by the sun. The cool weather was not really cold, but comfortable, while the many villages were each centered by a prominent church steeple that reflected strongly in the sun.

Further upriver, beyond Father Point, the river narrowed somewhat and one was conscious of heavily treed shorelines and a number of islands in mid-channel. After passing the entrance to the Tadoussac River, the channel narrows further when approaching Ile d'Orléans and then, there before you lies the city of Quebec. The Plains of Abraham tower over the city, which is located on the west bank of the river. Many of the fortifications from the days of French dominance are still standing, but the Château Frontenac Hotel dominates the lower city.

We proceeded alongside the wharf at Wolfe's Cove and commenced loading our designated cargo of pit props. It was the seventh of May and the Germans had surrendered, so we celebrated by firing off our bridge parachute wire rockets and almost set the entire bridge alight. A bunch of us then travelled to the Château Frontenac where we tested the goodwill of the security staff with a noisy celebration punctuated by yells of "la guerre est finie" which was the limit of our knowledge of the French language. We eventually dispersed and made our drunken way back to the ship.

Where we were tied up in Wolfe's Cove was close by the pathway climbed by the Highland troops that faced Montcalm on the heights and won a famous victory. I climbed the path to honour my countrymen these many years previously. The loading of pit props went smoothly, and fairly soon our holds were full and our decks were stacked high. When completed and secured, we proceeded down river but shortened our trip home by taking the Belle Isle route between Labrador and Newfoundland. Lots of thick fog and small bergy bits enlivened our voyage home.

Figure 43 - Herring drifter fleet off Cape Wrath

I had enjoyed visiting the St. Lawrence River and looked forward to seeing more of Canada in the future. We crossed the Atlantic quickly with our load of pit props and made land at the Butt of Lewis before closing with Cape Wrath, the most northwesterly of Scotland. As we approached Cape Wrath, *Cape Breton* found herself in the middle of the herring fleet. There were dozens of drifters operating their nets, with small lights marking their location just as dawn was breaking. I do not think that they were overly happy to see us.

We then traversed the Pentland Firth and made our way to West Hartlepool. Once again, the local lassies made us welcome, and I behaved as sailors do. I then went on leave to attend my father's wedding to Mary Fernie. It was a very quiet affair in Glasgow attended mostly by friends of Mary. I had a few drinks before the ceremony, which I do not think went over well with my dad. However, I wished them well and went on to Merseyside to see Wyn Murphy.

I arranged to meet her in Liverpool on a Saturday afternoon but never did make the date. Fate was taking a hand that day as, in Birkenhead Station, I bumped into Doreen and family heading into Liverpool for a dinner party with the family of Doreen's new boyfriend, another seafarer. Doreen's mother seemed to take it for granted that I was on the way to see her, and blithely added me to their family group. I weakly surrendered the present that I had intended to give to Wyn and presented it to Doreen. The dinner party was a great success from my point of view, but visibly a disaster from the point of view of the other family, the Givens. What was intended to cement relations between Harold (my rival) and Doreen turned into an imitation of an Italian operatic farce, with me leering at her, but being careful to dance only with her married sister Ursula. We had obviously re-established contact.

Cape Breton departed West Hartlepool in ballast in June 1945, bound for Montreal through the Belle Isle strait. The voyage opened up another part of Canada to my view, Trois Rivières, Sorel, Lac St. Pierre and the great city of Montreal. It was a very attractive city, with good parks, shops, cathedrals and churches, good food, and stacks of very alluring women. We made the most of our short stay.

One peculiar happening on the Atlantic I must mention was the sight of several American liberty ships huddled in a group who tagged on behind us to ensure safe navigation to their destinations. They missed the convoys, these ninety-day navigational wonders. There was also the sight of Swedish vessels all decked out in their peacetime colours bound for North America after being locked up in the Baltic Sea for the past five years. The world was changing!

Although the war in Europe was finally over, the war against the Japanese still had a way to go. In Burma, the Japanese were in full retreat down the river valleys and Mandalay and Rangoon were in Allied hands. In the Pacific, the Allied island hopping tactics had finally paid off and the Philippines and other islands close to Japan like Iwo Jima were captured after much hard fighting. The Japanese fought back ferociously, attacking the Allied fleets with suicide bombers.

In Montreal, we loaded grain and headed for sea, taking a shortcut through the Gut of Canso and passing through a myriad of lobster fishermen and their pots. We discharged our cargo in Newport News and loaded coal for the return trip to Montreal. We then loaded another cargo of grain for Barry in South Wales, arriving there just in time to celebrate the fall of Japan. Everyone spoke of a fearsome new weapon—the atomic bomb.

While in Wales I made contact with Hubert Jenkins' family, finding myself squiring his youngest sister Barbara to the swankiest and most expensive hotel in Cardiff. She was pretty and nice, but I did not pursue the attraction—I was in thrall to my love in Cheshire. I did meet Jenky's mother, a fine lady, and his older sister and her husband, all grand folks. Captain Jenkins was away at sea. We loaded cargo of bunker coal for the Cape Verde Islands while I was on leave with Doreen. In Chester on the River Dee, in a punt, I popped the question, and on the 22nd of August we became officially engaged. On the journey back to Cardiff I saw a heart-warming sight on a small Welsh country station platform. There, in front of my eyes, I saw the chief engineer of *Salween*, old MacDonald, who lost his family in the bombing of Clydebank, being greeted warmly by the chief nursing sister also from *Salween*. Love conquers all.

Chapter Nineteen

Cape Breton **(2)**

Cape Breton underwent a much-needed fumigation while in Barry, and we lived ashore at the Barry Docks Hotel (known as the Chain Locker). The hotel was locked up tight as a drum after ten PM. When a shipmate and I arrived back at the hotel after midnight, we had to climb the drainpipe and force a window to enter. We tiptoed through the darkened lounge, serenaded by the sighs and squeals of prone couples struggling on couches and upholstered chairs. We felt like joining in, but were not invited.

Figure 44 - Loading Coal in Barry Dock, South Wales

Once again, our voyage to warmer waters was uneventful. The Cape Verde Islands off the West African coast were surprisingly desert-like in appearance, but still fertile enough to support a moderately sized population. We discharged most of our cargo at Praia on Sao Tiago Island, the remainder at tiny ports on a couple of other small islands in the group. There was not much action ashore, and the discharging was a labourious task mainly accomplished by head-held baskets. However, I did see one remarkable sight—a naked woman dancing with an earthenware pot of beer balanced on her head outside a ramshackle bar bordello. A true magnet for all the sailors in town. The Cape Verde Islands were Portuguese territory and a sanctuary in the war years, unlike the Canaries further north owned by Spain and a haven for German submarines. We were made to feel at home.

Upon completion of discharging, we sailed for Abidjan in French West Africa, where we lay offshore outside the mud flats and loaded cocoa in gunnysacks. No chance for shore leave presented itself, and we had to content ourselves with viewing the Ivory Coast capital city through a pair of binoculars. Our next port was Takoradi in the British-controlled Gold Coast. Again, we loaded cocoa before moving along the coast to Accra where the loading was carried out from surfboats, a very dangerous but skilled endeavour. We completed loading in Lagos, the major port in Nigeria. Here we delivered our only passenger, a fellow called Tennant who was returning to Nigeria to resume his pre-war job as education administrator for the northern Nigerian city and state of Kano. He was good company and had a fund of stories about Nigeria and his wartime service in the army. It turned out that he was a Tennant of the brewing family and probably worth pots of money.

Lagos was a bustling noisy port city and as hot as Hades. The wharf at Apapa across the harbour was a little bit better with an Anglican mission close by where cold drinks were available in civilized company. Livelier night life was also at hand, but danger lurked in the shadows. Tales were told of terrible things that had happened to drunken sailors imbibing the local palm toddy. We largely paid heed to those stories and departed Nigeria with only fruit and bananas and several small monkeys. I could never see the need to purchase these small animals, which inevitably died in the ocean during stormy weather or perished from our winter weather in Britain.

Our port of discharge was the Tyneside port of South Shields. We arrived there in the early hours of the morning with heavy fog patches and black darkness providing the only welcoming canopy to our ship. At last, a tiny light appeared on the water, which turned out to be from an oil lamp on a rowboat. In the rowboat sat an old man who took our lines one by one ashore and made us fast to the quay. After the many occasions where we had been greeted by scores of workers pulling our hawsers ashore, supervised by screaming foremen, the South Shields response could truly be called "an economy of effort." We commenced discharging the cocoa later that day.

South Shields was no Shangri La, still bearing the signs of neglect of the great depression. It was however a friendly town, and we soon made friends in the local pubs. However, as an engaged man, I behaved myself as best I could in the circumstances, and went on leave to Merseyside. I had managed to smuggle bananas, cigarettes, and several bottles of booze out through the dock gates in South Shields, and was therefore greeted like a conquering hero by Doreen and her family. The liquor was supposed to be kept for our wedding day but was polished off long before. A tentative date had been established for the termination of my next voyage, which was expected to be in late March 1946. Meanwhile, I met some of Doreen's many relatives and began to realize what a huge family I was contemplating joining. The time with Doreen passed all too quickly, and I travelled north to Scotland to apprise my father of the coming event. I do not think that he was entirely happy about the news, but he was supportive, which was very reassuring to me.

Upon completion of discharging in South Shields, we prepared to sail south to Gravesend on the River Thames. Our captain, a nice man, decided to get very drunk before we had even cleared the mouth of the River Tyne and collapsed unconscious before the pilot departed. As we had a brand new first mate unfamiliar with the vessel, I found myself navigating *Cape Breton* all the way south through the hazardous minefields still protecting the east coast of England. I was very glad to see the River Thames pilot come on board off Foulness Point. We lay in the fogbound river at anchor for two days before going alongside a cement works wharf just west of Gravesend. There, we commenced loading packaged and barrelled cement products for a number of West African ports. The ship was chartered by Elder Dempster and Alfred Holt.

December on the River Thames is not the best time of the year. In addition to the rain, we were swept by cold winds. I visited London on two occasions, and while I enjoyed myself in the city, I missed the last train to Gravesend each time and had to seek refuge in the station waiting room, which was unheated. It was not a memorable experience. I did manage to see a couple of West End shows and cruised a few pubs. In one of them I met a New Zealander who tried to persuade me to join a New Zealand shipping company. He and I found ourselves in an expensive hotel bar where we were joined by several British Army officers, one of whom turned out to have served with a cousin of mine in the Fourth Gurkha Rifles. That led to a party which lasted until train time, which as I indicated earlier I managed to miss. The early morning train to Gravesend departed at six AM and was filled with miserable looking souls like me.

The loading of cement went on for several days, supervised by a shore captain from the Blue Funnel Line (Alfred Holt). He was an interesting man and tried to sell me on joining the Blue Funnel Line. I now could choose between New Zealand shipping and the Blue Funnel. I realized that I must be thinking about moving on from C.T. Bowring. However, I had to prepare for marriage first, and discuss my future with my bride-to-be. I therefore concentrated on the forthcoming voyage to West African ports.

We left the Thames in mid-December on a gloomy day and ran down the Channel in deteriorating weather until we reached the Bay of Biscay where the weather became most foul. By the time we were off Portugal the weather moderated and from then on *Cape Breton* was cruising in relatively calm seas and clear blue skies. Our first port of call was Dakar, the capital city of French Senegal. Dakar had been in the news in the nineteen forties as the scene of a naval battle between the Vichy French navy and elements of the Free French and Royal Navy. I could not see any sign of the battle, but extensive areas of the docks had obviously been repaired or reconstructed. There was considerable unrest in the port, and untrained workers from northern Senegal had been conscripted to unload our cargo. It was messy work with cement bags bursting in the holds and on deck. I tried to sort out the mess, but ended up shouting and screaming at the Senegalese in English and no doubt in a proper British sahib manner. I had temporarily reverted to my Paddy Henderson days of Indian crew control. How silly! Eventually, we hired some former French non-commissioned officers who sorted out the impasse.

Dakar did have a few bars and some night life. I became temporarily enamoured of a beautiful black goddess, but my shipmates saved me from myself by telling me I was drunk and hustling me back to the ship. Otherwise life was largely routine, although we did have some trouble with crew members drunk on the local arrack or firewater. We departed Dakar bound for Abidjan on the Ivory Coast. En route, a tragedy occurred, when one of our seamen went overboard. He was on my watch and I had noticed him behaving in a rather peculiar fashion by wielding his chipping hammer the wrong way around. I reported him to the master, who examined him and locked him in the ship's hospital for his own safety. After one night, he seemed better and was released with instructions to all hands to keep a close eye on him. After supper the following night, he left the mess deck and went overboard. An alarm was raised immediately and *Cape Breton* reversed course. However, the search in the dark was delayed by the need to free the lifeboat from its chocks, which were stuck to the sides of the boat. After some moments' frantic work, the lifeboat was launched and the search was underway. Searchlights were manned and the sea surface was scrutinized carefully, but no sign of the seaman was seen. After two hours the search was abandoned and *Cape Breton* proceeded on her way.

This event haunted me for a long time. Could we have done more to avert the disaster? Perhaps if we had been able to communicate with the young man and find out what was going on in his mind. Perhaps if we had kept him under lock and key in the hospital. Perhaps if we had not lost precious moments in releasing the lifeboat. All valid questions, and examined at the informal inquest when the vessel returned to the UK. The official verdict was death by misadventure and of an unsound mind.

We anchored off the Abidjan mud flats and commenced discharging our cement cargo into a series of wind-powered barges. Once again, we could only look at the city in the far distance. From Abidjan, we moved on to Accra for the spectacular view of the surfboats navigating their cement cargoes ashore. Our final discharging port was Lagos. It was as hot and dusty and smelly as ever, and we were quite glad to complete our cement contract and clean up the ship before heading for our first loading port which was to be Burutu in the Escravos River delta. There we would load cocoa and palm oil and some hardwoods.

The voyage from Lagos to the Escravos River bar was fairly short, and we were advised to expect a pilot boat off the bar. Instead of one pilot boat there were at least ten, all vying for our attention. It took some time to sort out who was the properly authorized pilot and who were the pirates. Eventually, the correct documents were produced and we headed up the Escravos River. The river was narrow and winding but certainly deep enough for a fully laden ship. Huge trees lined either bank, except where villages appeared with small plots of cleared land amid the forest. These villages were filled with people, most of whom seemed to be small black children and their mothers. Additionally, many dugouts plied the waters off the villages, conducting commerce and taking advantage of the good fishing. It was hot and clammy and altogether uncomfortable. We lay alongside in Burutu and commenced loading.

At this time we had two passengers on board *Cape Breton* who had joined the ship in the UK. They were a bit of a mystery, a mother and daughter from Montreal. Very much upper-crust Anglos who kept mostly very much to themselves. The daughter was fairly young and attractive and may have been inclined to greater friendliness but was discouraged by her mother. Gradually, on the voyage, we found out a little bit more about them. In September of 1945 as the world war concluded, a Russian cypher clerk in the Russian embassy in Ottawa named Igor Gouzenko defected and handed over to the Canadian authorities vast amounts of secret information implicating a number of Canadians spying for the Russians. The Canadians included respected members of the community such as a member of parliament and others of leftish leanings. Interrogations by the Mounties soon widened the circle of suspects, and our "daughter" was one of them. To avoid publicity and the possibility of a trial, the family had used their influence to spirit mother and daughter out of Canada.

I mention the above because it was while we were in Burutu that I saw a human side to our mysterious passenger. I was on the bridge deck minding my own business when a tall naked black girl propelled her dugout alongside *Cape Breton* and invited me to jig-a-jig in a loud penetrating voice. As I eyed up the temptress I heard a delicious chuckle from the captain's deck where the daughter was taking it all in. A communist with a sense of humour—what next?

We filled up our deep tanks with palm oil, and returned to Lagos and Apapa for final loading of cocoa, animal hides and hardwood. From there, we proceeded directly toward home, which this time just happened to be the Mersey and the port of Liverpool. It was now mid-March 1946.

Chapter Twenty

Marriage and the Sea

Cape Breton was warped into the Herculaneum tidal basin from the River Mersey on the 14th of March 1946. We commenced discharging cargo on the following day. The dock was rather old, being constructed in the late eighteen eighties and without shore-based cranes. Our derricks and winches came into full play. The dock was located upriver from the landing stage and fairly close to Aigburth.

I was delighted to see my bride-to-be once more and, after some hugging and kissing, we commenced planning the great event. The date was set for the 26th of March and we had to procure a special marriage license as time was of the essence. Between working on board and attending to the various preparations, I was a fairly busy and tense fellow. Even so, in the midst of all of the excitement, I managed to follow up on my plans to join a better shipping company. I contacted Cable & Wireless Ltd., as I had heard that they were keen on recruiting well-qualified young officers. They noted my application and advised me that I would hear from them shortly.

Doreen had many relatives and friends, so her invitation list was rather large. On my side there were not so many. My father, my stepmother and my brother would represent the Greenock contingent, while I had additionally invited the captain and chief engineer and their spouses. Most important of all, the third mate had agreed to be my best man. I wanted to invite my former girlfriend Wyn Murphy to the wedding but that suggestion was vetoed.

About this time, I began to get cold feet about the thought of getting married. Perhaps, if so many people were not counting on the big day, including my folks travelling down from Scotland, I might have scarpered. After all, I was only just twenty-one—why did I need to get married? The responsibilities I would be undertaking suddenly seemed overwhelming. But I did love her and wanted her to be mine so I prepared to meet my fate.

Figure 45 - Marriage, March 1946, Rock Ferry, Cheshire, England

New uniforms and other clothing were purchased, and I hosted a bachelor's party the night before the wedding and got slightly polluted.

The wedding day dawned clear and sunny, surely a good sign. The ceremony took place at St. Anne's Catholic church in Rock Ferry—my Presbyterian ancestors were probably turning over in their graves! My bride, however, looked absolutely stunning when she walked down the aisle on her father's arm. It was all worthwhile. The ceremony passed in a bit of a haze for me, and before I woke up we were signing the official registry and were man and wife.

The reception was held at the King's Hotel in Higher Bebington and lasted from early afternoon to about eight in the evening. It was good fun for all concerned but a bit wearing for the bride and groom who had to formally greet all in attendance. There was Aunt Mollie and all her family, Aunt Rose and her family, Aunt Jo, Aunt Harriet and her family, Uncle Willie and his family, plus scads of other relatives and friends of the bride's family. There were priests and gnarled old sea captains; all we were missing was a nun.

The usual toasts and speeches were made with both fathers doing a good job on behalf of their offspring. There were several impromptu recitals by slightly inebriated members of the gathering. Probably the most arresting of them all was one by Fred Settle who had been in the British Army in India. He told the story of "Mad Carew" and the green eye of the little yellow god, to a rapt audience. The bride departed the reception to prepare for her honeymoon, while the groom hung around the bar with ill-concealed impatience. Eventually we departed for the Central Station Hotel in Liverpool. There I discovered that my bride was still her mother's girl as she insisted on phoning her mother to tell her she was all right!

What occurred next is not for publication. The following morning, we took the express train to Scotland to begin our honeymoon. We arrived that afternoon in the Central Station in Edinburgh and made our way to Portobello where I had arranged to stay at a recommended bed and breakfast. The landlady was extremely pleasant and made us both very much at home. Explorations of the surrounding area took us to many parts of Edinburgh, including Holyrood Palace, the castle and the Royal Mile. Bus rides were taken to North Berwick and Dunbar, and to view the railway bridge over the River Forth that I had first crossed back in the thirties. We found beautiful gardens and out of the way places.

I discovered, however, that my countrywomen were very narrow-minded when I took my bride with me for a drink in a pub. In their eyes she was a scarlet woman.

One day, we visited a fascinating old church out in the countryside. It was the family chapel of the St. Clair family and its outer walls were covered with carvings of hundreds of gargoyles relating to the seven deadly sins. Inside were carvings and artwork of the Masonic Order. Most interesting of all were the references to the Templars (the monks of war) who apparently settled here in the early fourteenth century when the order was devastated and destroyed on the continent. Rumour has it that they brought the Ark of the Covenant with them and that it is buried under Roslyn Chapel. Could it be true?

After two wonderful weeks in the Edinburgh area, we headed for Greenock to have Doreen shown off to family and friends. It was all put in context when a distant cousin of mine met my bride and exclaimed, "She's a wee smasher!" Only the Scots can convey their feelings so bluntly but so truly. She was a Sassenach, but a definite hit among the porridge eaters. We had a grand time for a few days before heading back to Merseyside. Just as well, as I had realized that my money was fast disappearing. Two could definitely not live as cheaply as one. Thank goodness, my bride had come fully equipped with all the latest in fashion. Even her tall hats caused comment and stares in church.

We stayed with Doreen's folks in Higher Bebington while I awaited my orders to join another ship. Her family were very nice to the stranger in their midst, and visits were made to a number of locals to test the potency of the local brew. During this period, I must have done or not done something expected of me by my love, because I had a bar of soap hurled at me with great accuracy. This was some woman I had married, but definitely no angel.

I reported on board the *Benedick*, once more in Birkenhead. *Benedick* moved out into the Mersey to carry out minor repairs before sailing. I was able to introduce Doreen to life on board for a few days before our lives changed completely. I received a telegram from Cable & Wireless telling me I had been selected as a junior deck officer and to report immediately or even sooner. The salary was very much greater than I was presently earning and conditions sounded very much more attractive. I would be away for a long spell, but I was assured that there would be opportunities for my wife to travel to be with me in foreign parts. It all sounded good to me, but Doreen was not too happy. In retrospect, it was not too good a decision as far as our marriage was concerned. However, from a career and learning point of view, it was worthwhile. We had a sad farewell, and off I went to join my first cableship.

Chapter Twenty-One

Voyage to Singapore

I travelled to Portsmouth to join *HMS Queen*, an escort-type aircraft carrier built in the United States. She displaced about ten thousand tons and carried a crew of five hundred without air crew. I was the only merchant navy type on board. Apparently Cable & Wireless had persuaded the Admiralty that I was urgently required in Singapore and therefore could not possibly wait for space on a troopship. And so, I found myself sharing a tiny cabin below the main hangar deck, subject to every noise on the hangar deck, bosun's whistles, tannoy announcements, and all the general turmoil of a ship at sea.

Figure 46 - HMS Queen, en route from Portsmouth to Singapore, 1946

The first officer, a full commander, had previously served in the merchant navy. He surmised that I knew more about navigation than most of his officers, and conscripted me as an additional watchkeeping officer. I was watched with caution by the navigator but otherwise was able to conduct my self with distinction once I had mastered their bridge system. Too many bodies rattling around the bridge for my liking, but otherwise it was all as it should be on a well-run merchant ship.

In addition to the normal crew of *HMS Queen*, she had on board three hundred Royal Marine commandos bound for the South China Sea to mop up the local pirates who had become very active since the Japanese surrender. The commandos were fighting fit and their officers were a wild bunch of characters. They dominated the wardroom, and late at night indulged in raucous brawls with empty beer cans and their fists. One of their leaders was a nephew of Winston Churchill. He would lead the charge over settees and chairs, and heaven help anyone who got in his way.

The hangar deck was an excellent place to show the latest Hollywood films each evening. After every performance, the assembled officers would dissect the plot sometimes with hilarious results. Some of the more legal-minded reacted when we saw "Mildred Pierce," concerned about the American system of legal plea-bargaining. There was a great deal of talent and common sense displayed by most of the officers on board *Queen* and I participated in the discussions to the best of my ability.

The weather was relatively mild even when crossing the Bay of Biscay, and remained that way off the Portuguese coastline and through the Straits of Gibraltar into the Mediterranean. Our first stop was Malta, where we discharged naval cargo and spent some time at the Silema Beach. I also had time to visit the famous Gut and take in a few bars. There were some signs of the wartime bombing, but most areas had been cleaned up.

We departed Malta for Port Said and traversed the Suez Canal without undue trouble. *Queen* made fairly fast passage down the Red Sea and across the Arabian Sea to Trincomalee, the Royal Navy base in Ceylon. There, we loaded scrap aircraft parts and gave them a proper burial at sea in the deeper water of the Bay of Bengal. From there we set course for the Nicobar Islands and the Strait of Malacca. It was early July 1946 when *Queen* warped alongside her berth in Singapore.

Upon reporting to the Cable & Wireless office, I was informed that my ship was still at sea and that I would have to live in the seaman's hostel in the meantime. The first place I was taken to in the hostel was most unsatisfactory, with cockroaches and other bugs in evidence. A forceful confrontation with the management sorted that problem out, and I was able to rest in comfort. Singapore Island was full of troops awaiting a passage home to the UK and civilian life. They were mostly trained fighting men who had seen action in Burma and the Dutch East Indies. They were rowdy and noisy, and spoiling for a fight, either with each other or with the locals. Beer could be had at canteens but was rationed, so they consumed the local palm toddy in great quantities. The resulting chaos kept the military police and their naval counterparts extremely busy.

The hostel was practically next door to a canteen known as the Shackles Club, so I soon got to know the local scene. Indeed, at night the noise from the Shackles Club made sleep impossible. I soon discovered other interesting spots. There were large circuses or fairgrounds with names such as the New World or the Happy World. These places had eating establishments, Chinese theatres, dance halls, bars, and all sorts of fairground attractions. I tried out my dancing skills at the dance halls, where the dance hostesses charged a local dollar for three dances.

I took out a military membership in the Tanglin Club, a beautiful place with bathing pools, tennis courts and other attractions. There I met some wild Australians who made sure that I was introduced to lots of people. Among them was a lovely Dutch girl, about fifteen years old, who had spent almost four years in a Japanese prison camp. She loved to swim in the pool, but otherwise was withdrawn and sad most of the time. I often wondered in later life whether she managed to overcome her fears. War crimes trials of Japanese were ongoing in Singapore at that time, and I connected the guilty outcomes with my desire for revenge for this young girl. Such were the heated feelings of the times.

Chapter Twenty-Two

Cable Ship *Recorder*

At long last, my cable ship arrived back in Singapore. She was the *CS Recorder*, an elderly vessel, even older than the old *Mandalay*. She was built in 1902, and was one of the last ships constructed entirely of iron. Her displacement tonnage was about two thousand five hundred tons and she looked like a large yacht owned by royalty or some wealthy

Figure 47 - CS Recorder, Java Sea, 1946

eastern potentate. She was painted gleaming white from stem to stern with one yellow funnel. Her power was the usual triple expansion reciprocating engine. The crew was quite large, about one hundred and ten souls. The officers were all British, as were most of the petty officers. The remainder of the crew was a mix of Indian and East African. The captain was a smart little man called Frank Axtell to whom I reported on board. I was the brand new fourth officer, being paid much in excess of my previous second mate's salary in C.T. Bowring.

My cabin was located on the port side of the main deck, in a housing separate from the main accommodation. It was more than adequate for my needs. The captain resided immediately below the bridge deck, and below his cabin was the entrance to the officers' saloon, which opened on to twin staircases that descended to the dining area. The approaches were decorated with paintings of *Recorder* at various events in her career including, in pride of place, the official surrender of the German raider *Wolf* in the Cocos Islands in 1915. It was like magic after the utilitarian vessels I had sailed in since leaving *Salween* in 1943. The food was jolly good too.

A very fine wardroom was located off the dining area, fitted out with a bar, a grand piano and a small library well equipped with up-to-date periodicals. On the main deck, just forward of the bridge, was the cable working location, with hatches opening into the cable tanks where the repair cable lay coiled, ready for deployment. Further forward were the tanks containing the grappling gear, buoys and light anchors for cable operations at sea. A large windlass was placed so that it could control both grappling and ship anchoring drills as required. Forward of the windlass, grappling gear or cable could be lead to the bow sheaves and thence into the ocean. A wooden seat could be fitted to the line to enable the officer on watch to gauge the strain being subjected on the dragging equipment. A mechanical stress indicator was also available to assist the mate in his judgement. All of the foregoing I still had to see in action at sea.

In addition to the four mates, there were six engineer officers and four cable engineers who also looked after radio traffic. The main petty officers were the bosun, carpenter, donkeyman and cable electrician. Finally, and most important of all to those of us who love their comfort, a purser and a chief steward. In prewar days, the ship would also carry a fully qualified medical doctor, but in these days of shortage, those in need had to put up with the ministrations of the third mate.

The first cable repair jobs I witnessed were close to Singapore, not far from the Horsburgh Lighthouse and the Riouw Archipelago. They were in shallow water around ten fathoms in depth. The cable was easily retrieved from the sandy bottom by a simple grapnel shaped somewhat like an anchor cable but with open flanges. The cable was tested by the cable engineers for fault detection, repaired, and redeployed on the bottom. The cable would then be intercepted close to the actual fault, and the final cable repair carried out. In these depths, it was sometimes possible to find the fault by the towing of electrodes over the cable to detect signal change. A rough approximation of fault location could be obtained from signal strength advice sent by wireless from the nearest shore cable station.

Our first priority was to repair and relay where necessary the two Singapore cable lines to Batavia on the island of Java. They had been of course captured by the Japanese in 1942 and were diverted by them to include cable stations established on a number of small islands as defensive positions on the route between Singapore and Batavia. To assist us in locating these cable diversions, we occasionally had on board a Japanese naval officer supplied with cable charts constructed by the Japanese. He could not speak English very well and our Japanese was non-existent, which led to some hilarious misunderstandings. However, soon all the missing cable had been recovered and we were able to patch and relay where necessary.

Cable work off the Lingah Archipelago in the Northern Java Sea was particularly interesting and exciting. Sea snakes abounded in the area but were most visible at night in the glare of our bow working lights. The men in our workboats kept a wary eye about them as they carried out their duties. Additionally, the seas being shallow, the cable, when hauled on board at night, gleamed with a profusion of colours from the bottom vegetation clinging to its surface. It was truly spellbinding at times, with a clear tropical sky overhead showing countless stars, and the faint spice-laden smell of the nearby land.

We proceeded southward from the Karimati Strait to Tanjong Priok, the port for Batavia. Our main purpose was to refuel, water and provision before heading out through the Sunda Strait toward Christmas Island. Things were far from peaceful in Java at that time, and we found ourselves spectators in an uprising of Javanese rebels against the Dutch who were militarily supported by the British Indian Army, and even by two Japanese divisions kept armed to keep the peace. It was a very complex and dangerous situation, illustrated by the football pitch outside the docks, which was Allied territory during the day, but fell to the rebels each night.

As British visitors, we were not made to feel very welcome. The Dutch wanted to be left alone to sort out the rebels. The rebels wanted us gone so they could drive the Dutch out, as they eventually did. The Indians and the Japanese just wanted to go home, and the British military units just wished for a quieter posting. We kept our heads low, played on the football pitch by day and headed back to our wardroom each evening. It should be emphasized that not all the locals supported the rebels, who were ruthless in dealing with those they looked upon as traitors.

We were not really sorry to leave Tanjong Priok. Our destination was the cable from Batavia to Christmas Island that went on from there to Fremantle in Australia. These cables were all part of the old empire route and were vital to empire communications. The cable fault was in very deep water—about three thousand five hundred fathoms—and had eluded the best efforts of *Recorder* previously to bring the cable to the surface. We had similar bad luck over a period of several weeks of dragging. Pieces of cable were brought to bows but were mere strands of cable laid fifty years ago and known in the trade as "bread and butter" cable. It was surmised that earthquakes on the ocean bottom had torn up the cable. In the face of ghastly weather and disappointing results, we withdrew toward our main base in Singapore.

It was heavenly to return to this most interesting city with its racial mix of Chinese, Malay and Indian. I toured the city seeing all the sights, Raffles Hotel, St. Andrew's Cathedral, Orchard Road, Bugie Street and the centre of night life, Lavender Road. The Tanglin Club was visited again and I became a temporary member of the Singapore Swimming Club, which put on fabulous curry luncheons. Life was indeed good and I wished greatly that my wife could join me.

My Australian friend almost got himself lynched one night while visiting Lavender Road. As a joke, he stole a whore's panties as a trophy and was astonished to find himself being chased by a mob of very excited Chinese. He had not realized that there was a little pocket sewn in the panties containing money and other valuables. He was rescued by a British shore patrol before any damage was done and then apologized profusely to the indignant lady of the night.

Another infamous thoroughfare was Bugie Street, where transvestites congregated. Some very strange sights could be seen after dark. In order that I may keep the record straight for the uninformed reader, I visited St. Andrew's Cathedral in addition to the aforementioned dens of iniquity. Our travel was often by rickabike, a Japanese import that had replaced the old rickshaws pulled by sweating coolies, as in Rangoon before its surrender to the Japanese in 1941.

Inevitably, with tension in the air and people spoiling for a fight, I came in for my share of trouble. Accompanied by two engineers off *Recorder*, we visited the Great World amusement park, looking for fun and action. The Chinese theatre was incomprehensible to us, so we wandered into the dance hall to be besieged by a horde of taxi dancers who were having a slow night. After several dances and listening to as many propositions, imbibing great quantities of alcohol and probably getting noisier and more obnoxious by the minute, we wandered off to view the action in the vicinity of Lavender Road. Nothing there met with our approval, so we sought a taxi to take us back to the ship.

At long last, we managed to find an ancient open Buick with a Sikh driver who wanted to charge us double the normal fare back to the cable station at Number Nine Gate, Keppel Harbour. We ordered him to drive to the nearest police station where we could settle this dispute. Instead, he whipped the Buick into a warren of alleys and called for his mates to attack us. This they did with steel tipped lathis. There were six of them and three of us. It was a short but bloody battle. In the end, we three won the fight after the Sikhs fled the scene. We had managed to protect ourselves by seizing the lathis from our opponents and acquiring the engine crank handle as an additional weapon. We were victorious but in a bit of a mess. One of the engineers had a bad scar on one arm, the other had broken fingers on one hand and I was covered in blood from head to toe from a blow to my skull. A pyrrhic victory indeed, as we spent much time trying to persuade other taxi drivers to pick us up and finally had to pay one the double fare we had originally disputed.

I felt fairly good, but the third mate took one horrified look at the three of us and sent for an ambulance. We were soon in the emergency room, being attended to by efficient nurses supervised by doctors who had no doubt seen it all before. I needed thirteen stitches in my head and left there with a huge turban-like bandage covering the affected area. I was treated like a hero by our crew but felt an utter idiot. The chief officer, John West, gave me a few choice words of reprimand and some sage advice on the perils of overindulgence, which were obeyed for a while and then forgotten. Captain Axtell ignored the turban and its significance completely. I had better measure up in the future.

Recorder departed Singapore at the beginning of September 1946, bound for Mombasa. In normal times, cable ships were based at a home port for years, on call for immediate response to cable failure. Now, in the aftermath of war, each cable ship was faced with many cables requiring attention and our priority area was now the northwestern part of the Indian Ocean. Our first destination was the port of Mombasa, Kilindini, where I had spent time previously on the troopship *Salween*. It was pleasant to be back in East Africa. The coastlines of Kenya and Tanganyika were very attractive with their waving palms in the background and white reefs and silvery sands in the foreground. Although it was hot, being close to the equator, cooling breezes from the sea tempered the heat and made living on board and ashore quite comfortable.

One of my more attractive duties was the position of gin secretary. In addition to ensuring the honesty of my shipmates when they recorded their alcoholic purchases on board, I was required to visit the local clubs and issue invitations to members to visit us on *Recorder*. In turn we could use the facilities of these shore-based clubs, and even charge our expenses incurred to our shipboard account. You had to be careful and remember that shore prices were much higher than the duty-free prices prevailing on board ship. In Mombasa, I called on the Mombasa club and the yacht club, which provided us with lots of contacts and some lasting friendships.

However, our main task was to prepare for cable repair work in the vicinity of the Seychelles Islands. The bottom was expected to be a mix of rock, mud and sand, so a variety of grapnels would be deployed. Our rod and chain steering gear was overhauled. All cable ships used rod and chain exclusively due to the wear and tear on the steering gear in conducting cable operations. *Recorder* was a coal burner, so we travelled to Zanzibar to refuel before setting out for the cablegrounds. Once again,

I was struck by the beauty and tranquillity of the island and hired a bicycle to see more of it at leisure. I even climbed a palm tree to pick my own coconut. I also bought some perfume and make-up to send home to Doreen. It took several days to get on station, and it then became a boring routine of locating the cable-break area by a series of astronomical observations that determined the marker buoy position. The marker buoy was tethered to the bottom by a rope/wire combination fitted to a mushroom anchor. Operating depths around the Seychelles were of the order of five hundred to one thousand fathoms.

Figure 48 - A noon routine on *Recorder*

The ship would position itself from the marker buoy by magnetic compass bearings and rangefinder distances while conducting dragging operations. The charts used were specially drawn to show not just the position of the cable as first laid but also the positions and lengths of repairs carried out over the years. We were dragging for the original cable and found it in about a thousand fathoms of water. A Lucas grapnel was used to cut the cable at source, thereby enabling *Recorder* to lift the remaining cable to the surface without breaking. Deployment of workboats enabled the cable to be secured at bows during testing and in buoying it off while we went looking for the other undamaged end. From tests on board ship and from both shore stations, the cable engineers determined the actual location of the fault. The captain then commenced dragging operations after setting up another marker buoy. Operations could be controlled from either the bridge of the working deck.

Figure 49 - Cable operations, Indian Ocean, 1947

All these operations were carried out on a twenty-four-hour basis, with a full port and starboard watch on duty. The seamen were very competent, particularly those who manned the workboats under the control of the bosun's mates. Eventually, the cable would be hooked and cut and raised to the bow of *Recorder*. After testing the cable, the cable electrician would effect the repair to the copper wire and gutta percha covering. The splice would be made, encasing the gutta percha core in steel wiring and insulation material. *Recorder* would then steam back to the buoyed off cable, effect the final splice and lower it into the sea. From there, after a celebratory drink, we went looking for the next festering cable repair problem!

Rumour had it that we were shortly to go south to Durban for a major refit. I was anxious for this to happen, as communication with my wife had been spasmodic at best. I wrote every day, but the letters could only

Figure 50 - Doing a spot of navigating, CS *Norseman*, 1947

be sent off in bunches as we were seldom in port. I also looked forward to finding out if she could get a passage to Durban as the ship was expected to be there for several months and other officers were contemplating similar action. So it was with some expectation that I looked forward to arrival in South Africa. It was now October, and I had reason to celebrate as I had just been promoted to third officer.

Durban was as attractive as ever. The beach became a magnet for daily visits, as the major refit on board progressed. It was noisy and very hot and dirty on board, with most officers and crew choosing to live ashore at the owners' expense. I soldiered on, being a canny Scot, and collected my daily allowance for surviving the clamour. I was trying to save as much money as possible in case my wife managed to get a passage out to South Africa. However, she seemed hesitant, citing various difficulties.

Hoping to persuade her, I explored alterative employment ashore. I was immediately offered two jobs working either in the coal industry in Natal or in the copper mines in Northern Rhodesia. These were dirty jobs as a rigger but with extremely high pay. I was willing to leave the sea and change occupation so that we could be together. However, she was still doubtful about coming to Africa, so I had to drop the idea. Whether I would have made a good rigger with my seagoing experience was never put to the test. Perhaps I was a trifle relieved, as a land job far from the ocean was daunting to contemplate.

Figure 51 - Zulu warriors, Durban, Natal, 1946

Having made many friends ashore, there were always events to go to and parties to attend. A memorable event was celebrating Dingaan's Day out in the country. Dingaan was a Zulu chieftain who was defeated by the Boers in a famous victory. It was celebrated each year at a huge "briesfect" or barbecue. An enormous bonfire was lit and small trek carts were placed within easy distance of the fire. These carts were laden with chops, steaks, sausages and other cuts of meat. Each participant lay on his or her belly after selecting a piece of meat on a wire skewer and attempted a successful roast. Meanwhile, jugs of Cape brandy were being passed from body to body, and old Afrikaans songs were sung to the accompaniment of fiddlers and harmonica players. The combination of heat, brandy and music ensured that one's piece of meat was usually underdone or overdone. It was great fun at the time, out in the Natal hills but the stomach rebelled later.

All present at these affairs were white, with a mix of English-speaking South Africans, Boers, White Russians and recent immigrants from Europe. Blacks were servants or engaged in work that no white would undertake. Indians and Coloureds were in an in-between position, accepted reluctantly at times in the white preserve, but strictly excluded at other times and designated as non-whites. Public toilets were marked as whites and non-whites, and seats on trains and buses were also allocated by race. In Durban, these rules were not strictly enforced and the races could meet in some nightclubs and cinemas and other public places.

Although I liked Durban, I was missing my wife a great deal. The temptations of life ashore were also becoming more pronounced. There were many attractive young ladies around, and their availability was all too obvious. Added to that enticement was the conviviality enhanced by copious quantities of South African beer and brandy. I felt that I was on a downhill spiral and longed for the sea.

I discussed my dilemma with Captain Axtell and he very helpfully arranged a transfer to another cable ship, *Norseman*, which would be docking in Capetown shortly. He advised me that *Recorder* would be in Durban on refit for at least another six months, due mainly to the repairs required to her ancient iron hull. That news settled things; I knew that I could not survive such a spell in paradise. Accordingly, with a few fond farewells, I took the train to Capetown.

Chapter Twenty-Three

By Train to Capetown and Cable Ship *Norseman*

The journey lasted about thirty-six hours in comparative comfort. The first morning, I awoke when the train stopped at a station. I looked out the top bunk window and saw the name of the station—it was Bethlehem! I was astonished, and then realized that I must be in Orange Free State and not in Palestine. The entire staff of the train were white, all Afrikaners, and surly with the English-speaking passengers. However, they did serve a reasonable breakfast, which made some amends. In no time we were heading out across the Great Karoo, a great desert in December but apparently covered in lush grass and flowers in the South African spring. Some cattle could be seen in the distance and the occasional isolated farmhouse before night descended again. The following morning, we found ourselves in the treed area above the Wye River Valley, before wending our way by great loops of track down to the valley floor.

From now on, the scenery was pleasing to the eye with farms and vineyards on every side. The Cape Range stretched away to the southeast and soon we could see the landward side of Table Mountain in the distance. We crossed the Cape flats and very shortly thereafter we steamed into Capetown station. It was grand to be there looking up at Table Mountain and the Lion's Head. I made my way by taxi to the Mount Nelson Hotel where I had been reserved a room. *Norseman* was not expected in port for another few days.

The hotel was pleasant enough, but as usual in those days, the bathroom lay down the hall. The first morning there, I managed to lock myself out of my room attired with only a flimsy towel around my midriff. I knocked on the door of the room adjacent to my own, which was opened by a young lady in proper dress who eyed me most suspiciously. Before I could explain my predicament she closed the door in my face, forcing me to walk all the way down to the desk in my skimpy covering. What a start to the day. However, having time to spare, I set off to find my cousin Ailsa who had married a South African chap during the war and had settled in Capetown. They lived in a suburb called Orangezicht, which I tried to find with little success. I finally struck oil with a policeman who converted my Scottish pronunciation of the suburb to its proper Afrikaans.

Ailsa was delighted to see me and I met her mother-in-law and Jimmy Marais her husband. He had been attached to the Royal Navy during the war years but was now a Lt. Commander in the South African navy. I think that Ailsa was somewhat homesick, but she tried her best not to show it. I spent a very nice weekend with them and their young children. Swimming in False Bay was a treat; here the warm waters of the Indian Ocean take precedence over the cold Atlantic. We also watched a rugby match where the locals displayed their wild enthusiasm for the national game.

The following day *Norseman* arrived in Capetown and I went on board to meet my new shipmates. She had been operating in the South Atlantic and this was also her first visit to Capetown. The press were on board in strength and eager for stories. Next day in the Cape Argus there was overwhelming coverage of the *Norseman* story. It included stories of wartime adventures of various crew members on many ships. Very interesting, but not exactly the story of *Norseman*. I met the captain, Henry Lawrence, and a number of other officers and proceeded to make myself comfortable in an exterior cabin on the main deck.

Norseman was constructed in 1928 for the Western Telegraph Co. Ltd., now Cable & Wireless. She displaced about two thousand five hundred tons and was powered by twin-screw steam turbines. Her normal cruising speed was fourteen knots, and as in all cable ships could be controlled from either the bridge or the operating station on the bow. Two cable tanks lay forward of the bridge, with access to the working deck and the bow sheaves. Windlass, winches and dynamometer were laid out similarly to that of *Recorder*. Abaft the working deck, from below the bridge, a port and starboard interior alleyway ran the length of the ship to the quarterdeck, which was located close to the stern. Officers' cabin space was contained along the outer sides of both alleyways. The upper part of the engine room lay between the alleyways. Petty officer accommodation was on the boat deck, and the crew were located midships below deck, immediately abaft the cable tanks.

Figure 52 - CS *Norseman*, South Africa, 1946–47

Total complement was one hundred and twenty, consisting of master and four deck officers, six marine engineers, four cable engineers, purser, six petty officers of various trades, and ninety-eight crew members required for cable operations at sea, manpower essential to the conduct of over-the-side work and the deployment of open boats propelled only by oars. The master, as usual, lived in lonely splendour under the bridge deck. On the bridge were the wheelhouse, the navigational chartroom and the cable operations room.

The officers' dining room and wardroom were located below the quarterdeck and fitted out with grand piano, bar and reading room. All very civilized! Lots of visitors were well entertained within its bulkheads.

The officers were mostly British, with the normal sprinkling of Irish and the odd South African. The petty officers were a mix of British and Spanish, with the crew consisting entirely of Spaniards, mostly from Vigo in northwestern Spain. *Norseman's* homeport was Gibraltar.

For two weeks or so, I familiarized myself with my new home. *Norseman* was not as elegant as *Recorder*, but she was a comfortable ship and my new shipmates were an interesting bunch. The first mate was an unknown quantity who had just joined us after shore leave in South Africa. He imbibed a lot, but in the wardroom that was not unusual. The second mate, our navigator, was Bill Cross, a large man with a good sense of humour, who loved to live well. He was the son of an Anglican bishop, and a more unlikely Christian I have yet to meet.

Figure 53 - Sam Simpson and the author somewhere in the Indian Ocean, 1947

The fourth mate was Sam Simpson, a charming fellow but very English. The chief cable electrician was an older man known as Tikki Eastwood. He had earned the name Tikki years previously when he was stationed in South Africa and was constantly borrowing a tikki (three pence) to use the telephone to call his girlfriend. He and Henry Lawrence had been shipmates on the old *Britannia* stationed in Capetown immediately after the Great War. In those days, they lay alongside for months on end, with a spell in drydock the only break in routine. Today, we faced the prospect of much time at sea chasing after a multitude of cable faults.

Two other cable engineers were interesting characters. One was a quiet chap from the north of England called Ferrie who only really came to life after he had tossed back a few. The other fellow was called Mickey Quan, an Englishman of Irish background who became a good friend over the course of the fifteen months that I served on *Norseman*. Among the marine engineers were a few worthy of note. The chief engineer had a bad back and slept on a hard board and constantly let everyone know about it. The third engineer was a wild Liverpudlian called Colin Samples, who turned up much later in my life in unexpected fashion. There were two junior engineers from Ulster, both of the Protestant persuasion, and ready to fight at the drop of a hat. The most interesting one was Anderson. He had been in the Royal Navy on landing craft in the Adriatic in 1943/1944 assisting the partisans in Yugoslavia in its struggle with the Germans. He was not a big man, but possessed the bluest of eyes, which he could turn with great effect on the ladies. He was a man who was totally obsessed by sex, as I will attempt to illustrate later. His fellow northern Irishman was not so complex. He was a hard worker, blunt and outspoken, with little time for psychological discussion or debate. A good man in a fight, but an Orangeman through and through.

I almost missed out on probably the most interesting man in the wardroom. He was the purser, a Welshman named Morgan who had served in the Royal Navy during the air and ship battles in the Pacific in 1944/1945. He had been mentioned in dispatches for bravery when his aircraft carrier was damaged by kamikaze Japanese bombers in the late stages of the war. He was a small man with an easy smile who exuded enormous self-confidence. He was also a ladies' man who cut quite a swath through the visiting females. Actually, except for the older officers, the wardroom seemed to be a trifle preoccupied with the opposite sex. I had fled Durban's attractions only to be surrounded by temptation once more.

I got out and about as much as possible and travelled up to Signal Hill to view the area around, stretching from Sea Point in the west, through Green Point, Table Bay and Central, to Orangezicht in the south east, where my cousin resided. Immediately behind Signal Hill and the Devil's Peak lay the awe-inspiring Table Mountain, partially crowned with white halos of cloud. Most thought-provoking of all was the realization that the next closest land mass was the Antarctic.

There were lots of parks in Green Point and Sea Point to the west was an upscale neighbourhood of well-appointed homes, apartments and hotels. The train service was excellent to Rondebosch and Newlands where the University of Capetown was located. A huge statue of Cecil Rhodes dominated the approaches. Further on by train lay Muizenberg, a grand beach and swimming spot on False Bay.

South of Muizenberg on False Bay lay Simonstown, the former South Atlantic base for the Royal Navy, but now in the process of becoming the headquarters for the South African naval defence force. Further down the Cape peninsula, it self-terminated in the Cape of Good Hope and Cape Point. There was a monument in the Cape of Good Hope's nature reserve commemorating Vasco de Gama's sighting of the Cape in fourteen eighty-eight. The western side of the peninsula is very picturesque, with another nature reserve, the Silvermine, close by. From the reserve, a winding road takes one over Chapman's Peak and down into Hout Bay, a fishing paradise. The Cape is truly one of the most spectacular places on the globe.

With much fanfare and some weeping and wailing, *Norseman* departed the Victoria basin in early December 1946. For myself and perhaps a few others, there was a certain sense of relief to be going off to sea again, away from the hothouse atmosphere that was all too prevalent on board while in dock in Capetown. I will leave the reader to develop his or her conclusions.

Then fate struck, and off Danger Point, as we were about to turn into the Indian Ocean, we developed serious engine room problems and had to limp back to Capetown. Naturally, we were greeted with joy by the people who had seen us off with much sadness, while I pondered my situation.

The spirit was strong, but the flesh was weak. Let that be the record of *Norseman's* return to Capetown and my own in particular. Certainly the spirit was alcoholic, and that led to the other weakness, the fair-skinned ladies.

There was an abundance of available white women in port but some of our seagoing fraternity liked to live life on the edge and chased after the many attractive coloured girls. Some even ventured into District Six, the coloured enclave close to the docks in search of such forbidden fruit. Bearing in mind the law of the land, which denied inter-racial fornication, to be caught by the police in such a liaison could result in ninety days hard labour. Yet the gamblers were prepared to accept the risk. One of our engineers was even chased out of District Six with several slavering police dogs on his heels.

All good things come to an end, and after completing repairs we sailed once more out into Table Bay. Mickey Quan was very upset as he had fallen in love with a nice Afrikaaner girl. They wanted to get married, but her father absolutely forbid the marriage as in his eyes Mickey was a "roinek," a red neck, a descendent of the British that he had fought against in the Boer War as a young boy.

We carried extra cargo on the quarterdeck. Additional supplies for the wardroom—cases of brandy, gin and beer—all purchased at very reasonable prices and, of course, duty free. Obviously we were expected to be at sea for some considerable time. We passed Danger Point without any more engine trouble but, with increasingly bad weather, our supplies of booze had to be stowed below in a safer place.

Our destination was the vicinity of the British island of Mauritius in the Indian Ocean. The cable between Durban and Mauritius was defective and we commenced our search south of Mauritius but within sight of the French island of Reunion. It was a long boring procedure, dragging for cable in one thousand fathoms of water. The weather was foul most of the time and we often had to anchor in the lee of Reunion Island in force seven to eight winds. We could see some of the little ports and villages on Reunion, but never got a chance to go ashore.

Finally, we managed to complete the cable repair, with our seamen performing magnificently in borderline operational weather. These Vigo fishermen were truly professionals in handling the open rowed workboats in the ocean environment. In slightly calmer weather, they would hang nonchalantly from the bows, securing cable while huge sharks circled underneath their legs. These men were often scarred by their experiences in the Spanish civil war and were almost to a man strongly anti-Franco. They loved to have mock bullfights on deck with some taking the place of the bull and the matador and other actors in the drama of the bullring. When they got word that the famous matador Manolete had died, the entire ship went into mourning.

In addition to their courage, they also could display cruelty, usually expressed toward birds that they captured on deck or to sharks that they hooked by baiting with meat. They would then jam a two by four into the animals mouth so that it could not close it shut, toss the shark back into the ocean and watch with great glee as it would be attacked and then torn to pieces by its companions.

Norseman sailed for Durban to refuel upon completion of its repair of the Durban-Mauritius cable. We were about to get a change in first officer. The one that had joined us in Capetown was an alcoholic, who turned out to be a danger not just to himself but to the safety of the ship as well. Alcoholism was ever-prevalent on cable ships, what with very long periods of service at sea away from home and family, and a plentiful supply of cheap duty free liquor on board. His replacement was a fellow Scot called Rutherford from Dundee. He drank just as much as his predecessor but kept it under control.

Durban was a welcome sight after six weeks at sea. We tied up to the ocean terminal in the Bay of Natal, the inner harbour of the port of Durban. As usual in those days, we were given a warm welcome. I visited with friends who had a rather elegant home in Berea, Durban's most prestigious suburb. I also visited Amanzimtoti, a lovely hamlet that lay about fifteen miles south of Durban with both a fresh water lagoon and a fine beach fronting on the Indian Ocean. In those days, travel to Amanzimtoti was by slow train. Today it is no longer a hamlet and is connected to Durban by a first class highway. It sports many large apartment blocks and associated mega shops. It is also overrun with wild monkeys who steal everything in sight.

Duty visits were paid to the Durban Country Club and other private clubs with which we had contact. Gin secretary could be a most enjoyable duty. Finally, a visit to the beach front for old times' sake and a good swim out to the wreck still lying offshore of the Addington Hospital.

South Africa is a very pleasant place, but it is home to many wild animals, including a large variety of poisonous snakes. On the Bluff, close to the heart of Durban, black mambas can be found without too much difficulty. The black mamba is one of the deadliest snakes in the world. To be struck by one is an almost sure recipe for death. Nevertheless, we frequented the bluff from time to time, as it led to a nice little hotel and bathing facilities on the Indian Ocean. The hotel was used by Cable & Wireless as a place to treat staff suffering from stress, and we used to meet there with shipmates undergoing treatment. We saw a number of mambas and were careful to travel only in daylight.

Thieves were a hazard in Durban, particularly in and around the docks. Our chief engineer woke up one morning to find that his uniforms and suits had been pulled out of his wardrobe by an ingenious burglar using a pole and a hook, and spiriting them through his porthole out on to the wharf. All this was accomplished in the dark. It did not say much for security on the wharf or on the ship's gangway. An open porthole was an invitation to such thievery; thank goodness, my cabin was located on the offshore side of the vessel.

I mentioned earlier that one of the engineers was obsessed by sex. In Durban, he had invited a female companion on board, and was engaged in sexual activities when a troopship docked astern of us. Shortly thereafter, a female passenger from the troopship climbed up our gangway and demanded to see her husband, the aforementioned engineer. It became a bit of a French farce as we made the lady welcome while we warned our shipmate and attempted to smuggle his companion ashore. The outcome of all this subterfuge was a first-class marital row and then, to our surprise, reconciliation. Time and again, he would demonstrate such powers of persuasion as the voyage wore on. The rest of us viewed him with awe, tinged with perhaps a bit of jealousy.

Since my experience on *Mandalay*, I had not run into any other homosexuals. However, there were some drifting around on cable ships, and being back in Durban reminded me of their presence. A deck officer and a cable engineer on *Recorder* kept very close company, which was explained when I was made aware of their friendship with a full blown queer who was the organist at the most popular theatre in Durban. They would invite him on board frequently and it was soon obvious what was going on. A big shock—such handsome fellows! On board *Norseman* there appeared to be only one, and he was a harmless type who did not represent a threat to anyone. In fact, we worried about him and tried to watch out for him on shore where predators lurked.

The political situation in South Africa was changing. The old United Party formed under Jan Smuts was losing control of events. The National Party headed by Malan was striving for power and looked likely to win a majority at elections expected in 1948. The old easygoing attitude regarding race and colour was about to change. South Africa's laws regarding race, colour, property and movement had been on the books for a long time but were seldom rigidly enforced. Indeed, in cities such as Capetown and Durban, the barriers had seemed to be crumbling. Now that progress was threatened, as picked up from private conversations and in the newspapers. Apartheid was on the way.

We departed Durban in March 1947 bound for Mauritius and several cable repairs requiring immediate attention in the vicinity. I was happy to get back to sea, but unhappy to be receiving fewer letters from home. Something was wrong with our marriage, and I did not know how to put it right. All I could do for the present was to soldier on and fulfil my contract with Cable & Wireless.

Mauritius was a lovely island whose trade with the outside world in those days was mainly confined to sugar and rum. French influence was everywhere, even though Britain had occupied the island since the Napoleonic Wars, and much of the population was of British Indian origin. They had been brought into Mauritius to work in the sugar plantations. The capital and port was Port Louis, a well-protected harbour. There were beautiful beaches within easy reach of Port Louis, which was dominated by a large fort. A small steam train travelled up into the mountains and high valleys terminating at a lovely hamlet called Curepipe. Wild flowers grew in profusion everywhere and the valleys were a picture of colour. In Curepipe and the surrounding countryside, the population was largely Creole, and French was the language of communication.

From Mauritius, we proceeded again to the cable grounds south of Reunion Island to complete another repair. This time, we were lucky with the weather and soon had final splice at bows and then on to the next job. We did have another look at Reunion Island from offshore. This island had been British but was exchanged for Mauritius in the late eighteenth century. There were few harbours of refuge on Reunion so perhaps we got the better part of the bargain.

Figure 54 - Cable operations, CS *Norseman*, 1947

Our next repair job was the cable between Mauritius and the Seychelles, which took us longer than expected due to the condition of the existing cable. Break after break, leading to frustration after frustration. We were finally forced to retreat to Diego Suarez in Madagascar for fuel, fresh water and supplies. Madagascar was controlled by the French, and Diego Suarez was a French naval base situated at the northern tip of the island. It had been the scene of a fierce naval battle in 1942 between Vichy French forces and the Royal Navy. It was an attractive harbour. The people were friendly, the food was different, and the wine was a pleasant change. We completed our visit in too short a time and, at dawn the following morning, were on our way. It was an early start and I had stayed up most of the night carousing, and so was in pitiful shape as I helped navigate *Norseman* out of Diego Suarez harbour. It must have been that French plonk!

Our short stop in Madagascar must have been lucky, as we finished up several cable repairs around the Seychelles in short order. We then proceeded to Mombasa for supplies, fuel and to load additional cable for future cable operations. Kilindini harbour looked most welcoming as we settled in for a spot of rest and recreation.

With the impending loss of India, British East Africa was becoming important as a base for imperial power and as a source of supplies of food. Kilindini harbour was being fitted out with new naval wharves and shore establishments, while trade in and out of the port revolved around the groundnut project, a British government scheme to use masses of the British taxpayers' money to create a groundnut growing and processing empire in Kenya, Uganda and Tanganyika. It all sounded wonderful, but like most socialistic dreams, was eventually doomed to failure. The imperial base of power also vanished within a couple of decades as Britain gave these countries, and many others, their independence.

Mombasa itself was growing rapidly, and a small but growing tourist industry was exploiting the beaches on the Indian Ocean north of Kilindini and the old Fort Jesus, built back in the sixteenth century by the Portuguese. A few small resort hotels heralded the future. In Mombasa, there were several new hotels and restaurants. One in particular served fresh seafood that was much in demand. It was owned and managed by a rather exotic Seychelles beauty, who was the lady friend of a black sheep member of the Guiness family, whose product is consumed throughout the known world. He flaunted his association with the lady from the Seychelles, much to the disdain of the stuffier female members of Mombasa society. He also cruised around the waters of Kilindini and other harbours in a high-speed converted naval motor torpedo boat. He was certainly the talk of the town.

Figure 55 - Exploring the East African Jungle - 1947

Our second mate, Bill Cross, had to go to hospital for a minor operation and as a result met a number of local residents, who were eventually introduced to me and others visiting him. There was an attractive lady who helped nurse Bill back to health in the private nursing home. Bill liked her enormously but nothing developed further. There was a young Catholic priest who had a fine singing voice and a grand sense of humour. He needed it in dealing with our gang.

Then there was the episode in one of the Mombasa hotels. It was early evening, and I went for a stroll in the hotel gardens. I had forgotten that the hotel rooms opened on to the gardens and was astonished to hear loud voices and noises of passion issuing from one open door. An older Canadian woman, who was a permanent resident in the hotel, had a reputation for enjoying younger men. This apparently was her room, and she was entertaining the young second mate of a British India vessel that had just tied up ahead of us in Kilindini. She sounded so enthusiastic that I felt quite jealous, even if she was old enough to be my mother. I had been behaving myself, but it was at times difficult.

Through our temporary membership in the yacht club we had a visit on board from two young white Kenyan females. After showing them around *Norseman*, they were entertained in the wardroom. I freely admit that I had designs on one of them, but was taken aback to find out that she was barely fifteen years old. She looked totally bewildered as I prattled on about youth and innocence and escorted her off the ship. A question remains—was she naïve or was it I?

We departed Mombasa with some sadness and, after a quick cable repair off Rodriguez Island, headed north to work on the Karachi–Oman cable. Water depths averaged about one thousand fathoms and the bottom was mostly mud and sand. However, there had been much subterranean movement underneath the sea bottom, which thwarted our attempts to bring cable to bows. For forty-two days at sea off the coast of Persia we could only bring bits of cable to the surface. We were short of fresh water and of temper, and even resorted to building a mud ju ju on the bow sheave casing to placate the gods. All to no avail!

Norseman headed to Karachi for supplies and a few days' rest. Karachi in those days was not an attractive port, so we spent most of our time resting and drinking. There were so many opportunities to guzzle alcohol at duty free prices that it became a habit, even at sea, where pre-dinner gins were the habit, and other times when off duty. I had the eight to twelve watch and tried to go straight to my cabin to retire after midnight, only to be phoned upon arrival by the first mate Rutherford and ordered to join a group in his cabin who needed a fourth hand for bridge. That meant at least two more drinks before hitting the sack about two AM. I know that I was weak and so I worried about the situation. These senior officers that I drank with after watchkeeping were all two-bottle-a-day men and I do not mean beer bottles.

Off we went again to sea to try to pick up the Karachi–Oman cable, but this time much closer to Oman and the entrance to the Persian Gulf. It was now early June and the heat was becoming oppressive. No wind blew to help us cool off during the mornings and early afternoons, and the wind that blew off the desert in the late afternoon and early evening was fiery and miserable. For several days, we had to cease operations at mid-day while the temperature climbed to fifty degrees centigrade. Cool lemonade was passed around sparingly to assist us in coping with the weather. The problem was aggravated by the fact that Muscat, the main port in Oman, was off limits by order of the sultan, a real old despot.

We did manage finally to hook decent cable and were able to repair a fair portion of the Karachi–Oman line. It was, however, past time for our annual refit, so *Norseman* set course for Bombay. We arrived there in late June, just as the monsoon was breaking. There was tension and excitement in the air as the days of the British Raj were numbered and a handover to the Indians was anticipated by mid-August. One local rag with the appropriate name of the "Blitz" was issuing dire warnings and threats of blood on the streets, but most local residents seemed unperturbed, even indifferent or sad.

Chapter Twenty-Four

Norseman in Bombay

We went into drydock immediately in the steamy monsoon heat. The ship rapidly became a shambles as countless workers invaded our home and made life extremely difficult. To make it worse, I came down with a form of dengue fever compounded by sprouting water blisters all over my face and upper chest. I sorely needed rest and relaxation in cool quiet quarters, but it was not to be, as we were shorthanded and security watches were essential with the massive political and social changes underway throughout India. Almost daily, trips were taken in the early evening to Beach Kandy to cool off in the waters of the Arabian Sea. There I met Terry McCluskey, an old friend from Greenock who was in a senior position in the Bombay fire brigade. It was good to meet someone from home. He had been a firefighter during the Blitz on Greenock in 1941, and had followed his trade overseas to a number of British possessions. He told me about the *Fort Stikine* disaster, which almost destroyed the port of Bombay in 1943, and had other interesting tales to tell. Terry's younger brother Fred was closer in age to me and we played together as youngsters. Fred was a sergeant in the Welsh Regiment during the battles in Italy, where he won the Military Medal for outstanding bravery. The family lived in what was largely a Protestant enclave in Greenock but were brought up as Catholics, which must have been difficult for them back in the days when the Orange/Green divide hung over everything.

When we completed our sojourn in drydock, life on board became much more pleasant and we were able to entertain on board. Many interesting characters appeared, Parsees, dancers, singers, Hindus, and numerous ex-pats, just to name a few. One of the Parsees was a wealthy old retired businessman who lived in a large suite of rooms in the Taj Mahal Hotel. He invited some of us to a party in the hotel, where I met more interesting people, including Adrienne, the secretary to the general manager of the hotel. Without even thinking about it, I found myself vying for her attention while in competition with the first mate who was determined to exert his seniority. More on this matter later.

Our Parsee host was quite frail but did smoke while wielding a very, very long cigarette holder. I met his oldest daughter, an attractive lady, who had just scandalized her father by marrying a Moslem. Between this very personal matter and the British about to leave India after three hundred years, the old man was perplexed and worried, as indeed were many Indians who feared that a rupture of the status quo would mean unrest and trouble. The young were looking forward to the change but the older folks with something to lose saw the future in grimmer terms. Our visiting doctor on board *Norseman* was an elderly Parsee gentleman called "Engineer." As I was the guardian of the medical chest on board, we had many quiet chats between examinations of patients. He lived in a lovely old home on a secluded lane in one of Bombay's better districts with his large family. I hope that all went well for him after independence.

Among the singers and dancers mentioned were a mother and daughter act from Scotland who had been touring in the Far East since the Japanese entered the war in late 1941. They were good company on board ship but loosened up a lot under the influence of alcohol. The usual suspects among the officers buzzed around them like flies. Additionally, there were several people from a large British company based in Bombay. Their women were soon being looked after by our heroes of the wardroom.

There were of course a number of more staid and proper guests. The harbourmaster and his wife, the "Flying Angel" padre, the Royal Indian Navy base commander and others. The ship was certainly a magnet for the unorthodox, but sought after by members of the establishment. We were also probably popular because most of Bombay's private clubs were dry after an edict from the local government, controlled by the Congress Party of India. It was a deliberate act of revenge for many clubs' stupid practice of denying membership to Indians unless they were very wealthy or very powerful. One club that kept its bar open was the Radio Officers Club, which had always welcomed anyone with the proper qualifications. The past was coming back to haunt us.

In Bombay, there were many cinemas, some of them quite elaborate in structure and containing comfortable lounges that served drinks, alcoholic and otherwise. The cinemas were air-conditioned, which in the monsoon heat added to their attractiveness. Some showed the latest Hollywood extravaganzas, while many others showed only products of Bollywood, the local centre of Indian film in the Hindi or Urdu languages. These Indian films were wildly popular and featured historic events in ancient India, with unrequited love being a constant theme. Once I visited the lounge of one of these picture palaces and inadvertently drew attention to myself by sitting down in a chair that collapsed under me. There I was, in my best number ten's, sitting on the floor while nursing the remnants of a gin gimlet. I felt that I had let the empire down, but nary a soul paid any attention to my predicament. I went in to see the film, still wet and chastened.

As mentioned before, the contest between the first mate and me for the attention of Adrienne must have been obvious to all present in the Taj Mahal Hotel. Suffice to say that I won, but probably made an enemy of my senior officer. She was very attractive, well spoken, and I would guess probably in her late twenties. She was white but could have had some Indian blood in her from her great-grandparents. She had been educated in India at a very good school. She had a boyfriend of similar background who was away on business in Ceylon and acted fancy free. I liked her and being in her company and learned something of the Bombay scene from her. It was, however, a relationship based largely on physical attraction and when we parted it was all over. I hope she survived the transformation of India.

Indians had been agitating for independence from Britain for many years, but particularly in the nineteen thirties and into the nineteen forties. Opinion was divided in Britain about the wisdom of such a move, as India was perceived as not being politically mature enough and riven with racial and religious divides. In India, the politically active classes wanted independence but differed among themselves on how best to achieve it.

In 1935, the British government promulgated the Government of India Act, a constitutional milestone that could have led to Indian independence. It left the viceroy and provincial governors with some reserve power, but opened up the political arena to democratic action. Most of the provinces took full advantage of the opportunity, with the majority political party forming the provincial government in 1937. However, the Act was opposed nationally by the Congress Party and the princely states, and by the viceroy of that period, Lord Linlithgow, so it never came into effect nationwide.

In 1937, the Muslims in the Congress Party seemed favourable to the Act but by 1940, under Jinnah, were already talking of partition. They feared domination by the Hindu-controlled Congress Party and grouped themselves under the banner of the Muslim League. With India under attack by the Japanese in 1942, the British promised eventual independence, but the Congress and League rejected the offer. A "Quit India" programme mounted by the Congress Party was not a great success, as millions of young Indians volunteered for the British Indian forces fighting the common Japanese enemy.

At the end of World War II in 1945, the British Labour Government actively sought early realization of self-government in India. In 1946, the British government ably assisted by Lord Wavell, the viceroy, made a last-ditch attempt to bring about a political settlement. Jinnah was on side, but Gandhi rejected the offer. Religious riots erupted in Calcutta and spread to East Bengal and Bihar, with the Congress and League still far apart in their views.

With no agreement in sight and the situation deteriorating rapidly, the British government announced in February 1947 a transfer of power to take place no later than June 1948. This meant the partition of India and the creation of Pakistan. The new viceroy, Mountbatten, immediately speeded up the transfer of power date to August 15, 1947, in the face of widespread communal bloodshed in the Punjab and in Bengal. Massacres and massive migration followed. A quarter of a million people perished, and eleven million souls migrated to Pakistan and into India. It was a tremendous failure of statesmanship over many years on the part of the British and latterly the Indians. But two new nations were born.

Chapter Twenty-Five

En Route to Gibraltar

Norseman resumed cable repairs in the Arabian Sea without undue incident, but trouble was brewing among our Spanish crew. They had now been away from Gibraltar for more than one year and were getting mighty homesick. A deputation met with the captain to express their concerns. Our captain, Henry Lawrence, was a gentleman of the old school, who was sympathetic to their feelings but pointed out that he would require company agreement before returning the ship to Gibraltar. That agreement was not forthcoming and the problem was allowed to fester.

We moved south to the vicinity of East Africa to complete further cable repairs. Most of the crew worked with a will, but there was a dissident element that made its presence felt. We were no longer a completely happy vessel. We headed for Mombasa to take on supplies, fuel and cable, and there the entire affair came to a head. Some key members of our crew, quartermasters, donkeymen, etc., went ashore and did not return. They were eventually located but refused to return on board. Kenya, being a British colony, operated under the British system of law, so these crew members were designated as deserters and threatened with all the majesty of the law. However, an impasse was at hand, as these stubborn Spaniards announced that they were prepared to go to jail unless *Norseman* immediately set off for their home port.

The captain sought instructions from head office, while he recommended a return to Gibraltar as soon as possible. The crew remaining on board were loyal to their articles of agreement but obviously had great sympathy for the strikers. We sailed without a solution at hand, but returned alongside when Cable & Wireless sent a message that appeared to reflect a compromise. We were ordered to proceed toward Gibraltar but carry out a number of cable repairs en route. Would this satisfy the deserters? Finally, after much haggling, we sailed from Mombasa with our dissidents on board.

Figure 56 - The working deck of *Norseman*

Our first stop was off the coast of Arabia, east of Aden. It was hot and sandstorms swept in off the desert. These winds often deposited thousands of small birds on to our deck and rigging. Inevitably, they were followed by a number of hawks that pounced on their prey with great joy. Our Spanish crew loved to trap these predators and torture them to death. They were wonderful seamen, but cruel in ways that we found difficult to understand.

Our cable operations went well, although there was a mutinous rumble from our dissidents who wanted us to continue on our way home. We had a grand occasion in Aden, where we met up with *Cable Enterprise*, which had been sent to the area to take over our duties. She was a bit smaller than *Norseman* but of more modern vintage. Her captain was John West, who had been chief officer on the old *Recorder* when I joined her in Singapore back in 1946.

There was much coming and going between the vessels as we caught up on the latest news and gossip. As skipper of the captain's barge, I was in great demand and performed flawlessly. A very different story to my woeful display of seamanship in Port Louis, where I nearly decapitated the captain while manoeuvring under a hawser in the approaches to *Norseman's* gangway. I took a long time to live that one down and raised Captain Lawrence's blood pressure well above normal.

Trips were taken ashore to swim in a quiet cove some distance out of Aden. There were some nursing sisters present, which enlivened the affair. Evenings, there was an open-air cinema under the stars where cold beer could be had at a price. The perfume of jasmine permeated the cinema and clung to our clothes for hours after the performance. Even in September, the heat radiated from the rocks. The piping lament to "the barren rocks of Aden" was well named.

We were supposed to undertake several cable repairs in the southern Red Sea, but the surly attitude of some members of our crew persuaded our captain to advise Cable & Wireless that it would be appropriate to terminate cable operations with one more job. They concurred and *Norseman* departed Aden for Perim on the Straits of Bab el Mandeb at the southern entrance to the Red Sea. Perim was a small independent sheikdom that contained an unmanned cable relay station. Our task was to repair shore end cables where signal failures had been detected.

Before commencing our work, it was necessary to obtain the goodwill of the sheik. This was accomplished by attending a feast where suitable gifts were exchanged, numerous toasts were celebrated with sugary water drinks, and many sheep roasted and consumed. I managed to swallow a sheep's eye without blinking.

The shore end repairs were hard work under the blazing hot sun. However, our crew now knew that once the job was completed they were homeward bound, so they performed magnificently, and within a few days the job was completed and we were on our way northward up the Red Sea. As we approached the Gulf of Suez, the smell from the oil refineries at the head of the gulf hit our nostrils. It brought back memories of 1942/1943 and my days on *Salween*. The passage through the Suez Canal went relatively quickly. The big British base at Ismailia appeared busier than ever, and Port Said was its usual noisy harbour, filled with feluccas and bumboats selling everything from camel leather handbags and seats to French postcards and Spanish fly. There was one enterprising fellow on a bumboat who boasted of the name "Jock McGregor" with a respectable Glaswegian accent who would also sell you his sister if the price was right.

In no time at all, we were heading out toward the Mediterranean Sea, past the monument to Ferdinand de Lesseps, the French builder of the canal in 1867. The weather was cooler in the Mediterranean but still quite pleasant. Our Spanish crew were exhibiting signs of "channel fever" as we got ever closer to home port. I felt a trifle jealous, as my own personal affairs were still in turmoil. Letters from home were infrequent and cooler than I would have liked. It was October 1947 and we had now been apart for eighteen months—far too long a spell. I was lonely and beset by temptation. Exposure to unlimited quantities of alcohol was not a good thing. I felt adrift and in need of an anchor.

Off Malta, we got a welcome break when we were joined by the captain's wife who had been visiting one of her sons. She travelled with us to Gibraltar and brightened up our lives considerably. She was probably in her early fifties then, but very well preserved. She had obviously been a great beauty in her youth and exhibited graciousness and friendliness to all on board. She insisted upon inviting the younger officers to afternoon tea in the captain's quarters and made us feel appreciated. Even Captain Lawrence unstiffened somewhat under her spell. The son she had been visiting in Malta was a cable engineer on *Mirror*, our sister ship.

We reached Gibraltar on the twentieth of October amid great rejoicing among our Spanish crew. Fairly shortly thereafter, the majority of them had departed into Spain bound for Vigo. A few others stayed on and wanted to show us the attractions of La Linea and Algeciras that were close by. Algeciras was across the bay and had been a base for Italian midget submarines in World War II. They penetrated the boom defences in Gibraltar and made life difficult for Allied shipping. La Linea (the line) was located just across the border with Spain and was a lively town filled with bars, nightclubs and bordellos. It was a favourite target of the younger set from Gibraltar. Access from Gibraltar was simple during the daylight hours, but the border was closed tight from one AM to six AM. If you were caught in the no-man's-land between Spain and Gibraltar after closing hours, you had to patiently wait there until the borders opened up again. I did spend one miserable wet night in the neutral zone, staring longingly at the Gibraltar gates.

La Linea was a fairly basic sort of town. Algeciras was much more attractive architecturally, with fine churches and public buildings, and up-market hotels and cafés. There was a bus service from La Linea, but taxis were our usual mode of transport. Most items were inexpensive in Spain, and much brandy and red wine was consumed. The Franco government presence was all-pervasive, and one learned to watch what was said when the Guardia Civil were around.

Gibraltar itself was unique, very much an extension of the British Empire at the southern end of the Iberian Peninsula. The police wore Bobbies' helmets, the bars were pubs, and many of the shops bore the banners of their British heritage. The hotels were largely British colonial in style and decorum. Safe, dull even humdrum, but comforting to a weary traveller. However, although the locals were passionately pro-British, many of them were descended from settlers from other parts of the Mediterranean controlled by the British. Others were of course connected with the armed services or their descendents. A British governor ruled over all, except for a bunch of Barbary apes who dominated the heights and whose decendents had probably been there for thousands of years.

There were several bars that had a distinctly Spanish flavour, emphasising flamenco dancers accompanied by wild Arabic sounding music and song. They personified Andalusia and no doubt were inspired by their gypsy background and the long Arab occupation of Spain. A huge leap from the afternoon tea ensemble in the Rock Hotel.

CS Mirror, our sister ship, tied up astern of us after completing her work off Malta. There was a great deal of visiting to and fro, while we prepared for sea. Many of our crew had returned from Vigo, and fairly soon we were at full strength. On the second of November 1947, we sailed from Gibraltar, escorted by *Mirror* to beyond the harbour entrance. Our new tasks were in the Atlantic Ocean, beginning along the northern coast of Brazil and then working east to the Cape Verde Islands and north to Madeira. *Norseman* faced at least three months of hard work. As usual, there were eight or nine cable repairs before us.

Chapter Twenty-Six

The Amazon Coast of Brazil

Our first challenging task was off the mouth of the Amazon River. The cables led in through the vast delta of islands, mangrove swamps and mud banks to the city of Belem. The navigational charts were sadly out of date, and cables were found to now run across mangrove swamps and even in some cases over newly created islands. It was decided to visit Belem first and then work our way out through the delta, completing all repairs on the way.

Belem was a sleepy tropical city in those days, with a population of about three hundred thousand. It was the entry port for the Amazon River and served Manaus and other interior Amazon cities with a fleet of river vessels. A cable also ran from Belem to Manaus. Catholic churches with enormous cupolas dominated the city skyline when seen from the river. Around some of these churches clustered the red light district, a peculiar juxtaposition found only in Latin countries. Needless to say, it was not the churches that attracted our crew.

The streets were laid with cobblestones, and the city centre was well laid out, with good shops and public buildings. It even boasted a grand hotel where a four-piece orchestra performed every afternoon. There were lots of colourful paintings on sale, together with carvings of exotic scenes displayed on many types of hardwood. Trays inlaid with butterfly wings seemed to be very popular. The bars were the same as any others, but Brazilian beer proved to be a disappointment. A shipmate once claimed that there was no such thing as a bad beer. He should have joined us in Belem.

A circus was open most nights on the outskirts of the city, and much fun could be had there. However, many different animals were kept there in captivity and that was a chastening sight. To see large black panthers caged inside narrow confines and ill treated into the bargain was not my cup of tea. Anyhow, outside the circus were lots of wild animals, monkeys, sloths, snakes of every variety, for sale at the docks. We viewed this menagerie with considerable interest but declined to buy.

There was a tremendous explosion one day from across the harbour. An American welder accidentally set fire to an oil tank, incinerating himself and injuring several others. The photographs in the local newspaper were only too vivid. I met one of the welder's friends the following night while he was being obnoxious and a drunken menace to others. Not knowing who he was, I told him to shut up. He was a powerful fellow and tried to thump me. Luckily for me, others present intervened and, after the situation was explained, we became the best of drunken friends.

One day there was great excitement on board as an unusual delegation approached *Norseman's* gangway. There was a Brazilian policeman accompanied by the madam of a local brothel and one of her girls still dressed for night duty. It turned out that the girl claimed that her golden necklace had been stolen by someone from our ship who had accepted her favours the previous night.

Our chief officer, who was now Bill Cross, handled the affair with considerable panache by inviting the party into our wardroom to partake of morning coffee while he had the rest of us scurrying all over the vessel to track down the thief. There were of course denials from all and sundry, but eventually the thief confessed on the understanding that, if the necklace were returned to its owner, it would be the end of the matter. The necklace was given back to its owner and honour was maintained on all sides. Meanwhile, the madam was taking full advantage of the situation by issuing invitations to the entire ship's company to visit her establishment that night. If only major disputes in the world could be settled in such an amicable manner.

In all my rambling up to now, I have not given due attention to those on board whose job it was to minister to the comfort of the ship's officers. Without their dedicated service, our lot would have been more difficult and certainly much more uncomfortable. To be awakened each day to a cup of fresh hot tea, then fortified with fruit and cakes after a well-deserved afternoon nap was taken for granted. Additionally, stewards would launder clothing and press uniforms when required, while ensuring that the cabin was kept spotless and tidy. The meals served were usually acceptable, even on occasion spectacular. The wardroom was kept in immaculate condition, and our guests thoroughly pampered. Much of this success was due to the diligence of the purser and chief steward. But the most accolades must go to stewards such as Manuel who kept me in better shape than I perhaps deserved. My comments only apply to cable ships!

Another staple of shipboard life was the surgery. *Norseman* even had a small but well-equipped hospital attached to the surgery. In pre-war days, the surgery would be manned by a fully qualified medical practitioner, but wartime and post-war shortages of doctors lead to it being operated on a part-time basis by a junior deck officer, who often happened to be me. Many were the patients who appeared before me, sometimes with great faith in my ability to cure their ailment.

I dispensed black draught and calamine lotion with great abandon while dealing out other more lethal mixtures and pills with due care. Anything serious was referred to a shore-based physician for his action and advice. That often meant that I had to accompany the patient to a shore hospital or surgery, leading to encounters with interesting people. There were, however, many wounds and sicknesses that could be dealt with on board. I bandaged scrapes and bruises, even carefully treated several knife wounds that occurred among our volatile Spanish crew.

My reputation grew as a healer when I syringed out one donkeyman's ears and collected enough soil to grow a patch of potatoes. He could hear again and was duly grateful. Other cases involved venereal diseases—gonorrhea, syphilis and other combinations. These patients I could only examine and console while swabbing and cleansing the affected area. They were referred to the shore medical advisor who often prescribed pills or shots for my action. Crew members even came to the surgery door demanding extra large size prophylactics as evidence of their manhood and prowess. Luckily for the crew and me, there were no catastrophic events and my reputation remained intact.

On one occasion, I even attended an old Tarzan film while in Belem, which struck me as hilarious while surrounded by the Amazon jungle and its wild animals. I was living it, while Tarzan was in Hollywood! My companion at the film showing served me some roasted meat, which she swore was monkey, but I think she was kidding.

Eventually, we headed out of Belem for the mangrove swamps and the mud flats of the delta. The cables were easy enough to find, being in shallow water, but often took pathways that bore no resemblance to their charted position. Over the years, the delta had undergone great change, and new islands and swamps had appeared while others just disappeared. Repairs often had to be carried out from boat and barge under miserable conditions. Officers and crew were covered in mud while fighting off myriads of mosquitoes and every other bug imaginable. The crew slashed away at the mangroves and other vegetation, stirring up venomous water snakes. The captain ordered cold beer to be served to those heroes who manned the boats and the working barge. It was days before such arduous work was successfully completed, but one cable was found to transmit in only one direction, so we had to hunt further for this fault.

Luckily, it was located in slightly deeper water in a clear channel between two islands that were charted correctly. While seeking the fault, we were subjected to several unique visitations. The first, in daylight, was by masses of butterflies, yellow in colour. They were blown off the land and just used us as a resting place en route to another nesting place. The second was at night, by thousands of large dragonflies that were attracted by our working lights on deck. They flew into the lights before falling to the deck to be scooped up in shovels by the crew and deposited over the side. The third was again at night, when hundreds of bats flew on board and hung upside down in the working alleyways. At dawn, they departed all together, rising from *Norseman* in a black cloud that stretched over the monkey island while I sleepily checked our position by compass. The last visitation was terrifying, as nature was unleashed upon us. Thunder and lightening were followed by awe-inspiring displays of St. Elmo's fire. Giant balls of fire ran down the masts and exploded noisily on the deck. This was at night and carried on for some time, bringing all work on deck to a complete stop. It was a spectacular display!

The fault was finally located and repaired. It was caused by the tooth of a shark or other large fish, which was found embedded in the gutta percha covering the copper heart of the cable. We said goodbye to B
Amazon River and headed eastward down the Brazilian coast to Sao Luis.

Sao Luis lay a few hundred miles down the coast of Brazil from Belem. It was a small port, mainly engaged in fishing activities, but with a cable station that serviced both the cable to Belem and the cable to Fortaleza further down the coast. We carried out cable repairs as required, then docked in the harbour for fresh water and supplies. Shore leave was granted for the evening that we remained alongside. I had the duty watch, so did not go ashore. Just as well, as those who did reported little to see, except for one engineer officer who did not report back on board for duty. We anchored off the port while efforts were made to find him.

Figure 57 - Cable operations, 1947

After several anxious hours, he was brought on board by the American consul who had bailed him out of the local jail. There was no official British presence in Sao Luis at that time. Our engineer had caused a disturbance in a local brothel whose madam had called in the police. Judicious bribes no doubt obtained his release. He swore that he was robbed while in the house of ill repute, but he was disgraced in the eyes of our captain, and indeed did look a sorry specimen. For the American

Consul, it was a welcome break away from tedium, as he enjoyed our hospitality on the quarterdeck.

Our next cable repair was off the port of Fortaleza. The weather had been remarkably calm during our sojourn off Brazil, and so it continued as we located and repaired the cable fault. Minor repairs were required to our main engines, so upon completion of the cable repair we proceeded alongside in the port. It was larger than Sao Luis, but smaller than Belem, with the same cobblestone streets, ancient churches and public buildings constructed in the eighteenth and nineteenth centuries.

I visited the Cable & Wireless cable station there and was made very welcome. After a swim in the pool on the grounds of the station, I was treated to an excellent curry luncheon containing all kinds of delicious seafood and washed down with large whisky sodas. A siesta was then in order and I was deposited in a large, wide hammock to recover my strength. I dozed off and on, cooled by the onshore breeze, before something disturbed my rest and I opened my eyes to their fullest extent. There, in the tree branches to which the hammock was fastened, above my head, was a very large snake. It was looking at me with great interest, so I leapt out of the hammock and hared back to the buildings. It was a boa constrictor and well known to the cable engineers. They howled with laughter at my panic and assured me that he or she had eaten recently and was only curious about a stranger on the cable station estate. You could have fooled me!

My snake story was told and retold again and again on board *Norseman*. I viewed hammocks with considerable misgiving from that time forward. We sailed from Fortaleza shortly afterwards to conduct our last cable repair task along the Brazilian coast. It was the cable link between Fortaleza and Recife, the main cable station junction on the east coast of South America.

South of Recife, cable repairs were the responsibility of the *Lady Dennison Pender*, another Cable & Wireless vessel based in Rio de Janeiro. Many tales were told about her and her crew. It was said that they had gone native after being so long in South America and refused transfer to other vessels in the fleet. An officer on board was reputed to have married the madam of a very successful bordello in Santos, and then retired on the proceeds. Probably most of the stories were bosh, but she had that reputation. Unfortunately, our paths never crossed.

Chapter Twenty-Seven

Cape Verde and Madeira

We completed our cable repair on the Fortaleza-Recife line without too much difficulty and headed eastward across the Atlantic to the vicinity of Ascension Island and the Cape Verde's. We were back to dragging for cable in deeper waters, with all its boredom and frustration. The mountains of Ascension could be seen to the south, but we did not seek anchorage. With the repair finally effected, *Norseman* moved to the next job, which was just south of the Cape Verde Islands. This was a more difficult operation and we broke off from time to time to take on fresh water and fresh fish from the local fishermen. The fresh fare was much appreciated by all on board, as our food stores were greatly depleted.

When we left the South American coast, we had on board several stowaways that I neglected to mention. They were tiny pumas and panthers that were bought as pets by our crew members. They were tiny when they came on board but the size of their paws in relation to their bodies already gave some indication as to their future size. On board, they were allowed to wander around the decks freely as long as they did not get in the way of operations. They were attractive animals, but a bit messy at times as all youngsters will be. Unfortunately, their curiosity proved to be their undoing. At sea, while we pitched and rolled around, one after the other they disappeared into the deep. They should have been left in the jungle where they belonged.

It was now 1948, and I was extremely unhappy. Correspondence from home indicated to me that perhaps I had a rival for my wife's affections. I therefore decided to try and break my contract with Cable & Wireless and leave *Norseman* when she returned to Gibraltar. The matter was discussed with Captain Lawrence and it was so decided.

We continued to operate around the Cape Verde Islands until all cable repairs were completed. Our next operating area was in the vicinity of

Madeira, which provided a pleasant change of venue. Many cables were laid into Madeira, and a Finnish freighter had managed to drag anchor across all of them, thereby severing cable communications in and out of Madeira. *Norseman* anchored off Funchal, the port of Madeira, well clear of the damaged cables. Much of the work required repairs to the shore ends utilizing a hired tug and barge before new cables were spliced and relaid. It was a time-consuming job in heavy swells.

Figure 58 - CS *Norseman* off Funchal, Madeira, 1948

There were, however, compensations ashore as Madeira was a very pleasant place to take shore leave. *Norseman* could not lie alongside the quay because of the continuously running swell, so we had to run in by boat and judge the swell before leaping to the quay. We were told of many disastrous attempts to land safely, but accomplished the journey in safety several times. Mind you, the return journey to the ship was always easier as carried out within an alcoholic bubble of euphoria.

The first stop on shore was the ritzy hotel just outside the dock gates. It was called Blandings and had been very popular with the wealthy set in pre-war days. It was very opulent and sported a gambling casino. The city of Funchal was not large but stretched up into the mountains and was covered in all sorts of exotic flowers. Some of the floral bouquets stretched across deep ditches that were really open sewers washed down with the mountain rainfall. It was dry when we were there, so the stench of the sewers could not be hidden by the floral display.

From high on the mountain one could take a self-propelled fast sleigh ride into the heart of Funchal. The view from on top was magnificent, encompassing the entire island and other smaller islands belonging to Portugal. Our ship and the Finnish cable-destroying culprit looked mighty small from that vantage point. Down below, in Funchal, tourists were eagerly sought after, as the war years had hit Madeira very hard. The Union Castle liners that used to stop at Funchal en route to Capetown and return to Southampton spent the war years employed as troopships and armoured merchant cruisers. Now the Cape route had been revived, but it was still a shadow of its former self.

Perhaps that is why we were welcomed so warmly when we visited Blandings. Our waiter treated us like royalty, and we duly responded with generous gratuities for services rendered. Later that night, when the hotel lounge closed for business, we found the little seafront bars patronized by the locals where fado music was played and aqua vitae drank straight at prices about a tenth of what we had been paying in the ritzy hotel. They also served wonderful seafood and shellfish of every variety. In one of these bars, we ran into our waiter who insisted on buying all our drinks and taking us to view the local bordello. We must have really tipped him well.

Before we departed Madeira, I had a duty to perform as *Norseman's* gin secretary. I visited the local outlet of Saccone & Speed, the wine and spirits merchants, and purveyors to the Royal Navy. There I purchased, duty free, many a case of Madeira wine and Scotch whisky for consumption on board. I was well plied with wine while making these purchases and in addition arrived on board with several Madeira cane chairs, a gift to *Norseman* from the proprietors. A suitable end to my last cable repair job.

Chapter Twenty-Eight

Gibraltar and Home

We sailed for Gibraltar in early February, arriving there on the ninth. Amidst rather sad farewells, I signed off *Norseman* on the tenth of February and took up temporary residence in a small bed and breakfast hotel. I had served on *Norseman* for almost fifteen months and had really regarded her as my home. There had been rough times, but there had been grand times that I will always remember and the shipmates who made it possible. I loved the life, but the temptations of alcohol and the flesh were too much to handle in my present circumstances. A few days later, I watched *Norseman*, accompanied by *Mirror,* steam out of Gibralter breakwater. A part of my life was finished!

I visited my friends in La Linea and even took a drive up to Malaga to see the real Spain. In early 1948, the Costa del Sol was literally virgin land as far as tourism was concerned. If only I had invested some money in acquiring property, I would now be a rich man. I didn't but went to see a bullfight instead. Spectacular but barbaric. I think I understood the symbolism, but realized the large gulf in understanding that exists between the Spaniards and us, as noted before on the ship—a combination of bravery and cruelty. However, I did enjoy the music of the bullfight, the paso doble, and bought a few records to take home.

In mid-February, the Orient liner *Otranto* anchored in Gibraltar harbour and I moved from my hotel to the fairly spartan quarters on board. My cabin, shared with an army officer, was comfortable enough, but the ship was crowded with expatriates returning to Britain from the furtherest flung corners of the empire. There were demanding women, squalling children and choleric colonels all vying for attention. Added to the clamour was the dowdiness and rundown appearance of the vessel, long overdue for a refit. Food was plentiful but of marginal quality, and the worst attributes of colonial life permeated shipboard routine. Beef tea at mid-morning and tea and biscuits at mid-afternoon, announced by the ringing of bells and served only in the lounge. Similarly, coffee after dinner, again in the lounge, also announced with the ringing of bells. To me, it was an illustration that Britain's post-war recovery was a long way off.

At least a bit of a blow in the Bay of Biscay and the English Channel kept things under control. It was cold in the Channel and snow could be seen on shore as we approached the Isle of Wight. On the twenty-third of February, we came alongside at Southampton. After clearing immigration and customs, I boarded a train for Liverpool. Everything looked rundown to me, and I wondered what had happened in my absence, or perhaps I just had not noticed the squalor previously. In such a mood and with the marital problem to be faced, I approached Merseyside.

At my wife's parents house in Higher Bebington, I was welcomed with some warmth by her parents and more cautiously by my wife. After all, we had been separated for almost twenty-two months, and misunderstandings had arisen and festered. It was a difficult first few days, as we gradually unburdened our souls and tried to let nature take its course. I told her of my womanizing in general without going into details, and she told me of her boyfriend, who was an ex-Royal Air Force Battle of Britain fighter pilot. That romance was at an end, but she still recalled with a mixture of joy and terror the time that he had tried to teach her to fly a light aircraft. I was jealous and angry and would have attacked him if I had run into him. Indeed, when dancing at Hulme Hall, someone advised me that he was present. But when I went looking for him, he had vanished.

Without ever actually saying so in so many words, we agreed to forgive and forget the past and concentrate on the future. With substantial funds saved from my sojourn abroad and my unused clothing coupons, we were able to obtain new clothing for each of us so that we could take a second honeymoon. Naturally, it was to Scotland, and we arrived in Edinburgh mid-March 1948. No bed and breakfast in Portobello for us this time, nothing would do for us but a hotel located right on the Royal Mile. Like all Scottish hotels of that era, it had its peculiarities—a huge bathroom attached to the room, but with the toilet down the hall. The hotel itself was locked up at ten PM each night, making it essential that two lovebirds out seeing the sights of the town had to rouse the night watchman at the ungodly hour of eleven PM to gain entry. It did cause us many a giggle, much to the annoyance of the hotel's guardian.

Being on Princes Street, we were close to the Sir Walter Scott Memorial and, of course, the approaches to Edinburgh Castle. I did not forewarn Doreen of the one o'clock gun ceremony and she was ready to hit me with her umbrella when the gun fired almost over her head. The castle itself was impressive, even if it always seemed to easily be captured by the English in days gone by. The Scottish War Memorial was a beautiful hallowed place to the large number of Scottish war dead, particularly those slaughtered in their tens of thousands on the western front in the Great War.

One day, a Saturday, we headed for Holyrood Palace to lap up some Scottish history, but on spotting a tramcar marked football special we ended up at a game between Hearts and Midlothian. We were properly reconciled—we agreed that watching a good soccer match was much more important than lapping up some information about Mary, Queen of Scots, and her many lovers. We were getting back to where we had been on our first honeymoon in 1946.

From Edinburgh, we travelled by train to Greenock to see my father and stepmother. My brother was working on the Shaw estate, in preparation for his posting to Malaya as an assistant manager on a rubber plantation. Dad and Mary were keeping well and made us very welcome. We visited relatives and friends of our family, where my wife was hailed as a "wee smasher" by the admiring younger males. I introduced her to Cragburn, the dancing pavilion where I had learned to be a dancing success. Luckily, none of my old girlfriends were present.

Being late March, the weather was cool on the Clyde. Nevertheless, we set off for a trip down the river from Gourock to Dunoon and Rothesay. It was bracing but enjoyable, so we decided to do the circumnavigation of the island of Bute. The Kyles of Bute were lovely and the sky was clear, but the wind did howl. I thoroughly enjoyed the trip around Bute but I do not think Doreen was impressed, shivering and shaking in the cold wind.

Rothesay was, of course, quite different where she took pleasure in shopping and taking in the sights. It was a long day, but a good one when we finally wound our way back to Greenock. Another trip was by bus to Largs and a boat ride to Millport on the Cumbrae Islands. It was grand fun and reminded me of my childhood and the Clyde steamers. When the weather cooperates, the Firth of Clyde is truly scenic. To finish off our visit, I took her up the Cut, that famous Greenock waterway that flows out of Loch Thom. She appeared duly impressed as she scanned the river and the firth to the island of Arran in the far distance.

Chapter Twenty-Nine

A First Mate's Foreign-Going Certificate and Emigrating to Canada

Now we returned to Merseyside, where I had to prepare for my first mate's foreign going certificate examination. In addition, there was great excitement in my wife's family as we all prepared to emigrate to Canada. Doreen's sisters Ursula and Joan were already in Canada, living in Port Arthur, Ontario, the hometown of Ursula's husband who had met her when he was serving in Britain with the Royal Canadian Air Force. Doreen's folks were booked to leave for Canada in May on the Furness Withy liner *Nova Scotia* and we would follow them one month later. The extra month was to give me more time to prepare for exams.

The house on Withert Avenue was duly sold and we found ourselves house-sitting as items of furniture were gradually sold off. Toward the end, we were reduced to a card table and chairs and an old roll-up bed. Doreen was keen to go to Canada to make a new start in our marriage and to be with her family. I had liked what I had seen of Canada, and life in Britain was stultifying and mean, with little chance of improvement evident in the near future. I also wanted to make a new start in our marriage and Canada seemed to offer that promise.

With the house sold and occupied by its new owners, and Doreen's parents about to embark on their voyage of a lifetime, we moved across the river to stay with one of my wife's many relatives. She was Aunt Harriet, Doreen's mother's sister, a very jolly nice lady who looked after us very well for the remainder of our stay in the UK. Her husband, Peter, was a grand fellow, shore bosun for Canadian Pacific, with a grey moustache that he could use to advantage in chatting up the local barmaids.

It was a pleasant spot close to a convent retreat on a hill that afforded us many quiet walks. There was a restful park down by the river, known as Otterspool, where I honed my studies to examination standards. My wife helped me in these studies by questioning me closely on my knowledge, which helped enormously. Additionally, I took a mandatory course in lifeboat drill, which paid dividends. I wish I had taken such a course years earlier, it was such a seamanship thing.

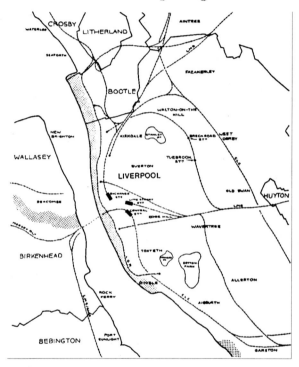

Figure 59 - The River Mersey

Merseyside is a subject all on its own. As I sailed from it and into it on many occasions, and lived ashore there for several months, it deserves a comment or two. Its people were irrepressible, always ready with a suitable quip, rendered in that unmistakable Scouse dialect. Thick and heavy around the docks and shipyards, but only slightly more refined in the business world and the suburbs. My wife was born in Bootle, so I learned how to interpret even the thickest of Scouse accents. Attendance at a local football match followed by a ride home on a tram was to encounter Scouse humour and irony in all its many forms. I was soon understanding the quick repartee and chuckling at the sharp minds behind the dry comments. Their attitude during the bombing and in coping with the post-war shortages was most commendable even if expressed in that inimitable nasal Scouse way. A great people!

One of the interesting things about Merseyside in those years, and probably still so today, was the many pubs scattered around the area. From Crosby and Bootle to Aigburth and Garston, from Wallasey to Port Sunlight and many places beyond, the selection of pubs was enormous. Some were absolute gems, others moderately attractive, and a few that compared well with the worst of dives that I had visited abroad. A pub-crawl through that part of Lancashire and Cheshire was not just a boozy affair but also a wonderful journey into the history and the varied ways of life of their people. A civilized way to imbibe and enjoy. It was instructive even to a Scotsman with a large appetite for the grain and grape.

My in-laws were Catholic as was my wife and her sisters. They had a charming custom on a Sunday after mass of stopping off at the local pub, the Prenton, for a drink before heading home for Sunday dinner. My Presbyterian ancestors would have been horrified, but I was most impressed. My mother-in-law was called Nellie by her friends; with blue eyes and blond hair, she must have been a knockout when younger. My father-in-law was known as Andy to his friends. He was a few years older than his wife and not given to talk unless he felt that it was absolutely necessary. I knew that Nellie liked me, but I was never sure about Andy. He would probably have preferred to have his eldest daughter marry a good Catholic boy. He worked as foreman mechanic for a large firm of haulage contractors in Liverpool. At their time of life, they were very brave to undertake the emigration to Canada. We were young and more resilient, and therefore felt more capable of adjusting to a new life.

We were leaving a place I had grown to like. A part of England that had a unique history, as I will attempt to briefly outline. The Merseyside I knew encompassed Liverpool and its environs in Lancashire plus the Wirral Peninsula in Cheshire, with the western shore of the River Dee and its eastern shore on the Mersey encompassing Birkenhead and the satellite ports of Port Sunlight and Ellesmere Port at the entrance to the Manchester ship canal.

The Wirral has a longer recorded history than that of Liverpool, with

Roman occupation since 70 AD centered on Chester, but with an extensive settlement in the Wirral at Moels. The Vikings invaded in AD 800 and settled along the western side of the peninsula. The Normans came in AD 1060 and made Chester a major base of operations while expanding the use of the River Dee for their maritime affairs. The Domesday Book of 1085-6 recorded four hundred and five heads of family in the peninsula. The Dee side of the Wirral dominated trade to Ireland from northern England for the next three hundred years, before extensive silting prevented meaningful enterprise.

Meanwhile, on the Mersey, a tidal pool called Lifer Pool or muddy pool was slowly growing to prominence, with the port of Liverpool being founded by King John in 1207. The port started trading in a small way with Ireland, exporting iron and wool for skins and hides in return. By the sixteenth century, a steady and growing trade with Ireland was the mainstay of the port. However, rapid growth did not come until the late seventeenth century with the expansion of British colonies in North America and the West Indies. By the eighteenth century, trade was booming, with ships departing for ports around the British coastline and to Norway, Hamburg, the Baltic and the Netherlands. The first tidal dock was constructed in 1715 and Liverpool grew to be the third port in Britain after London and Bristol.

From about 1730, the merchants of Liverpool began to make huge profits from the slave trade. They shipped goods to West Africa, slaves to the West Indies, then sugar back to Liverpool for refining, a truly triangular demonstration of the development of the immense wealth of Liverpool shipowners and merchants of the time.

By the end of the eighteenth century, this very profitable trade had been hard hit by the American War of Independence and the movement against slavery led by Wilberforce in England. The port soon recovered and expanded its trading partners to other parts of the globe. Many new docks were built. In the early 1800s, the port of Birkenhead on the Wirral, opposite Liverpool, rapidly expanded with new docks and added greatly to the trade of Merseyside. The world's first underwater railway (between Birkenhead and Liverpool) was opened in 1886. Liverpool became a city in 1880, with a population of six hundred thousand.

In 1911, the Liver Building was erected on the site of the former St.

George's Dock. Several other prominent buildings were built close by at that time. With the liver birds adorning the Liver Building, they still dominate the city waterfront. In 1934, the first road tunnel under the Mersey was built, even while the business recession was biting hard.

In 1939, we were at war once more with Germany, and Merseyside became ever more important to the successful prosecution of the war effort. From 1940 to 1942, Merseyside was bombed by the Luftwaffe, and mines were laid in the river and its approaches. The repeated attacks brought death and destruction to many. The ships in the docks, the shipyards and factories, the city centres and tens of thousands of homes were destroyed or damaged. The death toll was in excess of four thousand souls. Merseyside suffered and staggered under the blows, but quickly recovered and continued to play a key role in the Battle of the Atlantic.

In 1948, Merseyside had partially been restored to its former glory, but troubles were looming on dockside as the dockers' union imposed many restrictive practices on the employers with the full support of the socialist government in Whitehall. It was just one of many indications that Britain was under the control of the left, with all its levelling down instincts rather than wanting to build and expand that we might achieve our former strength as a nation. I was more than ever convinced that we could make a new start in another land, and Canada with its background of British emigration and history of Scottish exploration and settlement was certainly appealing.

My examination for first mate foreign-going loomed, and I sallied forth to the examination rooms on the Liverpool waterfront with a mixture of confidence and fear. As usual, the miserable examiners' clerk lorded it over us poor souls who dared to waste his time, thereby adding to our concern as we prepared for three days of written exams. I had prepared fairly well and managed to pass in every paper. However, I tripped up on the oral examination, failing to persuade the examiner that I knew what I was talking about. He told me to come back in two weeks and be more confident in my assertions. It was a blow, but hopefully not a fatal one. I was told by another aspiring candidate that the examiner, Jones by name, had probably had a bad lunch that day, and that I should try to persuade the clerk to schedule me for a morning session the next time around. As I am a morning person myself, that information made sense and I so arranged. I had no trouble with the oral exam the second time and became the proud possessor of a first mate's foreign-going certificate of competency. We duly celebrated my success with Doreen's Aunt Harriet in tow at a pleasant old pub in Mossley Hill called the Rose of Mossley. It was now time to think of moving on.

We had arranged our landed immigrant status with the Canadian government and had been accepted. We then sorted out all our affairs in Britain and awaited the sailing of our ship to Canada. On the tenth of June 1948, we boarded the Furness Withy liner *Nova Scotia* and late that evening set sail for Halifax. Our point of departure was the landing stage where I had returned to Britain on board *Stratheden* five years previously.

Figure 60 - My wife and I on board *Nova Scotia* en route to Canada, 1948

However, on this voyage I had to share cabin space with three other men, while my wife was cooped up in another cabin with three women and their squalling brats. It was hardly conducive to a prolonged honeymoon, but we did manage a bit of time to ourselves. The weather was not too good en route, but it was not an unpleasant trip. The food provided was mediocre, but the bars were open and the company of fellow passengers made time pass rapidly. There were many with interesting stories, and several people who appeared apprehensive about what they would encounter in Canada. It did make me think about what sort of reception we might encounter, but with relatives to meet us, we were sure that all would be well.

On the morning of the seventeenth of June, *Nova Scotia* sailed into Halifax harbour and docked alongside at pier 21. Without undue delay, we were inspected and processed by the Canadian authorities and became accepted as landed immigrants in Canada. Red caps assisted us with our luggage and we went straight on board the train that was to take us to Montreal. We were then advised that the train would not depart until evening and that we were free to see Halifax in the meantime.

My rambling now comes to a halt as we contemplate Halifax while sampling a huge banana split, unheard of and unobtainable back in Britain. If I am spared, as my ancestors would say, I will continue this yarn in another book that will describe what awaited us in Canada. Trials and tribulations there were, but also joy and accomplishment.

ISBN 141200071-8